PRAISE FOR *TRAVEL SEEKNESS*

Nobody wants to hear about how good your trip was. They want disasters, things gone wrong, rip-offs and scams. If there's a stomach upset, dysentery is always better than diarrhoea. *Travel Seekness* is a non-stop litany of messes, misadventures and misfortunes. The hostel from hell, endless swindles, even the bed bugs come in big numbers – 86 of them. **Lonely Planet co-founder Tony Wheeler**

Travelogues are generally not like this! It made me laugh out loud. So funny. So personal. If you want to travel abroad, save yourselves the bother and just read this instead! All the fun with none of the mosquitoes. **Diane Morgan, comedian & BBC Two's *Cunk on Britain* presenter**

Reading Lisa and Graham's book, I found myself excitedly adding items to my bucket list, as well as frantically crossing out others. It's a touching, honest and often hilarious collection of travel tales that will delight both seasoned travellers and armchair adventurers. **George Mahood, author of *Free Country* & *Travels with Rachel***

Despite their endless arguments, Lisa and Graham's passion for travel – and each other – comes across on every page. *Travel Seekness* is a love letter to two lives well lived on the road less travelled. **Anna McNuff, adventurer & author of *50 Shades of the USA***

Heart-warming and inspirational, this book made me laugh out loud – and cry, too. Lisa and Graham are evocative writers that put you right beside them on the plane seats. I feel like I've just travelled around the world! **Suzy Walker, Editor-in-Chief, *Psychologies***

As much an epic love story as it is a global whirlwind, Lisa and Graham whisk you off the beate churning food, the marathons, the the swingers – as if you were there. funny. **Esther Newman, Editor,**

GW00659200

What shines through as ever with Lisa Jackson's writing is a zest for life, an eye for detail and a keen sense of the ridiculous. Here she joins forces with her husband Graham to take us round the world. These heart-warming tales are splendidly told, reflecting our heroes' love for life, travel and ultimately each other. **Paul Tonkinson, comedian & author of _26.2 Miles to Happiness_**

Jump aboard this thrill-packed tour of almost everywhere. The two guides entertain with patter that's witty and acutely observant. **Roger Robinson, author of _When Running Made History_**

If you're the type of traveller who thinks 'What's down that alley' or 'What's that, and can I eat it?' on a trip you'll love _Travel Seekness_ – just don't read the Cuban toilet story before dinner. **Helen Foster, travel journalist & Differentville.com blogger**

A whirlwind adventure that will have you laughing and crying, Graham and Lisa's quest to find happiness in the hardest times of life's journey is an inspiring and heart-warming read. **Dion Leonard, author of _Finding Gobi_**

If you love David Sedaris, you'll love the observational humour in _Travel Seekness_, a laugh-out-loud travel memoir about one couple's quest to see the world without killing each other along the way. Lisa and Graham's tempestuous relationship with travel – and each other – will have you chuckling long after you've put this book down. **Christina Neal, Editor, _Women's Fitness_**

Life affirming and hilarious. Every chapter is a passionate homage to the wonder and madness of exploring the world. I loved it! **Amy Baker, author of _Miss-adventures_**

An absolutely fantastic collection of hilarious and often hair-raising tales, told in a way that makes you feel as though you are there. Who knew that queuing in India was such an art form? Loved it! **Mimi Anderson, author of _Beyond Impossible_**

To our astonishing parents, Irene 'Ma' and Reg 'Pa' Williams and Anthony and Leoné Jackson, and to our loving and supportive family and friends

To all the welcoming, considerate, generous and kind people we've met in some of the world's poorest countries and in some of its richest. It is they who turned travel into a life-affirming journey

The stories you are about to read are true. Only people's names, identifying characteristics, occupations, hair colours, blood groups and clothing choices have been changed to protect the guilty. If someone in our book sounds like you, then they probably aren't.

Madras, Bombay and Calcutta have changed identity, too, and are now known as Chennai, Mumbai and Kolkata.

CONTENTS

INTRODUCTION

Are there any do's and don'ts?' I asked the harried-looking doctor sitting opposite me and Graham in the rundown London hospital consultation room that was strangely large, like a classroom, only it didn't smell of chalk or crayons. The scuffed walls were painted a bilious shade of green, as if they too felt queasy after hearing so much bad news. I stared at the odd-looking green pipe resembling a section of vacuum-cleaner hose jutting out from the wall behind her and wondered idly why it was there as it didn't seem to come from anywhere or connect to anything. Perhaps it was an architectural appendix, a vestigial remnant from the building's past.

'We're not yet sure what it is,' the doctor replied.

Sitting there, looking expectantly at the doctor, we were hoping Graham's bout of extreme breathlessness was due to tuberculosis. It struck me how absurd it was to be actually willing someone to have TB, an illness that causes you to cough up blood, scars your lungs and, if left untreated, kills about half of those affected. But that's exactly what we were both doing. That's what an undiagnosed illness does to you: if you have to choose from a shortlist of completely shitty diseases, you're always going to opt for the least crappy one. It's like giving a condemned man the choice of how he wants to be dispatched – there are bad, and there are *really* bad ways to go. I sat there grimly reflecting on how much our life had changed in a week. Seemingly *overnight*, Graham had gone from a guy who'd been capable of running 27 marathons and ultra-marathons – reluctantly, as I'd enter him into my races and weather the inevitable tantrums when he found out – to someone who struggled to make it to the end of our road without gasping for breath. An X-ray had revealed something sinister, and we'd been called into the hospital to discuss the results.

'We're going camping with friends who have an 11-year-old son and we don't want to put him at risk,' I said.

'I'll know more when we analyse the fluid we're going to remove from your husband's lung,' the doctor said without looking up, shuffling Graham's medical notes into a neat pile as newsreaders do at the end of the news.

'So, it's okay for Graham to fly with me to Georgia, Armenia and Azerbaijan to celebrate my 50th birthday?' I asked, relieved that the 'sinister something' wouldn't kibosh our travel plans. The doctor shot me an alarmed look.

'With a lung like this,' she said pointing at an X-ray, 'he could die if he flew anywhere.'

The room spun. Graham's medical issue was clearly a heck of a lot more serious than either of us had anticipated, and it looked as if it had the potential to brutally wrest from us one of the things we most loved – travel.

Two weeks later, just before midnight, I called Graham from my hotel room in Yerevan, Armenia's capital. We'd decided that the procedure he needed to have to drain fluid from his lung wasn't reason enough for me to cancel our planned tour of the Caucasus. As the red illuminated numerals on the electronic bedside clock blinked away my final seconds as a 49-year-old, it didn't feel as though I was celebrating turning 50 but instead holding a solo wake for my 40s. Graham, invariably attuned to how I felt, tried valiantly to lighten my mood.

'You're now at the age where it's appropriate for you to buy travel sweets for the car *and* to forget where you parked it,' he joked.

Though I enjoyed the trip, it wasn't the same without him. The tedium of 14 hot and dusty hours stuck at the border between Georgia and Abkhazia, a pocket-sized breakaway state recognised by five countries, was immeasurably worse without Graham. I especially missed the humour he'd have brought to my experience of narrowly avoiding toppling over as I retched while squat-peeing on the reeking, excrement-covered floor of a deserted building when the border guards wouldn't let us use their toilet.

Once I was back in the UK, Graham and I attended another hospital appointment in the same green-tinged room, but this time with a different doctor.

'How much have they told you?' asked the kindly white-haired doctor from behind the desk.

'Not much,' said Graham, shifting uncomfortably in his hard plastic chair.

After knocking on the door, a nurse let herself in.

'Couldn't she have waited till we'd finished speaking with the doctor?' I thought, mildly annoyed that the nurse was interrupting our important consultation. She sat down.

'I'm really sorry to have to tell you that it's cancer,' said the doctor, attempting to smile reassuringly but not quite managing it. I looked over at Graham. He was deathly pale and staring at the doctor in disbelief. A sick feeling surged through my body as the desk, the piles of medical files and the unexplained green pipe coming out of the wall all seemed to expand in my vision, as if someone was playing with a zoom lens that suddenly brought certain objects much closer and into sharp focus. I recognised the feeling – I'd been in this place of terror and fear a few times before when travelling abroad. I knew I was dissociating, pretending that what was happening wasn't real to protect myself from the terrible news. We discussed the biopsy results and treatment options. I plucked up the courage to ask about the prognosis. It wasn't good, and the green pipe loomed even closer.

'Can I make you two a cup of tea?' asked the nurse as she handed us a sheaf of leaflets.

'No, I think we need to get home,' Graham said weakly.

'Yes, if I were you I'd want something stronger than tea. This must have come as a huge shock.'

Graham nodded dumbly. As we stood up to leave the nurse placed a reassuring hand on my arm and calmly said, 'I know loads of people who've lived longer than five years with this. Can I give you a hug?' Tearfully, we both embraced her. As I did so, I felt the dissociation dissipating and strength replacing it. Graham and I were going to get through this, together, using every means we possessed. I would read every book about cancer ever written. I would speak to every single person I knew who'd survived cancer to learn how they'd done it. I was going to use my hypnotherapy skills to encourage Graham's body to heal. I was going to research the hell out of his illness.

And in the weeks that followed I did all of those things. I read a pile of books a metre high; we attended a cancer workshop; I watched YouTube videos until my eyes burned; I read every research paper I could track down; we made lifestyle changes that would give Graham the best chance of remission.

'We aren't going to fight the cancer, Graham,' I told him, 'but heal it instead. We need to live in hope, not fear.'

I woke up thinking about cancer, I spent the day thinking about cancer, I went to bed thinking about cancer and I woke up in the night to think about cancer. I felt guilty doing anything that wasn't cancer related. It was when Graham forlornly asked, after opening the door to yet another delivery of cancer books, 'How many more books are you going to read, Leecy?' that I realised how his illness had taken over not only Graham's life but mine, too.

That's when I turned to travel to help me through. A few months previously, I'd watched the tail-end of a TV programme during which a seasoned travel presenter had cried on seeing the splendour of the Northern Lights, and I became convinced that we should go in search of the natural phenomenon that had so delighted and awed him. Researching the various options became a sanity-saving distraction. For an hour or so each day, I'd allow myself to fantasise about the fresh Norwegian fish we'd eat, the cosy cabin we'd stay in and the changing cast of people we'd meet as our intended cruise ship moonlighted as a local ferry. It spirited me away from a terrifying world in which we had to make life-or-death decisions. For those 60 minutes, Graham wasn't sick and I wasn't wading through a swamp of conflicting information and opinions; I was just doing what I loved doing, piecing a trip together.

In the end, the dates of Graham's chemotherapy clashed with the cruise, so we didn't book it after all. But the headspace I gained from planning, scheming and dreaming enabled me to continue with my research, despite its bleak predictions, which led to the breakthrough we sought. I tracked down one of the foremost experts in Graham's kind of cancer and, after 15 minutes in his hospital office, we knew we'd found The One. Until then, I'd been frantically trying to locate a holistic oncologist but even my health journalist friends couldn't name one. And yet here was this world-renowned surgeon talking about being humble in the face of the disease, suggesting dietary changes, herbal supplements and meditation. What's more, part of his 'prescription' involved drinking red wine. Every day.

'He had me at "red wine",' said Graham.

A week later Graham underwent a seven-hour operation so complex it was likened to peeling the skin off a grape with a scalpel, and the day after his surgery he was walking up and down the corridor outside intensive care, testing the patience of his physiotherapist with his persistent demands to be allowed to do 'just one more lap'.

Our next hurdle was the chemotherapy. I'd never been into a chemo ward before and the idea filled me with dread, especially as Graham would be on a drip for up to eight hours. How would we remain positive for such a long time? We considered downloading comedies to watch on his iPad, but worried that our laughter might seem disrespectful to the other patients. I toyed with the idea of wearing a hat from one of my fancy-dress marathons to keep our spirits up, but again we thought this would be inappropriate. And then I had my eureka moment: we could start writing that travel memoir I suggested a few years ago.

During the 27 years we'd been married, 25 of which we'd been living and working in London, we'd travelled to dozens of amazing countries, dashed off after work on Fridays for cram-it-all-in city breaks, run marathons all over the world and bolted leave onto work trips to squeeze in adventures prior to coming home. We had many a tale to tell.

Graham wasn't keen.

'Come on, it'll be fun,' I cajoled him. 'We can take our travel journals to your chemo sessions and use the time to decide which stories we want to include. Besides, if you won't be my co-author, I'll include all the funny bits you wrote and pretend I wrote them.'

'You can't do that,' protested Graham. 'That's plagiarism.'

'Oh yes I can. Sue me.'

And so for six emotionally draining dawn-to-dusk chemo sessions Graham put his feet up in a comfy recliner as the toxic cocktail that would blast the 'bad guys' slowly dripped into his veins. I sat in a chair beside him and read aloud from one of the dozens of travel journals I'd retrieved from our loft. Some were scruffy exercise books we'd purchased from roadside stationers, illustrated with Pritt-sticked postcards. Some were smart Moleskine notebooks. Still others were ring-bound manuscripts we'd put together after typing up scribbled notes into more legible text.

During the months post-chemo, as Graham gradually returned to better health, writing this book helped us to heal. We chuckled as we relived our misadventures and, when we struggled to find the correct word or agonised over the best adjective to describe putrefied shark, screamed at each other in frustration – and narrowly avoided scratching each other's eyes out – exactly as we'd done when backpacking around India 25 years earlier.

Once we'd finished a rough draft, we took it with us on the trips we went on as soon as Graham felt well enough to fly. We edited chapters as Graham steered a hire car along twisting mountain roads in the Balkans, and rewrote sections seated at a café on the ramparts of Dubrovnik. We added sentences in Albanian pavement coffee shops and removed paragraphs in a London hospital room while waiting anxiously to hear if Graham's fever was chemo-related sepsis (it wasn't). We revised chapter and verse during long summer days and long winter nights at home. We even cut short a wedding-anniversary weekend, where we stayed in a windmill in the medieval town of Rye, to dash back home to work on our manuscript.

And so, after more versions than there have been covers of The Beatles' song *Yesterday*, here it is. Finally finished.

It's been a long, tiring and difficult birth but, like all parents, we think our baby is beautiful.

CHAPTER ONE

1992: The Year of New Beginnings
Taiwan

A black petticoat, a chance conversation with a hippie and a fateful aerogramme postmarked Taipei are the reasons I became a traveller. Oh, and my desire to be bohemian, something it wasn't easy to be in parochial 1980s South Africa. Almost 40 years of repressive, religiously enthused apartheid governments had seen to that. South Africa loved rules, the pettier the better. Signs were posted to make it clear that post offices, public toilets, park benches, beaches, public transport, swimming pools and even graveyards were segregated. A film as innocuous as *The Rocky Horror Picture Show* had been banned by the overzealous Directorate of Publications in case it turned the country's impressionable young men into suspender-wearing transvestites precisely at the time they were most needed to man up, don khaki and fight the communist-backed 'total onslaught' on our borders.

I, though, fancied myself to be somewhat rebellious, a little avant-garde, and hoped to be a bit different – but not so different that I'd get expelled – from the other pupils at my prestigious, rule-bound all-girls high school. Had I grown up in Europe or America, no doubt I would have dyed my hair black, worn moody Goth make-up and smoked weed, but in Pretoria, the bastion of conservative Afrikanerdom, such overt defiance simply wasn't done. There were all of two nightclubs in Pretoria – Limelight and Jacqueline's – and even if I'd had the money to get in, my strict parents wouldn't have let me go. I even had to mute the *Grease* LP I'd clubbed together with my sister Loren to buy whenever my mum came into the room in

7

case she picked up on some of the risqué lyrics. Given my limited options, short of hopping the border and taking up with the ANC in exile, my greatest act of rebellion was buying a vintage negligee-style black petticoat from the Saturday flea market outside the State Theatre, Pretoria's monumental temple to state-approved high culture. And going barefoot whenever I wore it. This 'bohemian' look was harder to pull off than I at first imagined, as my mother would have grounded me if she'd seen me go out undressed like that. Whenever I left the house, she never failed to ask if I was warm enough, so going out unshod and in underwear definitely wasn't going to get the green light.

Hence, when I found myself lounging louchely across several tie-dyed cushions on the floor, sharing out-of-the-can ham and lukewarm Cold Duck sparkling wine with Loren and Viktor, a bearded, bead-wearing student we'd met at the flea market two hours before, I wasn't quite as cool as I looked, for beside me, concealed in a plastic carrier bag, were the shoes and the dress I'd worn over my slip to give my mother the slip.

'What do you plan to do when you leave school?' asked Viktor, removing his John Lennon glasses to clean them with the corner of his creased Nehru-collared shirt. It was almost accusatory, a test, as though Viktor had the correct answer and would enlighten me once I'd given him the wrong one.

I told him I intended to go to university the following year to study English literature.

'Why don't you go travelling? Maybe get a job overseas?' he asked through a rising wisp of musky patchouli incense smoke that was making my head pound. I'd never cared for patchouli, not since the aroma had been described to me as 'lavender's unwashed cousin'.

'I can't afford to – and my parents certainly won't pay for it,' I replied defensively. At that, Viktor got to his feet, stepped over Loren's outstretched legs, and disappeared behind the multicoloured beaded fly screen in the doorway of his bedroom. He returned moments later clutching a thick wad of brown twenty-rand banknotes held together by a broad rubber band.

He tossed the cash onto my lap. 'There!' he said. 'Now you have the money to travel. Where are you going to go?'

Embarrassed, and startled at seeing such a large sum of money, I muttered something about needing to give it some thought before hastily handing the roll back. In retrospect, it's hard to credit that this challenge from a hippie I barely knew, and can only assume was a drug dealer – though he didn't offer Loren and me anything harder than hard cash – forced me to confront the fact that it wasn't being a penniless, petticoated 17-year-old that was holding me back from travelling. It was fear. Fear of the unknown. And fear of how much hassle travel involved.

Thus far my life had been one of comforting predictability. We'd lived in the same house in Pretoria since I was two years old; went on holiday to the same place – my Gran's house by the seaside in Durban – three times a year; my dad remained in the same government job his entire career, and my mum stayed at home to raise three kids. Back then, in the mid-1980s, hardly anyone I knew had been abroad. Gap years hadn't been invented. Flying anywhere from South Africa was stingingly expensive, and bookshops and newsagents stocked more cute-cat calendars than travel guides. You had to write an actual letter in longhand with an actual pen to extract information from tourist boards, consult often-clueless travel agents, and book hotels either via snail mail or cripplingly costly international phone calls. And if your plans fell through, you couldn't simply go online and instantly make alternative arrangements. In those pre-internet days, organising overseas travel was akin to shampooing a cat: daunting and damn difficult.

I knew all of this because, aged 13, my parents flew our family to the UK for three weeks. It was our sole foreign holiday. My mother spent months meticulously researching and booking our trip and, with Loren's help, compiled a scrapbook of what we would see. I barely glanced at it before we departed from Jan Smuts Airport aboard a South African Airways 747. Spotty and horribly hormonal, I slouched from sight to sight wearing a brown plastic raincoat and rainhat no matter the weather, more intent on pulling faces to ruin my parents' photos than I was on appreciating the magnificence of St Paul's Cathedral or the quiet majesty of Loch Lomond.

'Lisa, if you spoil another photo with that sour face of yours, I swear I'm going to march you back to our hotel and leave you there,' warned my mother. 'We didn't come all this way and pay all this money for you to behave like a brat.'

I gave my parents every reason to wish they'd left me behind.

At the age of 18, I took the path of least resistance and did what I'd told Viktor I'd do and enrolled at the University of Cape Town. And one August day in 1986, as I sat in a stuffy philosophy seminar room wearing a tasselled ankle-length skirt, African-print T-shirt and yellow fez, someone who would change my life walked in. I was only there because I'd fallen ill with hepatitis and had had to drop out of French Intensive, a demanding course that involved cramming five years of schoolgirl French into a single year. I had an idealised idea of what studying philosophy entailed and had imagined myself wearing a black roll-neck sweater, smoking Gauloises, drinking black coffee and discussing existentialism. Instead, I was confronted with tedious topics such as 'the meaning of meaning' and 'what is truth?' Concepts that tied my brain into a double bow knot. I was, to put it mildly, very disappointed. This wasn't what I'd signed up for, and it certainly didn't fit in with my real reason for choosing the course, which had been that it agreed with my bohemian view of myself.

From the moment I met Graham I knew he was different, not least because he was from London. He was four years older than me and had come to Cape Town to further his philosophy studies. Despite our diverse backgrounds, I felt I'd known him my whole life and our first conversation lasted three hours, cut short by my need to use the loo. I almost left it too late! I bumped into Graham again the next Saturday at the local Rebel liquor store while buying semi-sweet sparkling wine for my 19th birthday.

'Hello Lisa, I see you've got a stash of fizz. Are you celebrating something?'

'Hi Graham. It's my birthday tomorrow so I'm having a few friends round.'

'That sounds like fun. Just don't get caught with alcohol in your res room.'

'I don't intend to. See you around.'

I wasn't brave enough to invite him to my party, but five days later Graham took me for sundowners on the rocks at Camps Bay beach where, huddled under my Paddington Bear duffle coat, we drank pinotage and ate smoked mussels from a tin, brie from a box and black olives from a bag. I was 22 when we got engaged, and a year later we were married at Roggeland, a Cape Dutch country estate near Paarl with soul-stirring views of the vineyard-clad lower slopes of the Hawequas Mountains.

By then I'd graduated, and had two jobs – one at South African *Cosmopolitan* magazine and another on the *Cape Times* newspaper – and seemed to be on the fast-track to living a conventional, grown-up life: marriage would be followed by a mortgage and then, assuredly, by motherhood. But as Graham came closer to submitting his PhD thesis we concluded that, with three philosophy degrees, which didn't qualify him to do anything other than teach philosophy, he had more chance of plaiting fog than he had of getting a permanent job in Cape Town. Following considerable deliberation – usually as we sat on our flat's balcony quaffing wine – we decided to emigrate to the UK.

It was at this time that the aerogramme from Taipei arrived. 'You can beg or you can busk or you can teach English,' wrote my sister's friend Robyn. I'm not quite sure why we started corresponding, but Robyn's letters about life in Taiwan were so full of tales of the fun times to be had – and how easy she was finding it to pay off her student loan – that it wasn't long before I became convinced that I should join her and earn as much hard currency as possible prior to heading to London. Taiwan would also be an adventure. In two short years I'd gone from graduate to employee to wife and, aged 24, though part of me loved being solvent and settled so young, another part of me feared I was in danger of acting 50 before I turned 30. Taiwan offered me the chance to do something different – something more substantive than swanning around barefoot in a petticoat – but simultaneously to play it safe. Robyn would be my soft landing: she'd show me where to stay, what to eat and, most importantly, how to find work.

The Taipei option seemed infinitely preferable to my sister Loren's travel experience. Unlike Robyn's tales of easy money and tropical nights, her letters were filled with stories of hardship and hunger. She'd flown to England where she'd worked as a cleaner for 70 hours a week to save enough to go travelling in Europe and America. She and her boyfriend had survived on a daily budget of £10 and in order to be able to afford Italy's museums and art galleries, for an entire month they subsisted on one meal a day of pasta tossed in olive oil and garlic. They'd bedded down with drug addicts on the filthy floor of Rome's Termini Train Station, and on other occasions slept with their backpacks secured to their ankles for safe keeping, their tent being too small to accommodate both them and their luggage. One letter even told of the terrifying night they'd camped on the central island of a four-lane highway as cars and trucks thundered past. Too broke to pay for Greyhound bus tickets, they had located a car-hire company willing to pay them to drive a vehicle from New York to Washington DC. Littered with chicken bones because the thief who'd stolen it had lived in it for a month while on the run, it smelled so bad they had to hold their breath for 400km.

Graham, too, wasn't exactly a poster boy for the joys of travel. Born in Accra, the capital of Ghana, he'd spent most of his life as 'diplomatic baggage' because his father was a British diplomat. By the age of 11, when he started boarding school in England, he had lived half of his life abroad. It sounds enviable, but he'd made and 'lost' many friends and suffered a disrupted education. When his father took a post in Australia, in the space of four years Graham endured 23 long-haul flights from Melbourne to London lasting up to 35 hours each, and those gruelling 240,000 miles had snuffed out any interest he had in travel.

'It was like taking six of the best six times a year,' he told me. 'In-flight entertainment consisted of two "family friendly", dull as ditchwater films screened on an overhead projector, and a few channels of tinny-sounding music that was piped through hollow stethoscope-style headphones. And although smokers were seated towards the rear, the air quality was bloody awful. Ironically, the freshest air was in the toilets.'

When I broached the idea of going to Taiwan with Graham, he heard me out but struck a cautious note.

'You don't know very much about Taiwan, Lisa, and there's no guarantee that you'll find work or enjoy living there.'

'If I don't like it, I'll come back to South Africa and we can fly to London together from here,' I replied. 'But if things work out, you can join me once you've got your PhD.'

Graham eventually conceded that my plan made financial sense, especially if Robyn could help me find a job. We agreed we'd do the responsible thing: work hard for a few months and then fly to England with enough money to give us a head start in starting over. It would all be over by Christmas.

With Graham's rather lukewarm blessing I made preparations. I applied for a Taiwanese visa, excitedly bought my first rucksack – in my naivety choosing the largest one Cape Union Mart stocked – and liquidated my savings to pay for my plane ticket.

Late one afternoon, before my nightly sub-editing shift at the *Cape Times*, I popped into a city centre travel agency. Its plate-glass window onto the pedestrianised street was covered with advertising posters and flight prices to destinations across Europe, North America and Asia. I couldn't see any for Taiwan. On entering, the agent seated nearest the entrance, a redoubtable-looking, impeccably coiffured and manicured woman, beckoned me in and gestured that I should take a seat while she finished her phone call.

'Sorry about that, my dear. I was booking flights for a family going to France. They'll love it. I'm Elzaan, what can I do for you?'

I said I wanted to book a flight to Taipei.

'Taipei in Taiwan?' she said. 'When do you want to leave?'

I didn't know. I hadn't thought about it. I needed enough time to let Robyn know I was coming.

'Um, how about a month from now?'

'And when do you want to come back?'

My visa was valid for 60 days from arrival but, unless things didn't work out, I had no intention of returning to South Africa.

'Two months from now, I guess.'

It took an hour for Elzaan to make the arrangements, but finally my ticket noisily emerged from the printer behind her desk. Retrieving it, and using a pen as a pointer, Elzaan went over the confirmed details.

'That's fantastic,' I said, tucking the ticket away in my handbag. 'Thanks for all your help.'

I rose to leave. And in that moment Elzaan, smiling goodbye, could restrain herself no longer. Having bitten her lip during the entire protracted transaction, she just had to say it.

'I can't really understand why *anyone* would want to go to Taipei,' she blurted out. 'It's not somewhere tourists go. In fact, it's a dump and a slum.'

'Fake news' & a phoney accent

 Like the coffee the hipster scalded his mouth with because he drank it before it was cool, in 1992 Taiwan wasn't in the least bit trendy. Not like it is now. Even my dad, echoing Elzaan, agreed.

'Taiwan is not exactly a tourist destination, my lovey,' he said when I told him my plans. He'd visited Taiwan many times on business and, though he'd made many wonderful friends there, had returned home with off-putting stories about the air pollution, gridlocked traffic and rivers bubbling with noxious gas. But nothing he could have said would've stopped me: I was determined to go. Maybe the challenge that hippie Viktor, whom I never saw again but also never forgot, had thrown down in that headache-inducing Pretoria flat had something to do with it.

In a flurry of focused activity I readied myself for Taiwan. I quit my newspaper job, we gave up the lease on our Cape Town flat and packed most of our belongings into 22 cardboard apple boxes, shipping them to Graham's parents in England.

The flight to Taiwan was long and tiring, so it was a relief to see Robyn outside arrivals at Chiang Kai-shek International Airport and not to have to find the airport bus on my own. As the bus made its way into town, we passed black-stained concrete apartment blocks that looked as though they'd been freshly firebombed.

'What the heck's happened here?' I asked, a touch alarmed.

'These are the city's exclusive suburbs,' replied Robyn breezily.

The traffic was horrendous. Hordes of helmet-less scooter drivers hurtled past wearing surgical facemasks in a futile attempt to filter out the smog and the choking dust from the Metro construction works, giving the bizarre impression that they were doctors with a death wish. Within days, I'd be wearing one myself.

'Taiwan is the one place on earth where smoking is actually good for you,' chuckled Robyn. 'At least there's a filter between you and the pollution. I guess that's why the most popular brand of cigarette here is called Long Life.'

Our Lonely Planet guidebook had warned about 'wild chicken' drivers, and it was just my luck that the very first bus I took was driven by a World Class Wild Chicken who was determined to spend as much time on the wrong side of the road as on the right one, and hell-bent on reaching 100km per hour, even for a metre or two, before simultaneously slamming on the brakes and hitting the horn. Robyn and the bus's other occupants were nonplussed but, with each near-miss manoeuvre, I let out an involuntary shriek, until a filthy look from one of the passengers made me realise I was behaving like a backseat driver, even though I was standing right up at the front.

We disembarked outside the glitzy Lai Lai Sheraton on Linsen North Road and made our way to a narrow lane between two rundown buildings covered in patches of peeling paint as if they suffered from structural eczema. At the end of the lane stood a shack built from discarded wood. The old man who lived there obviously had a thing for George Bush Senior and was doing his bit to get him re-elected: his home was festooned with US flags, red, white and blue bunting and posters of a benignly smiling Bush. Wearing sandals, trousers and a ragged white vest, he was sitting outside on a low stool. As we approached, he smiled in greeting, revealing teeth stained a deep crimson.

'What's up with his mouth?' I whispered to Robyn.

'It's betel nut,' she replied. 'Taiwanese people chew it as it gives them a buzz.'

As we walked past, the man spat a stream of blood-red saliva between his feet.

We turned left into the stairwell of the Taipei Hostel building and Robyn summoned the lift.

'Pray no one else wants to join us,' she said as we squeezed ourselves, my rucksack, daypack, bulky video camera and the guitar I'd brought for busking into the minuscule lift.

'But there are two of us, and the sign says it can take six.'

'Yes, but that's six *Taiwanese* people,' said Robyn. 'Whenever more than two or three Westerners get in, the overload alarm rings.'

The lift opened directly into the hostel's lounge-kitchen-reception. Behind the desk sat Ivy, Taipei Hostel's formidable but (if you stayed on her good side) friendly manager. Welcoming me as a new resident, Ivy told me she'd need to hold my passport hostage until I could change money to pay for my accommodation. I reluctantly handed it over, relieved to see Ivy lock it away with her cashbox in the top drawer of the desk. Then I set off in search of a bed. The first one I was offered was in a private room so small that I could touch both walls with my outstretched arms.

'This is fine, I don't need more space than this,' I said, until Robyn informed me that I'd be sharing the three-quarter bed with a complete stranger. A male one called Chinese Rob. Worried about how I'd explain this rather unorthodox and unappealing sleeping arrangement to Graham, I instead opted for a lower bunk in the female dormitory which looked out over a tall chimney from which white smoke rose lazily into a steel-grey sky.

'Oh yeah, that's a crematorium,' said Kayo, a burly six-foot-tall Aussie reclining on the bunk above. Seeing the worried look on my face at the thought of breathing in barbecued bodies throughout the night, Kayo confessed she'd been joking. The chimney belonged to a temple, and the smoke came from burning 'ghost money', not from incinerating the former hosts of the ghosts. Also known as 'hell money', this fake cash was tossed into a giant furnace in the temple grounds, along with cardboard models of cars, TVs and fridges to provide worshippers' ancestors with life's luxuries in the hereafter.

Jumbo jetlagged, I unlaced my shoes, swung my legs onto the

mattress and sank gratefully onto my bed only to sit bolt upright as the room began to shake.

'Don't worry,' said Kayo, 'this building is so badly built that it wobbles every time a bus goes by.' Little comforted by that, I drifted off to sleep.

Once rested, I felt ready to venture out into the noisy, smog-filled world outside. But first I had to brave the bathroom. It was wet from floor to ceiling because there was no shower curtain and the drain in the centre of the floor was choked with matted hair. I imagined athlete's foot crawling up the broken-tiled walls. A sign above the cistern ominously warned: 'No flush paper in toilet or will block'. Instead, to my disgust, soiled paper had to be deposited into an open wastepaper basket. The sight of a bin overflowing with shit-smeared loo roll – and a two-inch twitching cockroach beside it – was enough to have me screaming for help.

'Robyn! Come here! I need to use the toilet and there's a huge roach in here.' Robyn ambled over from the adjacent balcony, a cigarette in one hand and a can of Taiwan Beer in the other.

'Please get rid of it,' I begged.

'What's it worth?' she said, grinning evilly.

'I'll give you a can of deodorant,' I pleaded. The Lonely Planet had advised that this was one of several commodities, along with tampons and shoes any bigger than a size four, that were almost unobtainable in Taiwan, so I hoped it would prove a suitable bribe. Robyn coolly stepped on the monster bug and kicked its flattened corpse into a corner, allowing me to use the loo unmenaced.

I was still coming to terms with the bathroom situation when I took the lift down to street level and went in search of dinner. I hadn't realised that I'd come to Taipei at the worst possible time. The city was in the throes of constructing its first underground rail system, and four out of every six traffic lanes had been ripped up to excavate the tunnels. Water was sprayed over the roads to damp down the dust, turning the broken surface into sludge-filled potholes. This meant crossing the road was dirty as well as dangerous. The betel-nut-spittle-spattered pavements were no better: their loose slabs jutted upwards at crazy angles as if the undead had recently emerged from beneath them and there was a jumble of parked scooters whose jagged mudguards and rusty exhaust pipes made a hazardous obstacle course for anyone foolish enough not to have had a tetanus shot.

Nonetheless, I was thrilled to be in the Far East, a region I'd only seen depicted in Bond films and on travel posters. When I caught a glimpse of a garishly painted dragon on a nearby temple roof and inhaled the intoxicating incense drifting from enormous coils suspended from its rafters, I got goosebumps from the excitement and exoticism of it all. Coming from Cape Town I appreciated every difference, from the massive to the most mundane. It was liberating to be able to walk alone at night without worrying about my safety and a novelty to be able to buy beer from the 7-Eleven at any time of day or night. Scared of getting lost, I didn't wander further than the nearby McDonald's where I bought my first ever Big Mac, eager to try the iconic foodstuff that apartheid-related sanctions had barred from reaching South Africa. I was expecting a taste sensation, but my burger was vaguely minty, like toothpaste. Once I'd picked it apart, closer inspection revealed that the Colgate flavour came from its gherkin slices.

'How on earth did McDonald's become a worldwide phenomenon by selling such strange-tasting food?' I wondered.

Little did I know that, for hygiene reasons, I would soon become a regular.

My first paid job in Taipei saw Graham and I both becoming doctors at the same time. In the week he received his doctorate from the University of Cape Town, I awarded myself the title of 'Dr' at an international conference. Taipei Hostel acted as an informal employment agency for companies wanting to hire foreigners for promotional work, and for language schools desperate to find supply English teachers. Would-be employers would ring Ivy who would announce their request to the travellers gathered in the hostel kitchen-lounge-reception.

One phoned-in request was for a dozen or so hostel-dwellers to masquerade as foreign delegates at an alternative medicine conference. The chance to earn the equivalent of US$35 for three hours' work was too good to miss, and whomever happened to be around at the time scampered away to smarten up. As most of us were travellers, this proved something of a challenge. My 'Sunday best' was a brown handmade shift dress I'd bought at Cape Town's Greenmarket Square flea market and a pair of battered leather lace-ups so old that my pinkie toes poked out of the holes my feet had worn through them.

'This will have to do,' I thought. 'I'll have to pretend I'm a scruffy academic. There's plenty of them around.'

In the lobby of the conference centre we were fêted with orchids and jasmine tea served by smiling young girls in floor-length silk *cheongsams*, after which we were issued with sashes and rosettes and instructed to sit on the dais among the genuine delegates. Prayers were offered by a Catholic priest and a saffron-robed Buddhist monk, and we stood to attention as a couple of delegates warbled through their respective national anthems. It was then time to solemnly light the flame of eternal truth, which was ironic given that half of us were there under false pretences. We gathered round an over-sized copper oil lamp and one delegate after another tried, and failed, to ignite it with a plastic lighter featuring a mildly pornographic photo of a buxom, topless woman. After five awkward minutes of fumbling the attempt was abandoned and, the photo op ruined, we returned to our seats.

'Welcome ladies and gentlemen and distinguished delegates from around the world to the 24th World Congress of Alternative Medicine. We are so honoured that you are here with us today. Please can I now ask our distinguished foreign delegates to say a few words of introduction.'

'Shit, I wasn't expecting a speaking part,' I thought, panicking. 'We are so busted.'

When it was my turn, I had the inspired idea to speak in Afrikaans so that no one would understand what I said, or want to engage me in conversation afterwards. I introduced myself and said how delighted I was to be there.

'*My naam is Doctor Lisa Jackson en ek is van Suid Afrika. Ek is baie bly*

19

om hier met julle vandag te wees.'

I wished them health, wealth and luck and then made my way down the line, shaking the hands of the assorted alternative therapists. The other ersatz delegates also did us proud, claiming to be naturopaths, homeopaths, reflexologists and the like. Danish Magnus put on an especially impressive and daring performance. The sole hostel resident who'd managed to rustle up a jacket and tie, he boldly lied that he was a neurobiologist from Copenhagen and then recited a short impromptu poem he'd written about 'The park that is / Denmark'.

The introductions over, we were shown slides graphically illustrating how acupuncture had cured a man's haemorrhoids, gotten rid of another's man-boobs and been used to anaesthetise a woman undergoing surgery to remove a half-pound tumour from her face. We were also treated to an image of the organiser's bottom pin-cushioned with needles, presumably to show us what a 'good jab' his acupuncturist had done.

On the bus back to the hostel, delightedly counting the money in the envelopes we'd been discreetly handed on our way out, we congratulated ourselves on our Oscar-winning performances. We'd actually managed to pull it off. No one had been asked any tricky questions, and the real delegates had all seemed pretty impressed by our credentials.

The next evening, sitting on the balcony sipping some of our pay away, Danish Magnus ambled in, his guitar slung across his back, his trademark flat cap set back on his head and a roll-up hanging from his lower lip. He pulled up a stool.

'I have something to tell you guys,' he said sheepishly. 'I've just finished busking in the subway, and guess what? One of the *real* delegates from yesterday walked past and recognised me. I was really embarrassed and had no choice but to confess. I could hardly pretend that, as an eminent Danish neurobiologist, I'd need to sing for my supper!'

Singing along on the hostel balcony with Danish Magnus had made one thing as plain to me as a bowl of boiled white rice: I needed to be able to strum and squawk along to more than the opening three chords of ABBA's *Fernando* if I was to make it as a busker. I'd also ditched the idea of begging almost the moment I arrived as I'd seen several genuine unfortunates, such as the shirtless man who sat each day on the overpass bridge, his torso studded with marble-sized lumps. Instead, I found freelance work for five hours a day, six days a week as a sub-editor at the *China News*.

It was my job to render newspaper articles written in Mandarin – that had been translated into 'Chinglish' by Chinese interns with a morbid fear of spellcheck – into intelligible features in English. I soon concluded it was quicker to interpret what was meant than it was to track down and interrogate the interns as their English, though exponentially better than my non-existent Mandarin, was patchy. In desperation, I ended up manufacturing 'fake news' decades before that term was invented. Relying on guesswork, intuition and every scrap of knowledge I possessed, I did my best to decipher copy that covered concepts and subjects I'd never previously encountered. What in the world were the 'alcoholic bombs' that were 'a serious threat to social order'? Ten minutes of head scratching later I twigged the translator meant Molotov cocktails. The eight 'dummies' who'd 'burglarised' a home and used a baseball bat to mug a passing motorcyclist? Turns out they were criminals who were all deaf and dumb. And Sweet Potato Monkey? Apparently, it was the nickname of an armed gangster responsible for a one-man crime wave.

I lived in fear of the newspaper's forbidding owner from whose corner office, despite the closed door, I could often hear employees' sobs and wails. Working conditions were Dickensian and included no annual leave for the first year (and a mere five days per annum thereafter), no pension or medical insurance, and half-pay if one had the misfortune to become ill. It was, as one *China News* reporter told me, 'enough to plug your heartstrings'.

I landed an additional long-term job with the aid of the Taipei Hostel balcony, where hostel-dwellers congregated day and night. Whether you required help deciphering the bus timetable, wished to join in a sing-song or needed to get your hands on a doctored photocopy of someone else's university degree certificate (a prerequisite for some English teaching jobs) the balcony was where it was at. A stolen flashing roadwork sign and string of Christmas lights lent it a *Saturday Night Fever* ambience. When it came to my interview for work as a kindergarten teacher it was the perfect venue for practising the phoney American accent I knew was essential. Taiwan conducted most of its trade with the US, so the accent most in demand was not the Queen's English but the variant spoken across The Pond. Sadly the South African-accented English I spoke was not highly sought after. Several real Americans coached me in the nuances of the language and gave me tips on questions I might be asked about sports teams, politics and culture so that my cover story of having lived in America for a year would ring true.

'You need to remember to say "toe-may-toe" not "toe-mah-toe",' said Kent. 'And that your pavement is our sidewalk.'

'Our main sports are basketball and baseball,' Cheryl told me. 'If you're going to say that you lived in New York, the local teams are the Knicks and the Yankees. And the mayor is David Dinkins.'

In the event, I wasn't asked any probing questions. All I had to do was audition for the position by singing (with actions) nursery rhymes such as *Row, Row, Row Your Boat* in an American accent until I was hoarse. When I got the job two days later, I celebrated on the balcony – where else? – with a tin of Taiwan Beer.

I loved teaching at the kindergarten, probably because I had a lot in common with the three-year-olds. For starters, we couldn't read a word (or character) in each other's language – our shared vocabulary amounted to about seven words. And we all disliked Mercy, the petite, unsmiling Taiwanese teaching assistant assigned to mind me, who was unbelievably harsh, towards both me and the kids. If a child didn't grasp what I was trying to teach them, Mercy would prevent them from going out to play until they did. And on three occasions, when I was five minutes late due to gridlocked rush-hour traffic, she got the whole class to chant 'You're late, Miss,' five times before I was allowed to commence the day's lessons. I was actually rather surprised she didn't keep *me* in at break-time as punishment.

The children were adorable, and often made me laugh. The

favourite fruit of most of the class? Lemons! When I asked one boy, Eddie, what he liked to eat for breakfast, he said 'snake'. He may well have been telling the truth.

'Sounds more like a chundergarden than a kindergarten,' commented my dormmate Kayo upon hearing my tales of how frequently the children threw up, sometimes on me.

'Why are the children so often sick?' I asked Mercy as I mopped up beef-flecked vomit from the table.

'It's because they're not used to eating beef,' she explained, insisting the poor kid who'd vomited finish her food. Mercy by name, but not by nature.

I found it strange that the children were in the habit of crying soundlessly. Once, for example, when we were singing *Old MacDonald Had a Farm*, I suggested that on that farm he had a lion, as we do in sunny South Africa. The kids took this as their cue to violently maul each other (unprompted by me, I merely clawed the air), which inevitably resulted in a few injuries. But did the scratched and bruised children cry out in pain? No, they merely made agonised, tearful faces. The Silence of the Kindie Kids.

The major downside to my kindergarten job was my constant fear of losing it. One of the other English teachers, a *real* American, had been fired, and I wasn't too sure how long it would be until I'd be unmasked as an imposter and shown the door. So I did my utmost to impress the headmaster by serving the children chopped-up fruit on toothpicks to teach them the English words for orange, apple and dragon fruit, and wrapping individual chocolate Smarties in layers of newspaper for a game of pass-the-parcel so the kids could learn the English words for colours. I lived in utter dread of deportation, too. Whereas my position at the newspaper was semi-legal, this one definitely wasn't, and none other than Kayo had been arrested, fingerprinted, interrogated and forced to leave the country after she'd been caught teaching English illegally. Deterrence was big in Taiwan: photographs of suspected criminals, manacled and sobbing, were frequently published in the newspapers. I didn't want to end up like *that* in the *China News*.

Despite Kayo's assurances that deportation merely meant a three-day sojourn in Hong Kong while applying for another Taiwanese visa, I had daily visions of the kindergarten door being kicked in by the police and being led out in chains to a chorus of wails – silent, of course – from my much-loved three-year-olds.

The 'Dear John' letter

 It says a lot about Graham that he was happy for me to go to Taiwan on my own even though we'd only been married for 18 months. It wasn't because our marriage was so rock-solid harmonious: when we were wed, given the tempestuous nature of our relationship, I'm sure several of our friends thought 'I give it a year'. Even my mother was forever imploring us to stop that 'squaddling', as she called it. I was incredibly headstrong, having grown up idolising feisty literary heroines such as Sybylla Melvyn in *My Brilliant Career* and Lyndall in *The Story of an African Farm*. Despite coming from a country where at that time a man pushing a pram or supermarket trolley elicited disapproving looks, I was determined to have a relationship where I was treated as an equal. As a Brit, Graham was far better able to cope with my unconventional attitude than most South African men would have been, but it did lead to some heated 'discussions', some extending well into the early hours. While still dating, we broke up for several months but continued seeing each other almost every day – the main result of this altered relationship status was that I no longer accompanied him and his friends to happy hour at The Pig 'n Whistle student pub on Monday nights. In the event it was more challenging being apart than being together, so after a year-long engagement we got married.

A South African *Cosmopolitan* colleague had warned that the first year of marriage is the hardest. 'Why are you telling me this? It's going to be bliss,' I remember thinking. Thank goodness she did, as it was tougher than either of us expected. Graham and I fought about everything: how often music should be played ('All the time,' said Graham, 'Never,' said I), what we should eat (vegetable stew every single night suited Graham just fine), how often the flat should be cleaned (every 30 minutes, according to Graham) and about how we spent our spare time.

'You never suggest going anywhere, Graham,' I'd cry. 'If it wasn't for me, you'd stay indoors reading philosophy books all day. I want to go out and *do* things.'

'When was the last time you polished the bathroom tiles?' he'd reply, in an attempt to defend himself.

'We're not talking about housework right now, Graham, we're discussing how happy you are for our life to be boring.'

'Yes, but answer me honestly, have you ever polished the tiles?'

In an attempt to cajole him into becoming more adventurous, I took to calling him 'Pilot Light' because he never went out. Sadly, he never took the hint and simply said he found the nickname incredibly funny.

About the only thing we hadn't argued about was my reluctance to take Graham's surname.

'That's absolutely fine by me – I wouldn't want to have to change my name either. But what will we do when we have kids? Will they take your surname or mine?'

I hadn't thought of that, but we hit on a solution: we would double-barrel our names and become the Jackson-Williamses, which would give us an air of nobility and stop our children querying whether they had the same father. When we discovered that it was a legal requirement to publish a notice to this effect in the *Government Gazette*, which would be a costly bureaucratic hoop-jumping exercise, we agreed I'd keep my maiden name.

'Doesn't that show a lack of commitment on your part?' asked one of my varsity friends.

'Speak to me in 20 years' time,' I replied.

When I went round to say goodbye to Graham's friends before leaving for Taipei, one of them had looked somewhat surprised.

'She's going to Taiwan on her own? You're not getting divorced already?' he asked Graham when I was out of earshot.

I'd been blissfully unaware of his misgivings as I excitedly packed for my trip, but once I arrived in Taiwan, the first time I'd been away from Graham for any length of time since I was 19, it became clear to me how much energy I'd expended on arguing. In Taipei, I did what I pleased, when I pleased: I never had to listen to The Beatles, ate in McDonald's every day and never once polished a tile. And I was surrounded by people who did exciting things, dangerous things, hilarious things, and who were happy to tell me about them on the hostel balcony.

'I saw hundreds of people squatting down crapping together at dawn in Bombay,' Kiwi John told a group of us one balmy night up on the balcony. 'You have to go to Chowpatty Beach.'

'India's utterly amazing, it's so spiritual… and obscure,' agreed Melissa, a gorgeous ex-bar-hostess-cum-model who often wore chopsticks in her hair and to whom, I later discovered, almost everything was 'obscure'. 'And I adored Nagarkot in Nepal: you can see Mount Everest from there. You have to go to the Restaurant at the End of the Universe, it's an obscure café on the edge of a cliff and it has huge windows overlooking the Himalayas. When you're there, you feel like you're sitting right on the edge of the world.'

'Yeah, that sounds cool,' said Claudie, a brash American who told us she'd written a book called *A Thai Vampire in New York*. 'But my best trip was the trek I did in Chiang Mai. We got to go rafting and rode elephants. And we spent a very cold and uncomfortable night on the floor of a hill tribe hut. Whatever you do, don't smoke opium if they offer you any. My boyfriend did and he kept the whole hut awake all night with the sound of his vomiting.'

'How embarrassing,' said Robyn. 'That reminds me of the two Americans who came to Taipei after cycling around Vietnam. One of them had been sitting on the loo in a rural hostel and suddenly found herself wedged bodily into the bowl with her upper teeth embedded in the wooden seat.'

The balcony fell silent. 'What on earth happened?' ask Danish Magnus, lighting up a cigarette. 'Someone on the floor above had come crashing through the ceiling and landed squarely on her shoulders like a 140-pound human neck pillow,' explained Robyn.

We all knew that we shouldn't have laughed but we did, long and hard, picturing the poor girl trying to call for help with a toilet seat stuck to her teeth.

The more time I spent on the balcony, the more uneasy I became. When Graham joined me I didn't want to spend a few more weeks in Taiwan and then head straight to England. I wanted to have my own travel experiences instead of listening in slack-jawed silence or cackling as other people told theirs.

It was with a heavy heart, then, that I took out one of the aerogrammes I'd purchased to correspond with loved ones back home, and set pen to paper, writing my first-ever 'Dear John' letter.

'Dear Graham,' I wrote. 'I hope you're well and that you can see the light at the end of the tunnel with your PhD. Do let me know what date your graduation is likely to be. I'm still having a fab time in Taiwan – there isn't space here to write down all the amazing things I've seen and done so I'm keeping a travel journal so you can read all about my adventures. I know you're keen to find a job and get settled in the UK but I've met the most incredible people in the hostel and the traveller's tales they've told me have got me thinking. I don't really know how to say this, and I know I said we could go straight to England after Taiwan, but I really, really want to go travelling in Southeast Asia. It's the one time in our lives where we won't be tied down by our jobs, a mortgage or children and I truly think we should seize the chance while we can. Once you get here, you'll see that what I'm suggesting makes sense. Please give it some serious thought. Good luck with the thesis. Get here soon! Missing you like mad. All my love, Lisa xxx'

Two-and-a-half weeks later, I received a reply.

'I'll think about it.'

The 'group sex' pencil

 I had to sell Priscilla to pay for my airfare to Taiwan. After seven years of faithful service it was hard bidding goodbye to our trusty white 1974 Volkswagen Beetle. For the first three years I hadn't the money to get her professionally serviced and, though I drove her until her exhaust corroded away and her tyres wore through to the canvas, she never once let me down. I got more than I paid for her, which was enough to cover a flight to Taipei.

Five weeks after Lisa flew to Taiwan – weeks spent tying up loose ends in Cape Town and attending my PhD graduation ceremony – I joined her.

Lisa met me at the airport. 'It's so good to see you again Leecy. The past few weeks have been really tough without you. I've missed you so much.'

'I've missed you, too,' replied Lisa, taking me by the hand. 'But it's been such fun here. You're going to love it.'

Lisa brought me to the hostel, where she'd bagged a private room so I didn't have to relive boarding-school dormitory life, and familiarised me with the location of the most important facilities: the pavement 'slop shops' where most hostel residents ate and the 7-Eleven for beer. I immediately threw myself into the business of finding as many hours of work as I could. Thankfully, it didn't take me long to land two regular jobs teaching English, one at the main Post Office and the other at Learing Powep, a language school across the road from Taipei Hostel. Learning Power, which charged US$750 for a three-week business-English course, had clearly not deemed it necessary to spend a single cent on proofreading its enormous advertising hoarding.

One of my students was Peter Lin, whose enthusiasm for learning English was matched by his devotion to promoting the 'revolutionary' Oggi pencil that, he assured me, represented the cutting edge of propelling-pencil technology.

'This pencil cost over US$2 million to develop,' said Peter, 'and it available in 39 shapes and colour. It will be big-time success.'

Peter proudly demonstrated how it worked. I couldn't discern anything revolutionary in it. He clicked the top and it propelled fresh lead, as a propelling pencil should. It wasn't exactly going to grab a flag and start singing *La Marseillaise*. There was one hiccup, however. Peter, not being a native English speaker, had a most unfortunate difficulty in pronouncing the name of the invention he was employed to sell: 'Oggi' came out as 'orgy'. He couldn't fathom why his customers would blanch noticeably before asking, 'You mean you called your pencil "Group Sex"?' I successfully corrected his pronunciation, but it wasn't enough to salvage the group sex pencil, which sank without trace.

Peter's classmates were Joseph, Jenny and Sarah – Taiwanese helpfully adopted English first names to make it easier for Westerners to address them without getting tongue-tied. I didn't have any teaching materials, so I ad-libbed. A lot. We'd talk about Western customs and etiquette, such as how to shake hands (which we practised), how to eat a multi-course meal (outside-in with the cutlery) and which glass was for red wine and which for white. That sort of thing. I believed it would be genuinely useful for them to know and they lapped it up. Joseph had visited the US on business and it transpired he had slept under the bedspread but on top of the blanket, which was my cue to discuss how hotel bed linen was layered and should be used. They asked all sorts of questions and questioned my answers.

I learned a lot from my students. My class taught me, for instance, that Mandarin speakers pronounce 't's' as 'd's' and 'p's' as 'b's'. Therefore 'Taipei' was 'Daibei', which finally explained why my fellow hostellers affectionately referred to the city as 'Diapers'. I'd mistakenly thought that nickname had been inspired by the shitty state of its streets. The students also taught me that Taiwanese people were uncomfortable with the English 'th' sound, not only because it was difficult for them to pronounce (coming out closer to 'zse') but also because it needed them to protrude the tip of their tongue between their teeth, a social no-no, like blowing your nose on a linen napkin in a restaurant. When I asked them to repeat 'The American couple went to the theatre' they'd put one hand over their mouth and muffle 'Zse American couple went to zse zseatre'.

One evening we discussed humour. Joseph asked me to explain what people in England found funny. I struggled to answer. Not everyone is a Monty Python fan, bawdy humour is not universally appreciated and puns are a minority taste. I did my best. My students then wanted to test their appreciation of Western jokes and asked me to tell them one or two. I played it as safe as I could while still giving them a genuine flavour of English humour – so no lame 'knock-knock' jokes but something less ribald than might be heard in a rugby-club changing room.

'What's brown and sticky?'

They looked at one another as though it was a joke one of them might sometime, somewhere have heard. Then they looked to me for enlightenment.

'A stick,' I told them.

Perplexed silence. Not a snigger or a smile. Okay, I thought, I'll try another one.

'Why did the chicken cross the road?' Silence again, though Peter looked contemplative and Sarah slowly shook her head from side to side.

'To get to the other side. Why did the baby cross the road?' I expected at least one of them to refer to the need for the infant to get to the other side, but again they were mute.

'Because,' I went on, 'it was stapled to the chicken's leg.'

Peter, Joseph and Sarah looked mildly quizzical, but Jenny's face clearly showed that she was processing what I had said. She looked up at the ceiling, frowned and put her forefinger to her lips before declaiming, using her hands to capture the relative sizes of babies and poultry: 'No, no. Baby big, chicken small. *Turkey*! Turkey big. Turkey can carry baby.'

Oh, how I laughed.

Two tribes

 There were two distinct camps in Taipei Hostel: the slave-and-save tribe and the work-and-wizz-it-up-against-a-wall tribe. The former, whom we dubbed the SAS, had come to Taiwan to earn as much money as possible, whereas the latter drank, drugged and partied away whatever they earned. Back in the early 1990s, teaching in Taiwan was lucrative: an hour's wages were enough to pay for accommodation, bus transport, a daily tin of beer and eat-as-much-as-you-like slop-shop nosh from the row of four street-food shacks across the road from the hostel. Every additional hour we worked was pure profit.

Luke was a member of the SAS. A lanky strawberry-blond Brit

with the direction sense of a mole, he was in Taipei to study Mandarin as part of his degree. Luke could tell you what 'thermonuclear warfare' was in Chinese but struggled to translate the more useful 'Turn left at the traffic lights' and 'Beef noodles, please'. He revealed the limits of his linguistic ability when he got us hopelessly lost on a Sunday outing to tick off some of Taipei's sights: the National Palace Museum, housing almost 700,000 Chinese cultural treasures that had been relocated ('looted' the Chinese Communist Party would say) to Taiwan when Chiang Kai-shek's Nationalists fled Mao's Communists on the mainland; the Taiwan Provincial Museum, whose most extraordinary exhibit was a panda with a 'Made in Taiwan' label on its bottom (the first and only time we'd seen a stuffed toy in a natural history museum); and the Taipei Fine Arts Museum, where a half dozen upturned Perspex tables labelled 'Disjointed Harmony' were 'art'. Despite Luke repeatedly asking for directions, in the end it was Lisa who figured out how to get to both museums by poring over our guidebook's near-incomprehensible map.

Derek was a nicely brought up, well-educated hostel guest. Originally from South Africa, he was backpacking solo around Asia. One evening, after relaxing with a few beers, he disclosed why he was travelling alone and would soon be heading home. In Thailand he'd met Paloma, an alcoholic, suicidal, violent, vengeful Spanish divorcee. Theirs had been a brief but tempestuous relationship.

'During our final fight, Paloma burnt all my clothes, stole all my money, smashed up my Walkman and camera, hid my passport and tried to stab me,' Derek confided to the balcony.

Yehuda, a mousy-looking, bespectacled 20-something Israeli, was another hostel stalwart. He'd lost his English-teaching job when too many students complained they couldn't understand his heavily accented and often ungrammatical English. We suspected it was Yehuda who'd penned a reply to someone's advert on the hostel's whiteboard behind reception, which was used both as a 'jobs vacant' noticeboard and to sell second-hand items.

'Lonely Planet travel guide to Japan for sale — NT$150 [US$6] or nearest offer'

'If you can't afford NT$150 you shouldn't go to Japan you frugle [sic] bugger'

To which a third hostel inmate had added: 'This person teaches English in Taiwan?!'

Yehuda's hobby was hanging around the hostel lounge waiting for 'victims' on whom he could practise his kung-fu. The unwary would emerge from the lift to find a whooping Yehuda in full flight as he perfected the roundhouse and scissor kicks he hoped would be his ticket to movie stardom in Hong Kong.

Other SAS members included Swiss Andy and Marianne, a couple from a small Alpine village near Zurich who funded their world travels by making and selling jewellery crafted from coins. Marianne had a wicked sense of humour and a raucous laugh to go with it, and her linguistic malapropisms were legendary. Fascinated by the English term 'lager lout', she kept misremembering it as 'bottle lout' and 'stout lout'. And she always referred to vomiting as 'throwing over'.

'The first time I ever eat salted butter I threw over,' she said in her charmingly Swiss-German accented gravelly voice. 'We don't eat butter with salt in Switzerland. And this one old man, in our willage, he threw over so many times after drinking that he lose three sets of dentures.'

But, of course, the work-and-wizz-it-up-against-a-wall tribe were far more colourful. Kim, who worked as a hostess in a karaoke bar, was rumoured to be a heroin addict. When in the hostel she spent all her time vacantly staring out of a corridor window and applying concealer to her face, which was covered in black, cigarette-burn-shaped sores. Kim didn't talk much, and people tended to avoid her. She looked slightly piratical because she wore a headscarf and kept a large, scary-looking knife tucked into the back of her Thai fisherman's trousers.

Susan, a Mormon from Utah, was another alleged addict who'd fried her brain by doing too many drugs. She often retired to her room for a week at a time, emerging occasionally to fetch drinking water from the cooler.

Then there was Jeb, a genial 45-going-on-70 American who'd

paralysed half his body in the 1960s – possibly through drugs – and who told us he enjoyed reading the introductions of books. He'd read the intro to *Great Expectations* no fewer than seven times. Likeable Jeb may have been, but he had an unstable streak, and had once brandished a machete-like kitchen knife and threatened to stab anyone in the hostel lounge who tried to change the TV channel. No one dared. But no one tried to take the knife from him either. Jeb also had a secret: he struggled to control his bowels. Until she twigged that it was all Jeb's doing, Robyn spent several weeks cleaning up trails of diarrhoea in the bathroom and the passage outside in the mistaken belief that Walter the Devil Cat, the savage stray she'd adopted, was responsible.

Robert, Jeb's sidekick, was an unpleasant drunk who sank a can or three of Taiwan Beer for breakfast. He once memorably asked another hostel inmate whether he knew what it felt like to be shot with a shotgun and, when the reply was negative, slung a handful of small change in the unfortunate man's face, exclaiming 'Well, you fucking do now!'

Khalid, a Pakistani 'painter and labourer', was an enigma. He had the smoothest hands we'd ever seen and never had a fleck of paint or speck of dirt on him. We suspected he worked in 'import-export', possibly of the snuff he kept sniffing. His preferred hangout was the wild nightclub FUBAR (fucked up beyond all recognition) where he spent many hours buying all and sundry eye-wateringly pricey drinks, supposedly on a labourer's wage. A Muslim, Khalid told me that he only ever drank alcohol when in Taiwan and spent his days in fear of accidentally eating something that had been cooked in pork fat.

'That kind of food's no good,' he'd say, giggling.

Khalid always seemed to be avoiding someone: the police because he'd overstayed his visa by one-and-a-half *years*; his Pakistani friends since they were forever trying to cadge money and booze off him; his Pakistani enemies, a gang of whom had lain in wait for him for a week at the end of the hostel lane; and his father, who'd managed to track him down in Taipei after three years of radio silence. Lisa and I didn't much care for Khalid's friends. Two of them had allegedly been clever enough to escape from Taiwanese jails and stupid enough to get recaptured when they stopped to ask a policeman for directions.

The most notorious hostel inhabitant was Aussie Cliff, whose criminal exploits made it into the pages of the *China News*. A craggy 50-something, his deeply pock-marked complexion made him a doppelganger for the Panamanian strongman Manuel 'Pineapple Face' Noriega. A 'friend' of his had broken into a hospital pharmacy to steal drugs but, off his face at the time, had been quickly apprehended. Unfortunately for Aussie Cliff, the police figured out that the pharmacy didn't stock marijuana, a small pouch of which was discovered among all the stolen painkillers. The 'friend' promptly confessed that Aussie Cliff was his dealer and helpfully informed the police of his whereabouts, which led to the ill-fated chap being arrested in Taipei Hostel at 2am one morning and charged with possession. Released on bail, he promptly skipped the country and fled back to Australia where, hostel hearsay had it, he went to live with his mum.

The police raided the hostel again one evening in an attempt to root out those who'd overstayed their visas. All that can be said of their efforts is that they were thoroughly un-thorough. Unfailingly polite, they asked everyone to fetch their passports, but neglected to prevent anyone from leaving the building, giving any visa violators ample opportunity to slip away. English Fred – dubbed 'Dead Fred' because of his almost translucent pale visage, nocturnal lifestyle and soap-dodging habits, which lent him a faint whiff of decomposition – couldn't be bothered to do even that. Having slipped out of reception, he simply crammed himself under his bunk bed until the raid ended. Hostel inmates with nothing to hide posed for photos with the smiling officers. The police left empty-handed even though, by rights, several people including Khalid, who'd left early for yet another night in FUBAR, should have been cuffed and carted away.

Besides the odd day of sight-seeing, festivals were just about our only respite from slaving and saving. The calendar was peppered with occasions for Taiwanese to perform lion and dragon dances and paint the sky with fireworks. It was astounding how flags, bunting, posters and millions of fairy lights could transform Taipei from a drab, gritty building site by day into a brilliantly lit, neon-splashed carnival by night.

One sticky evening we attended the Pudu Festival, a celebration held to appease the 'hungry ghosts': as there's no food in hell, the souls of the departed are let out one day a year to feast among the living. The Taiwanese counterpart to Halloween, Pudu didn't involve costumed kids risking early onset tooth decay by trick or treating but rather thousands of water lanterns floating down the Tamsui River, deafening processions of drummers and bus-length dragons made of strings of lanterns dancing amid a rain of ghost money. It was fascinating to see the way that Taiwan, a country known for its robust economic growth and technological prowess, could meld modernity with a centuries-old belief in ghosts with the munchies.

Voodoo vendors

 Grandma Mary used to jab me in the back with a knife if I dared to slump when eating— okay, it was a butter knife, but a knife nonetheless — and placing my elbows on the table was, in her eyes, a crime akin to mugging old dears like herself. It was just not done. Not ever. So my paternal grandmother would have passionately disagreed with Jeff 'The Frugal Gourmet' Smith when he wrote: 'I prefer the Chinese method of eating... you can do anything at the table except arm wrestle.' Fresh off the plane from South Africa, on my first foreign foray since I was 13, I was taken aback by Taiwanese table manners. Burping, slurping and tossing bones and seafood shells onto the table were all considered perfectly polite, as was lifting your bowl of noodles to your mouth all the better to shovel food speedily into it.

My maternal grandmother, whom we affectionately called Oumie, wouldn't have batted an eyelid. Oumie was big on indulgence and not all that concerned with discipline, and would remonstrate with my mother whenever she had the temerity to chastise me and my sister Loren, her angelic blonde granddaughters. Oumie's favourite story, which I now know to be fictitious, involved Paul Kruger,

President of the Transvaal Republic during the Second Boer War, taking tea with Queen Victoria. Kruger horrified the Palace courtiers by pouring the tea from his cup into his saucer and drinking from it. Victoria, in a show of gracious good manners, followed suit. As children, Loren and I loved drinking tea sweetened with condensed milk, seated with Oumie on *riempie* (rawhide) chairs round the dining room table, giggling away as we took tea like royalty, sipping straight from the saucer. It was an act of micro-rebellion we revelled in. I'm sure Oumie's advice would've been, 'In Rome, do as the Romans do, and in Taipei it would be rude *not* to slurp your food.'

Taiwanese devil-may-care table manners were the least of it; the foodstuffs I encountered often turned my stomach. If she'd seen the food on offer, Graham's Aunty Doreen – who back in 1970s London had refused to eat spaghetti 'because it's foreign' – would have been, quite frankly, terrified. Especially if she'd encountered the 'voodoo vendors', locals manning mobile carts selling skewered duck hearts, congealed blood jelly, sautéed squid beaks, stewed milkfish intestines, grey-green thousand-year eggs supposedly boiled in horse urine and ghoulish bowls of chicken-scrap soup: clawed feet, oily strips of pimply skin, and shrunken gelatinous heads, Mohican combs and all. By far the most nauseating foodstuff they served was stinky tofu: brown squares of fermented tofu that looked like chunks of fatberg scraped from a sewer and smelled like a blend of toe cheese and rotting rubbish. The only carts I bought from were those selling satay-style chicken and whole grilled squid, which were both lip-smackingly tasty.

The police were constantly playing cat-and-mouse with these unlicensed vendors because, quite rightly as it turned out, they were viewed as a health risk. One day, as I walked from the bus stop to the kindergarten, I glanced into a double doorway and saw a street-food cart alongside a massive axe embedded in a wooden chopping block thick with congealed blood and feathers. It was obviously used to slaughter and chop up chickens. As I stopped to peer in, countless cockroaches the size of small mice scuttled from the doorway towards me, pursued by a wispily bearded man, bent nearly double with age, who was using his walking stick to crush as many as he could. He'd been fumigating his food-preparation area, and very likely the food in it, too. I didn't eat from a Taiwanese street cart ever again.

My encounters with the so-called 'slop shops' were similarly unhappy. Here, portions of freshly cooked meat and vegetables could be ordered using the 'point and pay' system and then enjoyed at one of several rickety tables set up on the pavement. Parisian boulevard-style eating this was not. Mangy and crippled dogs nosed through the garbage piled up alongside the stalls. In Taiwan, dogs were often bought by parents to amuse their kids over the holidays and then callously tossed out onto the street at the end of the summer to fend for themselves. The *China News* reported there were a million 'strayed dogs' on the island. I could have told the newspaper that a considerable number of these mutts lived by the slop-shops on Linsen North Road.

It was after seeing one stallholder giving each greasy plastic plate a cursory dunk in a bucket of filthy water before issuing it to her next customer that I became a convert to McDonald's, right next door. I preferred eating my meals out of clean polystyrene boxes in air-conditioned surroundings where the food was prepared out of sight, even if the burgers tasted like toothpaste and the fries, once cold, like ear wax. Inevitably, after eating McDonald's three times a day – washed down by one-litre cup-buckets of Coke – for four months, I became the proud owner of the complete collection of wind-up Happy Meal toys and had gained so much weight that I could barely see over my plump cheekbones. I was the original *Super Size Me* and, as Graham charmingly put it, by the time we left Taiwan I looked like 'a Big Mac in boots'.

Even buying food or drinks from the 7-Eleven could prove hazardous. If you weren't careful you could end up with beer tea, papaya milk or pumpkin drink. Or Kaoliang fermented sorghum 'wine': 58 per cent proof, 100 per cent disgusting. Selecting ice cream was a lottery: the lollies all masqueraded behind innocuous wrappers waiting for the hot and unwary. You'd purchase one, take a bite, discover it tasted of avocado, or beans, or pumpkin or corn on the cob, and nine times out of ten rush from the store to spit it out into the gutter. Then there were the hot dogs with cream sauce – lovely to look at but in reality a revolting mixture of anaemic, gristly sausage 'meat' and semi-sweet white sludge. About the only 7-Eleven food I could tolerate was *gua bao*, white steamed buns filled with pork. The inmates in the hostel joked that they were stuffed with 'pork fur', so that put me off them a bit, too.

Pork fur paled into insignificance when compared with what was on offer at the Huaxi Street Night Market. A charnel house better known as 'Snake Alley', it was famed for its snake-meat restaurants. There were several venues in this arcaded market in the middle of a red light district where customers could select a live snake for supper. Once chosen, the reptile was suspended by its head from a wire hoop and, with one hand holding its tail end and the other a scalpel-sharp knife, the 'chef' slit the creature from top to tip, wrung its blood into a shot glass of strong liquor and squeezed the bile into a second glass. The blood and bile were then drunk as an aphrodisiac. Snake Alley also boasted several dildo shops.

'It's a unique take on one-stop shopping,' quipped Graham.

The still-living snake – if it was dead it put on a bloody good show of looking alive, coiling up like a spring when its tail was released – was then disembowelled and skinned, chopped into small pieces and whisked off to the kitchen to be rendered into soup. I'm not exactly a fan of snakes, but this 'spectacle' was truly sickening.

Sandy and I bonded during an earthquake. One night, the *China News* building started to sway, causing the calendar on the wall above the news desk to swing from side to side and the electric fans to rock back and forth. I'd jumped out of my chair, unsure what was happening, and surfed the floor as it shifted beneath my feet. Rushing from reception, Sandy came over to reassure me that we were perfectly safe.

'Earthquake happen a lot in Taipei,' she told me, 'but this baby tremor. You not be scared.'

One weekend Sandy invited me to her family home. Her apartment was at the top of a grungy flight of steps and she had to unlock several heavy steel doors to get there. Removing our shoes, we entered the sitting room, the centrepiece of which was the family's brightly coloured shrine: a demonic-looking God surrounded by gifts of incense, fruit and candles. Sandy gave me a biscuit and left me watching *Star Trek* dubbed into Mandarin with her mum, who didn't speak a word of English. Emerging from the curtained-off kitchen 20 minutes later, Sandy offered me a glass of milky liquid with what looked like oversized frogspawn in it.

'What is it?' I asked warily.

'Bubble tea.'

I eyed the glass. 'What does it taste like?'

'Nice.'

I brought the lukewarm liquid to my lips and tasted the contents, inadvertently sucking in one of the slimy balls. Trying hard not to gag, I tentatively chewed. It resembled stale jelly.

'But what is it?' I asked.

'Tapioca. You finish it.'

'I'll try.' But hard as I tried, I couldn't stomach it.

Sandy was adamant. 'Finish it!'

'I can't, I'm full. From the biscuit,' I pleaded.

And so it went all afternoon long as I made very stilted conversation and answered a barrage of questions of a personal nature. Did I have a husband? What about children? What was my star sign? And what exactly did I earn at the *China News*?

'Not enough,' I said, hoping to deflect the question.

'Yes, but how much?'

'More than I earned in South Africa.'

'Yes, but how much they pay you?'

I didn't want to offend Sandy but I feared that, as a foreigner, I was paid far more than she was.

I declined to answer.

'OK, if you not tell me that, tell me your blood group.'

As social chit-chat went, that was a new one on me, but I felt this time I had to answer, even if it was a lie, as I had no idea.

'O,' I said.

'Oh,' said Sandy.

The bucks start here

 After four months in Taiwan, our job was done: four adults could tell but not comprehend at least one English joke and a dozen kindie kids knew how to let any future English teacher know she was late for class, in English. But by now our plans had been FUBARed.

Although we'd stuck to our strategy of saving as much money as we could, inspired by the enthralling tales we heard on the balcony I'd concluded that, not for the first time, Lisa was right: the UK could wait. If we didn't seize this opportunity to travel, then we'd regret it. So we agreed that we'd make our way to London in an unplanned, deadline-free, hop-skip-and-jump kinda way. Providing our general direction of travel was more or less westwards, we were UK bound. We confidently assumed this would get travel out of our systems, something that turned out to be as delusional as piratical Kim's attempt to kick her heroin habit by going to Thailand, slap-bang in the middle of the Golden Triangle, one of the world's largest opium-producing areas.

We'd secreted more than NT$200,000 in cash all over our hostel room. It was stashed away in so many places that we couldn't be sure that we recovered it all, and long after we'd left Taipei half-expected to come across Taiwanese banknotes stuffed into a roll of socks, inside our alarm clock or in the lining of Lisa's guitar case. Shit, like forgetful squirrels who bury acorns and can't later find them, we may have left a few thousand dollars for the next occupants to discover.

The proceeds mostly of hard-earned but illicit employment, our earnings needed to be changed into a hard currency that we could exchange outside Taiwan. We could do this in one of three places: a regular bank where, if we couldn't explain how we'd come by such a large quantity of Taiwanese dollars the stash might be confiscated; Hong Kong, where we'd get a poor rate; or at a nearby 'gold shop'.

Like many of Taipei's money-changing shops, this one masqueraded as a jewellery store and may have sold the occasional item of jewellery – there was plenty displayed in the windows and in the cabinets inside – but in reality it functioned as a foreign exchange.

Unofficial and illegal, it was no less a bank for that. The exchange bureau was at the far end of the shop behind a 'secret' locked door and you were admitted by the staff once you'd been scrutinised via CCTV. We spent what felt like ages staring up at the camera with pleading faces, trying to look legit enough to be allowed to do our illegitimate transaction.

Inside, it looked exactly like a bank: there was a counter, several counting machines and the various exchange rates were posted electronically. We asked for US$8,000 and the woman behind the counter brought into view a brick of US$100 bills in serial order that was probably still warm from the US Federal Reserve press. The notes were so new that she had to slam the brick sharply on the counter to break it into more manageable chunks, then riffle through the notes to separate them prior to feeding them into a counting machine. She passed 80 bills to me. I insisted that Lisa and I inspect each note.

'Do we have to do this in front of her?' asked Lisa. 'It's making it obvious that we don't trust her.'

'If you'd rather risk losing it all and being arrested at Amex for possession of counterfeit money then let's take the cash and get out of here,' I shot back.

Lisa got the memo and we proceeded to inspect the banknotes, holding up each one in turn to the overhead light. We'd heard a rumour that the Iranians were forging US dollars but that theirs didn't incorporate a 'USA' strip and microscopic-but-legible writing around Ben Franklin's head. Ours all seemed good, but the real test would come when we used them to buy travellers cheques at the Amex concession several blocks away. It was a nerve-wracking ten minutes as the Amex staffer subjected each bill to scrutiny under an ultra-violet lamp, but she was eventually satisfied that they were the real deal. If they hadn't passed muster, we'd have exchanged four months of hard graft for 80 pieces of worthless paper.

As we said our final goodbyes, swapping addresses and promises to write, two hostel inmates asked if they could take our photo. It was during this impromptu shoot in reception that Swiss 'stout lout'

Marianne raised her concerns.

'I think you bust your luggage limit, Lisa and Gray-ham,' she said.

'Do you think we might have?' I asked, wondering if the hostel had a set of scales anywhere.

Another inmate wandered in and rushed out to get his camera. It seemed our departure for Hong Kong was creating quite a stir.

'Tell me you're not going to travel the world with all that shit,' guffawed Kiwi John, pointing to our two overfilled rucksacks, daypacks, bumbags, sleeping bags, mosquito net, guitar and bulky video camera. 'Rather you than me, mate.'

Heedless of our folly – we were two feet wide, five feet deep and as agile as astronauts – we congratulated ourselves that we were the best-provisioned travellers, ever. We had a shirt for every occasion, trousers for every day of the week, a library of travel guides, and enough underwear to last us two weeks. We staggered into the lift, praying the overload alarm wouldn't ring. It was time for Lisa and me to *Star Trek* and boldly go forth on our own.

CHAPTER TWO

1993: The Year of the Banana Pancake Trail
Hong Kong, The Philippines, Thailand

 'Would passenger Lisa Jackson please come to the baggage counter,' a voice in arrivals at Kai Tak airport boomed over the intercom. My heart froze. Had the authorities in Hong Kong been tipped off that we'd been working illegally in Taiwan? Did they know about the dollars we'd bought in the gold shop? Worse still, were they suspicious of how much luggage we had and did they suspect we were drug mules? I braced myself for an interrogation, and the cavity search I feared was coming. We'd heard sensationalist tales about such things in Taipei Hostel. I prayed I'd be searched by a woman with petite hands.

'Relax,' said Graham, which I took to be advice to prepare for my cavity search and which ramped up my anxiety even more. 'It's probably nothing.'

'If it's nothing why are they calling out my name for the whole airport to hear?' I whispered, casting anxious glances at the other passengers waiting at the baggage carousel.

We located the counter.

'Is this yours?' asked the burly uniformed official, holding up my guitar case.

'Yes,' I barely managed to squeak.

'Good. It was labelled "Fragile" so we wanted to make sure you got it safely.'

'See? I told you it was nothing,' said Graham, turning and leading the way back to the carousel.

While I took some time to descend from 50,000 feet of fear,

Graham stood calmly watching the conveyor belt for the rest of our luggage. I realised at that moment that travelling with Graham was going to prove a lot more challenging than I'd anticipated, given my 97 per cent risk-aversion score in the psychometric career test I took as a 17-year-old, part of my parents' attempt to determine whether, given my severe needle phobia, I was really cut out to be a doctor. No doubt in preparation for a lifetime of cowering indoors behind electrified fences and risking a car-jacking every time you pulled out of your driveway, South African aptitude tests didn't only assess literacy, numeracy and general reasoning, they also asked detailed questions about your attitude to fear.

'Would you enter a cave if you didn't know what was inside it? Would you swim off a beach without lifeguards? Would you pat a dog you didn't know?'

'No, no and no again,' had been my emphatic answers.

Graham, on the other hand, though not exactly Braveheart – he's scared of flying, heights and cockroaches, though thankfully okay with buttons, one of the many phobias I now use hypnotherapy to help my clients overcome – views authority as a sparring partner, something to be playfully boxed about and outsmarted if you are quick-witted enough. In his last term at boarding school he and three friends brewed homemade beer, fermenting the batch in a teacher's vacant apartment. It was discovered and reported to the headmaster by a snitching cleaner. Summoned to explain himself, Graham – three months from turning 18 – had to sham contrition as the headmaster lectured him about how 'disappointed' he was, and about how Graham had 'let down' the school, and most especially himself. Then, foolishly, the headmaster had declared his hand: he would phone Graham's mother and ask her to fetch her errant son and keep him at home until the end of term. Graham was having none of that. Back in his boarding house, he'd used the public payphone to tip off his mother and brief her on what she should say.

'That is naughty,' she'd lied when the headmaster rang. 'But I can't have Graham home now as we're redecorating,' she'd lied again. 'It would badly affect his A-level revision and' – this time telling the truth – 'he's got his heart set on going to York University.'

Rather than make himself the villain of the piece, the man who'd wrecked a promising young man's life chances over 20 litres of home brew, the headmaster backed down. Graham and his friends had gone to the nearby Sandrock pub to celebrate.

We waddled through Hong Kong Customs. I was convinced we'd be stopped and searched. Sure enough, a stern-faced official beckoned us over but, clocking the amount of clobber we were carrying, changed his mind and waved us on. He probably suspected that, unless he radioed for reinforcements, by the time he finished with us and got home, his dinner would be in the dog.

The Chungking Challenge

 The airport bus dropped us off a couple of blocks away from Chungking Mansions, a backpacker hangout legendary among the Taipei Hostel balcony crew for being both affordable and a fire hazard: the worst fire had occurred four years before, when a Danish tourist died. The name sounds rather grand, but we'd been forewarned that Chungking Mansions most certainly wasn't. Known to travellers as 'the armpit of Asia', the Lonely Planet described it as 'two words for dirt cheap accommodation in Hong Kong'.

I was too scared to disembark directly outside Chungking Mansions as I'd heard alarming stories of touts strong-arming travellers into taking hugely overpriced rooms or forcing them to pay a finder's fee even if they didn't take the room they'd been shown. I also reckoned we'd be less vulnerable and better able to bargain if we weren't buckling under the burden of our luggage. So I stayed to guard our Himalayan pile of belongings and tasked Graham with finding us affordable accommodation. He returned after 45 minutes.

'I couldn't find anything.'

'Really?' I said dismayed, wondering where else we could look if Chungking Mansions was full or unsuitable. 'What rooms did you go and see Graham? Were they all disgustingly dirty?'

'Er, none,' admitted Graham sheepishly. 'I felt intimidated actually, and I didn't know where to start looking.'

'You mean you didn't see a *single* room?' I asked, furious that I'd sat in the hot sun for almost an hour for nothing.

'No. You'll see what I mean when you get there, Lisa – it's all a bit… scary.'

I gave him hell. I couldn't believe he'd been so spineless and that I'd hitched myself for life to an A-grade scaredy-cat. What on earth could be so bad about the Mansions? Wobbly-legged under the weight of all our gear, I frog-marched Graham back from whence he'd come.

Comprising five blocks of 17 floors apiece, each served by two small and slow lifts, Chungking Mansions was packed with hostels, restaurants and electronics shops that, it was said, supplied 20 per cent of sub-Saharan Africa's mobile phones. Its labyrinthine lobby-cum-shopping-arcade teemed with traders selling everything from samosas to laptops and thronged with so many different nationalities that it felt as if we'd parachuted into the Mos Eisley cantina *bar* scene in the first *Star Wars* film. There were turbaned Sikhs, Europeans (mostly scruffy-looking backpackers) speaking a Babel of languages, West African women wearing flamboyant, brightly coloured prints, elegant east Africans and a smattering of Pakistanis in pyjama-like *shalwar kameez*. The noise was deafening and the queues for the lifts depressingly long.

'Good morning, sir, how are you?' said a well-dressed Chinese man to Graham, thrusting something shiny at him. 'Copy watch?'

'No thank you,' said Graham, pushing away the fistful of fake Rolexes the man was holding out.

I conceded that it was all a bit overwhelming and felt a knot in my stomach at the prospect of not knowing what the lift, once we'd taken it, would open to reveal. I had a horrible vision of stumbling out into a drug den or brothel – Kiwi John had warned of them – or into some smelly hostel teeming with rats.

I knew, though, that we couldn't afford other accommodation, so there was nothing for it, we simply had to brace ourselves and take pot luck, picking from one of the guesthouses listed on the information panel next to the lift. We chose one and waited for ten minutes in bad-tempered (me) and chastised (Graham) silence, before squeezing ourselves into the lift. The impatient scowls on the faces of those denied entry because of our voluminous luggage spoke volumes. Shuddering under our weight, the lift let out a strained groan as it slowly ascended to the 11th floor.

'Copy watch?' said the lift operator, holding out another clutch of fakes. We shook our heads.

When we stepped out into our chosen guesthouse's reception, there wasn't room to swing a cat. And there was a cat to swing, a freakishly muscular beast the size of a lamb, stretched out asleep on the counter. It stiffened and stretched its imposing physique as Graham stroked it from head to tail.

'This is one brute of a cat. Incarcerated in a high-rise hostel it must have taken to bench-pressing the desk phone and doing chin-ups on the towel rails.'

I ignored him.

'Good afternoon. Do you have any double rooms?' I asked the desk clerk. He nodded.

'How much are they?'

'One hundred and sixty Hong Kong dollars.'

'We'll take it,' I replied.

'What happened to shopping around?' said Graham peevishly. 'That's 20 US dollars. I reckon we can get a room for less than 15 US dollars.'

'Graham, don't breathe a word. I am absolutely livid with you. I told you it would be hard to bargain under the weight of all this luggage. I don't know about you, but I'm staying put.'

Our room was shoebox small – the width of a three-quarter bed plus my childbearing hips – and the bathroom was the size of a phone box. But at least it was clean as can be, not that there was much to clean.

'This really is wonderfully convenient. I can shit and shower at the same time,' said Graham after inspecting the bathroom.

'Hmm,' I sniffed, unamused.

This being Hong Kong and a civilised part of the British Empire, we could flush the loo paper.

'When the Chinese take over in 1997, the first thing they're likely to do is put waste paper bins in every bog and prohibit flushing,' said Graham, who'd never quite got his head around why Taiwan had plumbed itself into a sewerage infrastructure that couldn't cope with a two-inch turd invading its one-inch pipework.

My dark mood didn't improve when, after Graham had taken his seated shower, I used the loo and found he'd left the toilet roll atop the cistern. It was now a swollen, soggy, unusable mass.

'Go to reception and ask for another roll,' I barked. 'And buy me a cooldrink while you're there.'

I was still seething at Graham's cowardice as he reached into my bumbag to fetch some cash and accidentally set off the rape spray I'd carried with me on my keyring ever since leaving South Africa. The room instantly filled with a cloud of acrid smoke that singed my eyes and made me gag. I'd avoided being teargassed by the police when taking part in anti-apartheid demos while at university, and yet here I was, in the tiniest room in Hong Kong, gassed by my own clumsy husband.

'Graham! What have you done, you idiot?' I spluttered, looking for a window to throw open. The window was screwed shut so, crying and chocking on the teargas, we rapidly fled the room and took the stairs three floors up to the Healthy Mess Restaurant, chosen for its extensive choice of vegetarian Indian fare rather than its unappetising-sounding name.

During our meal, I deliberated whether to continue being angry with Graham, but he won me over by promising that, if I wanted to, I could order dessert.

Shoot me in the temple

 'Lisa, what have you been up to?' I asked, as she emerged from a supermarket near the Star Ferry.

'Nothing,' she said innocently, holding out the carrier bag of provisions she'd bought for our picnic on Stanley Beach. I hate crowds and so had sent her into the packed store while I waited outside.

'Spit it out.'

'What?'

'You've gone and bought yourself a Mars Bar ice cream and scoffed it inside the store, haven't you?'

Lisa burst into guilty laughter. 'How on earth did you guess?' she asked, once she'd composed herself.

'I just know you so well. You had that "I've done something naughty" look on your face. When you had your first one yesterday, I saw how excited you were that your favourite chocolate bar had been turned into an ice cream and knew you'd want another.'

'And *I* knew you wouldn't let me have a second one as they're so expensive.'

'Too bloody right they're expensive. I'm not letting you out of my sight again when you've got money in your hot little hands – you can't be trusted. And anyway, the least you could have done was buy me one, too.'

'Ah, but that would have been *twice* as expensive,' observed an unrepentant Lisa.

It was at this moment that I took the executive decision to appoint myself our trip's accountant. If our round-half-the-world journey wasn't to telescope into a Hong Kong-plus-one holiday then I needed to keep a beady eye on our finances.

Lisa was hell-bent on seeing every single sight Hong Kong had to offer and after studying our guidebook had drawn up a list so long I felt tired before I finished reading it. My heart sank when I spotted several temples: after Taipei, where I'd been dragged along to so many that even my underpants smelled of incense, I was bored of them. This incensed Lisa.

'How can you be bored of temples?' she berated me. 'They're absolutely stunning and they're all different. We don't have anything like this in South Africa.'

'Once you've seen one, you've...'

'Don't dare say it, Graham. This is the start of our trip and already you're getting all blasé and lazy. We are doing temples whether you want to or not.'

And so we did Hong Kong on two temples a day, against my

better judgement.

Thankfully, Hong Kong – or Hongkers, as we affectionately called it – turned out to be more than a templefest, and by the end of two weeks I'd grown to appreciate its modern-meets-time-immemorial vibe. Below towering skyscrapers such as the brand-new Bank of China Tower, which had scandalised the locals when its architect IM Pei failed to consult with *feng shui* experts prior to designing it, the city's rickshaw pullers plied their trade. Mummified men who looked too old to pull a loo chain, let alone a rickshaw, they were a dying breed, the last licences had been issued in the 1970s. We also saw a few boats belonging to Hong Kong's 'boat people' in the Yau Ma Tei Typhoon Shelter off Kowloon, most of whom had by now moved to safer and more sanitary public housing on dry land. As a child Lisa had been fascinated and repulsed when her mother told her that these fishermen used the harbour as both a toilet and a food source.

'My mother said they used to tie their children to the boats with string,' said Lisa, 'so that if one of them fell in and drowned, it would be easier to recover their body.'

We spent a happy half an hour at the Hong Lok Street bird market, which was alive with the cheeping of birds in intricately carved wooden cages. All manner of birds could be purchased, and the market also functioned as a concert venue as dozens of locals thronged there, cages in hand, to allow the birds they owned to sing with those for sale.

'I'll give you some money so you can buy live maggots and grasshoppers to feed them,' I offered.

'No thanks, I'd rather spend the money on another Mars Bar ice cream,' Lisa replied.

Midway through our time in Hong Kong we caught the ferry to Macau, a sleepy backwater maze of winding cobbled streets, tiled colonial buildings and cheap and good Portuguese wine. We delighted in what the Lonely Planet described as 'a sermon in bad taste', the pineapple-like Hotel Lisboa, with its smoky ground-floor casino where miserable-looking Chinese came to have fun losing their money. A ruined gabled façade featuring a pensive skeleton, depicted as 'a sermon in stone' (was the guidebook author a priest, we wondered, or simply someone who'd run out of metaphors), was all that was left of the church of São Paulo, once one of the largest Catholic churches in Asia, that burned down during a typhoon in 1835. From the hill it stood on we caught tantalising glimpses of China, at that time off-limits to South Africans owing to Pretoria's close ties with Taiwan.

Drowning lessons

 By the time we reached the end of Lisa's Hong Kong and Macau mother-of-all-must-do lists, all I wanted to do was hit the beach. And where better than Boracay, famed among Taipei Hostel backpackers for its palm-fringed beaches and lime-cordial-coloured waters. But in order to get there, we first had to fly to Manila, a giant, crime-riddled, overpopulated fiasco of a city.

'Blimey, they're unlucky,' I thought on hearing the tales of woe of a British traveller we bumped into during the wait for our flight. In the five weeks he and his wife had spent in Malaysia and Thailand they'd had more than their fair share of accidents. They'd both been hit by a bus when motorcycling, but luckily got away without any broken bones. He'd had the squits for five days and been put on a glucose drip in hospital. She'd walked into a lamppost and gashed open her head. He'd stepped on a poisonous spiny urchin in Koh Phi Phi. Now they were leaving the safety of Hongkers for the mean streets of Manila. It looked like a decidedly poor choice for them. Come to think of it, given how green we were, and Lisa's attitude to risk, it probably wasn't the best choice for *us*.

Our guidebook didn't pull its punches when it came to security in the Philippines capital, cautioning that 'the rush to pick your pockets ensues whenever you go for a walk in Rizal Park,' so we walked Manila's streets, which were riddled with potholes full of foul-smelling, scummy water infested with mosquito larvae, on high alert. Whenever we stopped anywhere to puzzle over the map, one of us kept watch.

'Suspicious character at nine o'clock,' Lisa would warn, which meant power-walking to three o'clock as fast, but as nonchalantly, as we possibly could.

Lisa had three heart-in-mouth moments when red-eyed, surly-looking youths rose from where they were loitering, strode too quickly towards us, and then, when they were within touching distance, abruptly peeled away. We became so paranoid that we started trying to move our lips out of time with what we were saying, like a badly dubbed movie, in a clumsy attempt to confuse any out-of-earshot lip-reading muggers.

The guard who courteously opened the door for us when we lunched at Pizza Hut, instead of reassuring us, alarmingly toted an enormous rifle. Christ, was Manila so dicey that armed guards were needed to deter desperados from robbing 12-inch pepperoni pizzas? Half a day after arriving we were eager to bolt for the exit, our nerves more frayed than the brim of an old straw sombrero.

The traffic in Manila was manic, a crazy melee of horse-drawn carts, pedicabs, madly honking cars and impossibly overcrowded jeepney taxis that shoved and butted their way along the city's littered streets. Gloriously kitsch, festooned with prancing chrome horses, pennants, tassels, aerials, multiple air-horns and clusters of headlights, their nameboards proclaiming 'I love Jesus' and 'Praise God', Manila's jeepneys were the vehicular version of a drag queen wearing every single item of colourful costume jewellery they'd ever bought while simultaneously loudly professing their faith. In that hair-raising traffic, you really did want God riding shotgun.

The cheapest accommodation in town was in Ermita, an ill-lit, run-down neighbourhood overrun with touts offering to change money on the black market for very tempting exchange rates. It was here that a smartly dressed money changer had scammed Swiss Andy and Marianne out of US$150 using a sleight-of-hand trick – and a hint of menace. Our hostel wasn't the haven we'd hoped it would be. In fact, it was downright dodgy: there was often no running water and there were power cuts – 'brownouts' – for several hours a day. We'd arrived during a brownout and had been shown to our room by torchlight.

'Oh my God,' said Lisa, when the lights came on. 'We've checked into Alcatraz. I didn't realise that this room doesn't have any windows. And I think that's a mouse dropping on the floor.'

The hostel's Filipino occupants, staff included, liked nothing better than to clear their throats incessantly and hoick the risen phlegm into cups, bins, sinks, toilets and out of the windows. Each morning at 6am there was a dawn chorus of throat-clearing hacking that was impossible to sleep through. Unless you were Lisa who woke, of her own free will, at 9am each day, blissfully unaware of the discordant and unhygienic alarm call I'd been subjected to.

Worst of all, the hostel was overrun with cockroaches. In my hierarchy of loathsome insects, cockroaches are king and their existence is proof that this is not the best of all possible worlds. They're Usain Bolt-fast, able to run up to 80cm per second – that's like 'Lightning Bolt' covering 50 metres in a second. They fart 45 times their bodyweight in a year and they don't need their heads to breathe, meaning they can survive decapitation for up to a week before dying of dehydration. And roaches get absolutely anywhere and everywhere. I had a five-centimetre-long one run up my leg as I sat on the hostel loo; one joined me in the shower; and the 90-litre plastic kitchen bin vibrated under the weight of rampaging roaches feeding inside it.

We saw all of Manila's sights in a couple of days, and a thorough reading of our guidebook revealed that the Philippines boasted not only a town called Sexmoan somewhere on the island of Luzon but a senior Catholic official called Cardinal Sin. The one thing we weren't able to tick off Lisa's to-do list, however, was offload her guitar, and not for want of trying. Never once used for busking it hadn't earned us a penny, and we'd lugged it everywhere since leaving Taiwan. We'd left Taipei weighed down like two brick-kiln donkeys and, quick to see the error of our ways, had sent the bulk of our luggage ahead of us to England from Hong Kong. We tried to do the same with the guitar, but the post office said we couldn't mail it back to South Africa unless we found a container for it, which proved impossible. So we flew with the bulky embuggerance to Manila where we paid to have a box the size of a Hobbit's coffin made to take it. I would have happily buried it in an unmarked grave, but we hauled it to the Central Post Office, set across our laps, about a foot of each end protruding into the street, in a pedicab. Following a half-hour ride in the crazy traffic we were dropped off at what we were told was the CPO, which of course it wasn't, forcing us to spend 20 sweaty and sweary minutes walking hither and thither until we located it.

The CPO was a very large and imposing neo-classical building, with the international parcels counter down the stairs at one end. There the box was weighed and measured. It was six inches too long. It couldn't be posted. No matter how passionately we begged and pleaded and told the impassive post office worker how the guitar had become our proverbial albatross, an ever-present reminder of a much-regretted decision, the answer was no.

Despondent, we retraced our steps, stopping at a 7-Eleven to buy a six-pack of San Miguel to dull our frustration. Displayed behind the till were a dozen or so mugshots of thieves holding the goods they'd been caught heisting, a public shaming intended to be a salutary warning to would-be shoplifters. I half-expected to see a picture of Aussie Cliff with 200 Marlboro Lights. Most of those pictured had gone for high-value booze and fags, though one had tried to make off with three bars of soap. It's possible he was just a dirty teetotal non-smoker.

'Let's leave the bloody guitar in the hostel for someone more musically talented than you to appreciate, Lisa,' I suggested.

'Absolutely not. Mrs Daniel taught me to play on this guitar and you know how much I loved those lessons. And I taught my dad to play *Mama Tembu's Wedding* on it – there's absolutely no way I'm abandoning it.'

So the bloody thing journeyed with us all the way to Boracay – now out of its coffin-box which we did abandon – back to Manila and on to Singapore where, hallelujah, we were able, finally, to post it back to Pretoria.

Getting to Boracay was a bit of a schlepp, like assembling a flat-pack wardrobe. It needed to be done methodically, in steps, because if one screw or bolt was left out the whole complicated thing would collapse. First there was the hour-long flight from Manila to Kalibo aboard a plane with a strict dress code: 'It would be appreciated if our passengers did not wear shorts, singlets, thongs or slippers on Philippines Airlines flights'. Did anyone ever, anywhere, board a flight in a thong? It must have happened if Philippines Airlines had banned them. Too much sweaty cheek on the seat is bad at the best of times, but ghastly if the air-conditioning fails. It was a number of years before I realised that Philippines Airlines had banned what my English education had taught me was a form of underwear, but what Filipinos confusingly call flip-flops.

Next was a two-and-a-half hour, hair-greying bus journey over pot-holed roads from Kalibo to Caticlan, considered so hazardous by our driver that he recited fervent prayers to Mother Mary over the public address system as we set off. Throughout the bone-jarring trip we were ceaselessly badgered by a press of eager touts who hung over the back of the seats in front of us, showered us with brochures depicting wood-and-rattan bungalows to rent and urged us to 'Take a look, take a look'. It was like being trapped into viewing someone's caravan-holiday snaps, only worse, as the touts constantly and loudly squabbled with each other to win our business.

'You come with me, okay? My name Angelo. Best room on Boracay. What your name sir?'

'No sir, look sir, my place the best. Cheapest, too. You come with me I am Jejomar.'

'Don't go with Jejomar, come with me, look at my room. Better than his. What's your name – you come to mine? My name Arturo.'

From Caticlan we caught an outrigger to Boracay, the ocean spray soaking us and our rucksacks as we puttered through the waves before wading ashore in the transparent shallows holding Lisa's guitar and all our belongings above our heads, careful not to lose our footing and dunk everything we owned into the brine.

For a brief moment I contemplated whether I should 'accidentally' drop the guitar but wasn't feeling strong enough, after the bus ride, to cope with Lisa's ire.

We took accommodation in a bamboo-and-rattan bungalow set in lush gardens. It featured an en suite with a sit-down loo, a balcony and breakfast brought to the room, all for US$6 per night.

'This is *so* nice,' Lisa told me, 'I'd even let my parents stay here.' Praise indeed from someone who continually begged me not to divulge too many details about the places we'd stayed in when I wrote letters home.

Back in 1992, long before it became the world's most notorious island, Boracay was paradise. There were very few concrete buildings, none more than two storeys high, and the only things bobbing in the waves were sinuous strands of seaweed, not the untreated effluent that turned its clear waters into a 'cesspool' and in 2018 forced the Philippine government to close the entire island for six months. When we visited, Boracay didn't host 1.7 million visitors a year as it did in 2018. The well-heeled fly-and-flop brigade went elsewhere.

So enchanted were we by Boracay that the day after we arrived we extended our stay from one to two weeks, not knowing this would turn out to be a near-fatal decision.

But for the fact that there were no jet-skis, powerboats or overwater bungalows, to us Boracay was Bora Bora, only better as we could actually afford to stay there. Life on the island was like waking up each day and walking onto the set of every cinema advert we'd seen that glamorised alcohol and tobacco, the ones where toned-'n'-tanned men and women imbibed cirrhotic cocktails and took long draws on slender cancer sticks against a backdrop of achingly beautiful shores. Our lazy days invariably started with breakfast in bed that included half a papaya each. That was enough tropical fruit for me, but Lisa would go on to order every possible variation of fruit shake from the gaily decorated beach stalls – papaya, dragon fruit, banana, mango, pineapple. If she carried on this way our backpacking budget would be blown, so I limited her to two a day. Either that, or no beer in the evening. The choice was Lisa's. She chose fruit-shake mornings, and beery evenings. It was, I think, the correct choice. Lisa wrote rather touchingly in our journal: 'My only sad moments on Boracay were when I came to the end of a fruit shake.'

But every paradise has a serpent, and Boracay's came in the guise of its small, whining and preternaturally tenacious mosquitoes. Every night we'd encase the bed in the mosquito net and then, as Lisa sat inside naked acting as bait, I'd prowl around outside it fully clothed hoping to swat the buggers that had somehow got inside. The idea was to hit a book against Lisa's outstretched hand and, in so doing, create a bloody book-net-hand sandwich with a mozzie filling. It was satisfyingly effective whenever we co-ordinated our actions, but mostly a ridiculously divisive comedy of errors.

'You're supposed to put your hand *there*!' I'd berate Lisa as I swung the book at the mosquito only for it to impact harmlessly on the flexing material of the net where her hand was not.

She'd bark back at me that I hadn't specified *which* mozzie I was going to splat, or that I hadn't given her enough time to position her hand properly.

'You're too impatient. I wasn't ready. And tell me *exactly* where you're going to hit because I can't always see what you see!'

'By the time I've pointed at it, and you've put your hand in the right place, the mozzie will have long gone!' I'd snap in frustration.

And so it went. Often till one in the morning.

A couple of evenings later we were given some mosquito coils, which solved the problem and didn't involve Ivan Lendl lunges and matrimonial bickering.

Besides the mozzies, Boracay was utopian but, even if you're Lisa, there are only so many fruit shakes you can enjoy, only so much snorkelling with tropical fish you can do, only so many sunsets you can savour while wriggling your toes in sand so fine it felt like freshly sifted icing sugar before you get slightly bored, a little restless. Which is why one morning, we gave languid indolence a holiday and explored the island.

On a map, diminutive Boracay resembles a half-gnawed bone cast into the Sulu Sea. The island's coastline comprises rocky promontories punctuated by stretches of white beach that cling to its sides like morsels of uneaten meat. It's a mere 7km from top to bottom, so we set out that day to walk its entire circumference, starting midway up White Beach. We'd gone about 2km when the sandy beaches petered out and our way was blocked by a rocky headland. A local boatman, sitting on the spar of his outrigger mending a net, looked us up and down and claimed it was impossible to continue on foot.

'Many big stones,' he said emphatically. 'Sharp stones. You can't go that way. I will row you there. Twenty-five pesos.'

We'd been backpacking for a month and at this point suspected that anyone offering unsolicited services was most certainly out to cheat us. In fact, so careful (alright, tight) was I with our money that I'd insisted we drink the smelly water from our bungalow's well – with a dash of iodine to make it safe – rather than buy cheap bottled water. When Lisa demurred, I'd explained: 'It must be okay, the islanders drink it.'

To which she'd caustically replied: 'Yes, but have you seen an islander older than 40?'

I hadn't. So, instead of getting ferried dry and safe to Puka Shell Beach for what amounted to a dollar, we ignored the boatman's warning and cut inland over the rocks. At first we encountered unthreatening smooth stones.

'You see, I told you he was saying that to get us to pay him an extortionate price to row us round,' I crowed.

My smugness was extinguished within a minute. Ahead of us was a rise carpeted with volcanic rocks so sharp and spiky that they pierced our cheap flip-flops and painfully pricked our feet. Loathe to lose face by retreating past the boatman who would, I was sure, smirk a knowing 'I told you so, you cheapskate' smile, I hit on the brilliant idea of launching ourselves off the rocks into the sea and swimming around the headland to Puka Shell Beach. It seemed a very simple, elegant and face-saving solution. The fact that the waters off White Beach were placid and calm and yet the sea on this side of the island was wind-lashed wild didn't worry me one jot.

We spent a few minutes planning our act of foolishness. Inflating the travel pillows we'd brought with us in case we found a stretch of deserted beach on which to snooze, we stuffed them into our daypacks for buoyancy. Agreeing that it would be clever to wear our flip-flops on our hands as paddles, we selected the least bad spot from which to enter the water: a spit of rock several feet below us and two above the surf and swell. Finally, we counted the waves. Five small ones are always followed by three bigger ones, we'd once been told by friends whose parents owned a cottage by the sea.

'I'll go first. I'll launch myself after the third larger wave and you must follow right behind me.'

I half-fell, half-dived into the water and thrashed furiously in a straight line out to sea against the waves and the wind that threatened to dump me back onto the jagged shore and split my stupid head open like an overripe watermelon. I'd made barely five yards before it dawned on me how bloody hard this jaunt of ours was going to be. Turning to look back at Lisa and warn her off, I saw she'd already leapt in. Like the pig in the business fable who jointly set up a bacon-and-egg restaurant with a chicken, we weren't just involved, we were both committed.

Held back by the flip-flops on our hands, which far from helping us swim faster were an encumbrance, and the blow-up pillows which created a significant amount of drag and pushed our faces down into the water, we struggled to get beyond the breakers into calmer water. I wasn't going backwards, but my progress forwards was slow and I was already tiring.

'Swim, bloody swim, Lisa!' I exhorted.

Lisa was 15 metres behind me. I hoped she could hear me, and draw strength from my encouragement. I heard only the odd word or two from her. Whatever she was shouting, the wind and the noise of my own clumsy floundering drowned it out.

'Keep going! Keep swimming!' I hollered, coughing and spluttering as the wind forced choking gulps of seawater into my mouth and lungs.

After what seemed an eternity we broke through the surf and began to swim a long rightward arc towards Puka Shell Beach, still several hundred yards distant. Our energy rapidly depleting, we laboured on. I was now very scared. I swim like a brick. If I stopped paddling, I'd perish. I wasn't worried that Lisa would sink as she floats like a cork, but I was increasingly concerned that she hadn't the strength to make it to shore. I imagined the story in the next morning's newspaper: *Police puzzle why drowned tourists had flip-flops on hands*. If Lisa drowned and I survived how could I explain that she'd died because of my misplaced pride and desire to save a few pesos? Maybe I couldn't. Maybe I'd have to live with the lie that it was her idea, not mine.

Above the frothing tops of the waves I could see holidaymakers on the beach, sitting in deckchairs, reading. They were completely oblivious to our existential plight. Had they looked up from their books and seen our bobbing heads they would most likely have mistaken us for two sea-faring coconuts. I thought about shouting for help, but the noise of the wind and the sea would have muffled my cries and I needed to conserve energy. I considered trying to signal our distress and in that moment Stevie Smith's poem 'Not waving but drowning' came to mind. Had I waved, the sun-bathing tourists would probably have cheerily waved back. No one was going to save us.

'Swim, for God's sake swim!' I mentally urged Lisa on as my own strength ebbed away. I kicked harder, frantically pulling at the water with my be-flip-flopped hands. Lisa was now 40 metres away from me, and barely visible.

And then the tide turned, literally. The current and the wind that we'd had to fight now came to our aid, pushing us in towards the beach and easing the strain on our weary muscles. About 20 minutes since leaving land I swam up behind the breakers and with their help clumsily bodysurfed up onto the beach, where I lay panting and suffused with adrenaline, trembling with fear and exhaustion. Five minutes later, Lisa washed up.

Lying flat on our backs, chests heaving for air, we turned our heads to look at one another. It was a look of humbled idiocy. Of two people who thought they knew better than they did, but who'd grossly miscalculated and had been lucky to get away with it.

'Please, please, promise me you'll never tell anyone about this,' I pleaded with Lisa. 'It's by far the stupidest thing I've *ever* done… and I have no excuse. For Christ's sake, I wasn't even drunk.'

For the rest of our stay on Boracay we played it safe, lazing under the palms drinking fruit shakes with Swiss Andy and Marianne, whom we were overjoyed to bump into at a beach café one morning. Lisa loved Marianne for dubbing me 'The Little Scottish Boy' because of the limit I'd put on her fruit-shake consumption.

'Come on Gray-ham,' Swiss Marianne would chide me, 'don't be so stingy. Let Lisa have another fruit shake before you go back to your boon-galow.'

Singapore and Malaysia proved a doddle. 'We're really getting the hang of this traveller thing,' we thought. Even Lisa was surprised at how well we'd navigated overnight bus rides and haggling with taxi drivers. The ferry ride to the Thai island of Koh Lanta, however, was less plain sailing. Packed like pilchards below deck as the vessel bounded across the waves, we queasily eyed the tiny portholes knowing that if the vessel sank, there was no way anyone would get out alive. A particularly large wave crashing against the bow had everyone hastily donning their lifejackets, which gave the journey a terrifying *Titanic* air.

No sooner had we set grateful foot on terra firma and booked into our beach chalet than Lisa faced a new challenge to her peace of mind: the exposed rafters were a highway for scurrying rats. I wasn't particularly fazed by them, but Lisa was a lot less relaxed about it.

'I won't be able to sleep a wink tonight in case their droppings drop on us,' she told me anxiously.

'Unless the rats have the squits, the mosquito net will protect you,' I tried to placate her.

Somewhat reassured, Lisa settled down in bed to read our guidebook. Climbing in next to her, I slipped under the sheet and found my place in *American Psycho*. I bided my time, waiting a good 20 minutes before making my move. After stealthily licking the back of my hand, I turned it towards Lisa.

'Look!' I exclaimed, feigning disgust and showing her the streak of saliva. 'A rat just peed on me!'

Lisa's jaw dropped and her eyes widened. I leaned closer and, before she knew what was happening, swiftly wiped my hand on her bare arm.

'Ugh, that's absolutely disgusting!' she shrieked. 'Why the hell did you do that Graham?'

'Well I don't want rat piss on *my* hand.'

Saying that was like chucking water on a chip-pan fire. Lisa's flames of righteous indignation exploded.

'Get away from me! Now I'm going to have to shower again. I'm really upset. I can't believe you did that. When we get to England, I'm going to report you to your parents.'

I was convulsed with laughter, hardly able to breathe.

'It's not fucking funny. I hate you.'

It took me a while, and immense willpower, to recover my composure and pacify Lisa. Once she'd stopped berating me I explained the prank, and eventually Lisa calmed down. I considered it prudent not to mention that rats are doubly incontinent and therefore, despite the mosquito net, there was a high risk of intermittent golden showers during the night.

Death porn

'Oh my God, what the hell *is* this?' I asked Graham fearfully as I paged from one distressing image to another. I couldn't begin to imagine who would buy repulsive 'reading' matter such as this, the print equivalent of taking a road trip with the sole intention of rubbernecking.

'I have absolutely *no* idea,' said Graham, 'but it's giving me the heebie-jeebies. I was wondering why we haven't seen or heard any other guests. Perhaps this is why.'

We'd been dog-tired and, finding most of Koh Samui's hotels fully booked, had plumped for the first one that had a vacancy and wasn't exorbitant. Thrilled to have a private room on the second floor, we were less delighted when we discovered the magazine that had been left on a chair inside. Behind a cover depicting a coquettish Asian woman were 50 colour pages of mutilated corpses of people who'd been killed in eviscerating road accidents, their bloodied limbs hanging at obscene angles out of car windows and their shattered heads protruding through windscreens. Other images depicted people who'd been shot, axed or battered, their lifeless bodies spread-eagled on floors and pavements.

The concrete floor of the corridor was painted a deep crimson. All the better to mask spilt blood, I thought, as my imagination went into hyperdrive. No one knew we were staying here except the manager. Graham and I could be dragged from our room in the middle of the night, slaughtered in the corridor and no one would ever hear from us again.

'Please can we go and find somewhere else to stay?' I begged Graham, doubting I'd sleep after what I'd seen and fearful that the death-obsessed owner of the magazine would return to reclaim it. Or that we'd end up featured, in grisly full colour, across a double spread in a subsequent edition. Or worse still, star in a Koh Samui snuff movie.

'Lisa, it's midnight and it's too late to leave. Besides, all the places we saw on the way here were full. Trust me, I don't want to stay here a second longer than we have to, so we'll definitely move on in the morning.'

'If we're still alive,' I reflected grimly. 'Picture kittens playing with balls of wool. Picture bumblebees alighting on buttercups,' I recited to myself, hoping to expunge the grisly images. But some things just can't be unseen.

Graham tried to make light of our situation. 'Welcome to Koh Samui's Hotel Slaughter. On the front desk tonight is The Boston Strangler, behind the bar is Jack the Ripper, and providing room service is Mr Ted Bundy.'

'Graham, stop it! I'm scared enough already.'

Throwing the creepy magazine under our bed, Graham began pushing a chest of drawers against the door.

'What are you doing?'

'Making sure that if someone wants to get in, they'll have to force their way in, which will wake us up and give us a fighting chance.'

I helped Graham barricade the door by heaving a weighty teak chair onto the chest. Anyone who tried to break in would now have to do some noisy shoving. I didn't want to turn out the light but Graham said that by keeping it on we might advertise our presence, so I reluctantly flicked the switch and plunged the room into a still, eerie darkness.

With visions of Jack Nicholson's deranged, axe-wielding 'Here's Johnny!' scene from *The Shining* playing in my mind, I drifted off into an uneasy sleep. Inevitably, in the middle of the night, Graham needed to go to the toilet, and began pulling the chest away from the door. It couldn't be done quietly.

'I can't hold it in any longer,' he said, apologetically.

'Can't you pee into your water bottle, Graham?' I pleaded. 'Or out the window?'

'I would if I could. But I can't piss a quart into a pint pot and someone's bound to see me if I stand at the window and pee onto the street below.'

Cursing him, I helped Graham lift, rather than drag, the chest of drawers out of the way. Graham opened the door and peered into the dark corridor. He switched on our torch, shone it onto the floor and, barefoot, stepped stealthily outside. I feared for him as he padded into the darkness, the beam of light showing his passage. He turned a corner and the light was gone.

'How quickly can G pee?' I tried to recollect. In this place, with a full bladder, the answer was always going to be 'not quickly enough'.

With the room door unsecured I feared for myself. It was black dark and deathly quiet. I *so* wanted to see the torchlight illuminating Graham's return. Then I thought that if he'd been attacked and chopped up in the toilets his murderer could return to find me using the torch and I wouldn't know it wasn't Graham behind it until it was too late. After many heart-thumping minutes, the turn in the corridor showed a light, which swung round the corner and came towards me.

'Graham?' I whispered. 'Is that you?'

The light drew closer, lifting once to shine directly into my eyes and ruin my night vision. 'Graham?' I challenged a second time.

'Shhh,' he cautioned. 'Be quiet.'

He stepped inside our room, shut the door and together we rebuilt our barricade.

'Boy, I needed that,' he said contentedly.

'Well I bloody didn't,' I shot back. 'Next time, tie a knot in it.'

Years later, once the internet had been invented, we learned that snuff movies are an urban legend. It's true that the Italian director of *Cannibal Holocaust* was charged with the on-screen killing of its stars, but he was acquitted when the deceased actors, miraculously risen from the grave, made a surprise court appearance for the defence. 'Uncle Google' also informed us that mangled-and-murdered magazines are quite popular in Thailand. Just like some people in the West revel in viewing 'slasher' movies featuring chainsaw dismemberments and hapless teenagers being suspended from meat hooks, there are Thais who derive an obscene thrill from paging through 'death porn'.

Monk-ey business & crickety teeth

 Bangkok has the reputation as Southeast Asia's Con Capital. Almost every traveller on the Taipei Hostel balcony had warned us to be careful, cautioning that some sharp characters with well-honed scamming skills saw travellers as *über*-wealthy walking wallets and that their patter could be persuasive, their smoothness disarming. The juiciest tales seemed to involve unwary backpackers accepting drugged snacks and being robbed of all their belongings, or being duped into paying gemstone prices for cut glass. Forewarned, we were on high alert when we set out to see the Grand Palace and the temple within its grounds that housed the Emerald Buddha, Thailand's most sacred object.

It was so hot that we had to stop every 400 metres to buy a big bottle of iced water, which we'd down in one go while sheltering in a shaded doorway, before reluctantly plunging back into the dazzling sunlight. Despite drinking so copiously I never once needed the loo: any excess fluid was simply sweated out where it soaked my cotton T-shirt and khaki shorts and ran streaming down my legs into my new hiking boots.

It's hard to conceive of it now in these 'Google it' times, but we had absolutely no idea what the Grand Palace looked like. Fighting our way through Bangkok's crowded, smog-choked streets, wilting in the intense heat and humidity, we passed the entrance to a *wat*.

'What *wat* is that?' I asked myself, peering into a shady courtyard. An elderly bald monk in a robe with one shoulder exposed, beckoned us over. 'Grand Palace?' I asked.

He nodded. 'Grand Palace closed today, but I can show you round. Special tour.'

Wow, a special tour. Lady Luck was smiling down on us.

Relieved that we'd see the Palace without needing to trek all the way back when it re-opened, we stepped inside.

The courtyard's outer walls contained the crypts of people who'd paid to be entombed there, including a Canadian tourist knocked down, we were told, as he read a map. The monk rapped on the door of the temple's inner sanctum and we were let in. Believing we were going to be given special access to the Emerald Buddha we ducked through the narrow doorway and entered a gloomy room where a young man dressed in shorts and a T-shirt was scraping gold leaf from a Buddha statue. Bending down, the monk selected a shard of gilding and solemnly handed it to us with both hands. We weren't sure whether it was a good idea to be making off with such a big chunk – he'd told us it cost about US$2,000 to gild a life-size Buddha – but felt it would be rude to refuse.

Dominating the temple was a large seated Buddha.

'Tallest in Bangkok,' said our guide. And it may well have been, for we hadn't yet seen any others with which to compare it.

Ten minutes later, we were back at the exit.

'Donation? You give gift for the Buddha?' demanded the monk as he pressed two miniature plastic Buddhas painted gold into our sweaty palms.

'How much should we give?' I asked, awkwardly.

'One hundred,' he decided, looking at me slyly. 'Each.'

I looked at Lisa.

'That's eight dollars, Lisa.'

'*Eight* US dollars for two small figurines? One is fine,' she said, swiftly handing hers back as I dug around in my money belt for some money before handing over a sweat-dampened red note. The monk snatched it eagerly.

'Something for food?'

I looked at Lisa, who gave her grudging assent. Resignedly, I passed over another 20 baht.

Back in Bangkok's baking hot bustle we consulted our map and it very soon became apparent that we were still several kilometres away from the Grand Palace. To add insult to ignorant injury, the tacky gold figurines could be picked up for 30 baht at almost every roadside souvenir stall. We'd been ripped off to the tune of US$5, and boy did that hurt. But not as much as the massage Lisa had that afternoon at the Wat Pho Thai Massage School, where a seriously sadistic Thai masseur used her bony elbows, forearms, hands and feet to torture Lisa for 30 minutes as I, almost doubled over with laughter, took photos of Lisa's agonised expressions.

Bangkok proved to be full of such photo opportunities. When Lisa first tasted durian, a fruit the late celebrity chef Anthony Bourdain wrote would make your breath 'smell as if you've been French kissing your dead grandmother,' I was poised to capture her gurning on film. Lisa had to agree with Ant, the durian's reputation for smelling like faecal matter and tasting like a mix of melon and flatulence, was entirely deserved.

Durian sweets weren't the sole unusual delicacy Bangkok had to offer, however. Besides the ubiquitous traveller fare of banana pancakes and granola with yogurt, it was also renowned for its fried finger food. Or fried insect snacks, to be more precise. One evening, as Lisa and I exited Lumpini Park, where we'd watched mass outdoor aerobics and old men practising tai chi like hypnotised herons, we chanced upon some food stalls set up in a car park. Here, along with chilled jellyfish, quick-boiled pig's liver, duck webs and wings and stewed beef with tendons, it was possible to purchase crispy critters: bamboo worms, ants, crickets, beige-grey grubs and locusts. I bought two crickets as a taster, one for me, one for Lisa – but Lisa was off her insects and didn't want hers. I rather enjoyed them, so I went back and, for ten baht, bought a small paper bag of crickets plus seven grubs and a locust. Bargain.

'I don't think I can manage more than one grub as they're not that nice,' I said. 'I can't help but think I'm eating capsules of pus.'

The locust and the crickets, however, deep fried and sprayed with a condiment of unknown provenance, tasted like bacon, although the spurred legs kept getting stuck between my teeth.

'Can I have a sip of your pineapple shake to rinse them away?' I asked Lisa.

'Not on your life!' she snapped. 'Keep that crickety mouth of yours away from my drink!'

Back in our hostel I remarked that I was curious about the mysterious but moreish sauce they'd sprayed onto the bugs.

'I know *exactly* what it was,' Lisa exclaimed. 'Raid insect spray!'

CHAPTER THREE

1993: The Year of No Loo Roll
India & Nepal

 Like a baby bawling inconsolably on a plane who can't be ignored, India frazzled our nerves like no other country we've visited before or since. Though we fancied ourselves as streetwise veterans of the Banana Pancake Trail – we'd backpacked through Hong Kong, the Philippines, Singapore, Malaysia and Thailand for 13 weeks prior to landing in New Delhi – nothing could have prepared us for India. Its unending noise, gaudy temples, over-crowded and polluted cities, magnificent forts and sumptuous palaces, the islands of riches alongside grinding poverty, its ubiquitous litter and excrement, the dazzling saris shimmering in the dust-bearing heat, the insistent beggars and the wretched lepers, its serene deserts and mist-wrapped tea plantations. Almost 200 million cows, 110 million goats, 75 million water buffaloes and millions of mangy stray dogs – all of them shitting and pissing and choking up not only the fields but the streets – India was disorientating, delightful, demanding and depressing, often at the same time.

Despite the amazing stories we'd heard about India on the Taipei Hostel balcony it hadn't figured in our original plans because, thanks to apartheid, South African passport holders could visit India solely on a 'grace and favour' basis, if they could find a friendly consular officer, or *make* a friend of a consular officer, at an Indian embassy. Melissa the Obscure had done exactly that. She'd wangled her Indian visa by 'gifting' a bottle of Johnnie Walker to an official. And, no doubt, by smiling sweetly and coyly batting her eyelashes as she submitted her application. Lisa wasn't up for bribing and flirting – frankly, neither was I – so we'd initially discounted visiting India and instead contemplated taking a coast-to-coast road trip across America as Loren had done.

Fortuitously, the death throes of apartheid and the power of 'cricket diplomacy' opened up India to South Africans just in time. We were in Bangkok when we heard the exciting news that, with the Indian national cricket team touring South Africa for the very first time, getting a visa had become routine. So we bussed to the Indian Embassy dressed in our best 'please sir, can I have a visa?' clothes to lodge our application for a 180-day visa. The Embassy thronged with Westerners, some in grubby singlets and shorts, sharing biros pulled from handmade fabric satchels and counting out sticky baht recovered from neck wallets kept safe against their perspiring bodies.

'They've dressed to impress,' I muttered to Lisa.

We weren't to see groups of Westerners in India until we got to Hampi, by which time the shorts and singlets had been discarded in favour of orange or purple *dhoti* trousers and candy-striped waistcoats, their hair was unwashed stiff and their wrists and ankles encircled with leather, silver and woven bracelets. No doubt they'd gone to India to 'find themselves'. And they had literally succeeded: they'd found themselves dressed like every other Westerner who'd gone to India to find themselves.

Motorcycle madness & a man called Pinky

It was not obvious who was driving the antediluvian bus we'd caught from the airport to downtown New Delhi for two rupees. There were four men, shawled in heavy grey blankets to fend off the chill of a February dawn, crammed into the driver's cab, all talking 19 to the dozen and not one of them had his eyes on the road. None of that 'don't speak to the driver' health and safety nonsense here. Perhaps it was driven by committee, with one working the accelerator, another the brake and the remaining two sharing steering and horn duties.

We got off at Connaught Place, New Delhi's circular Imperial-era commercial centre modelled after Bath's Royal Crescent, and sought out Ringo's Guesthouse, as recommended by our guidebook. It was still before seven in the morning but the staff were up and about making *chai* and frying omelettes for the gaggle of Westerners who, to save a few rupees, chose to sleep on the roof over the dormitory and had been woken by the weak, early light.

'Welcome, sir, madam. You are wanting a room? For dormitory it is 42 rupees and for private room – no toilet – it is 140 rupees,' the young man behind the reception counter informed us.

I asked if we could see the double room.

'Persons is in there sleeping, sir. Checking out is 11. Then you can see. Please, have some tea.'

Tired from the late-night flight, Lisa said that we'd take dorm beds. If Ringo's had ever had good days, they were way back in its past. It wasn't dirty – the liberal sloshing of sudsy water about the floors and toilets ensured that – as much as it was tired, broken down and gloomily lit. The first thing I spotted when I popped my head into the semi-subterranean, prison-like dormitory was a large rat standing on its hind legs on one of the beds. I knew Lisa wouldn't mind sharing a room with shower-shy backpackers but sleeping with a rat that big was a step too far, so I hotfooted it back to reception and booked the still-occupied double room.

Dumping our rucksacks behind reception we retired to the rooftop courtyard where we were served hot, sickly sweet *chai*. Then I left Lisa to snooze while I set off through the city's unfamiliar streets in search of the main post office. In the days before email, Poste Restante (or Post Restaurant as my mother repeatedly misspelled it) enabled friends and family to send mail to foreign post offices for travellers to collect as they passed through. To save money, I walked. I didn't dare stop to refer to our map as each time I did, an auto-rickshaw driver would pull up alongside and insist that I take a ride. As vultures and black kites wheeled overhead in the misty cold morning I had to step over and around bodies wrapped from head to foot in sacking. It was distressing not knowing if they were corpses or destitute homeless people sleeping rough. It took me over an hour to find the post office and retrieve a small bundle of mail. Footsore, and unsure of the way back to Ringo's, I splashed out on an auto rickshaw. Whenever we stopped at a traffic light, someone would seize the moment and try to sell me something – a chess set, fruit, maps, or rather amusingly, fake moustache and beard sets – and gaggles of begging street urchins would reach in and pinch my arm to get my attention.

When I re-joined Lisa at Ringo's, we sat in the courtyard on wobbly plastic chairs and spent an hour keenly devouring our post in the feeble sunshine.

'My parents finally let Mark have a kitten,' said Lisa. 'It's white and he's going to call it Kietsie. They went to my gran's house in Durban for Christmas.'

'My sister says her eldest is already going to kindergarten and her youngest is learning to walk,' I told Lisa. 'Ma and Pa are enjoying life back in England. They say Houston was too hot and humid.'

News update over, it was time to compile a list of chores for the day. The list read as follows:

Buy tea

Buy milk powder

Buy a sink plug

Buy an Enfield

The final item was added because doing India on an Enfield motorcycle had a romantic ring to it. I'd once had a Yamaha 125 and the prospect of owning this classic 1940s British design, now manufactured in India, was irresistible. We would be independent, going where we wanted when we wanted, and seeing sights way off the beaten track. The staff at Ringo's recommended going to the Karol Bagh district to buy one. Lisa and I got an auto rickshaw there and, sure enough, in one of the crowded streets we located half a dozen small shops with ranks of second-hand Enfields parked outside. I tested a couple, and plumped for a British racing green model. I loved its retro looks and the echoing sound of its 'thumper' engine. I spent an hour negotiating with Pinky, Laxmi Motor's salesman, a young man with a slick side-parting, a neatly trimmed moustache and a sales pitch that, unlike most in town, didn't involve him tugging insistently on my shirtsleeve. I was tempted to ask him how he came by his unusual name, but thought that asking him might prejudice my negotiations. His opening price was, as expected, grossly inflated, and I immediately made a counter offer of half that, which Pinky dismissed out of hand. Hearing this exchange, Lisa claimed she had urgent business elsewhere and disappeared. In the preceding three months of backpacking I'd discovered that Lisa would rather agree to a vendor's opening offer, no matter how patently absurd and said-for-a-laugh it was, than be party to the awkwardness of haggling. I, however, saw it as an enjoyable ritual, and happily engaged with Pinky in bargaining banter. Following some good-natured to-ing and fro-ing, we settled on 24,000 rupees (US$775).

Pinky told me to collect the bike the next day, but said that for some inexplicable reason I needed to bring a letter from the British High Commission stating that they had no objection to me buying a motorcycle. What possible concern could Her Majesty's Government have about a Brit buying a bike, I wondered? When I put it to him, Pinky couldn't answer that question. It took an hour-and-a-half to get to the High Commission in an auto rickshaw as we had to weave our way through New Delhi's anarchic traffic. In the midst of the melee, holy cows calmly grazed on discarded fly-blown rubbish, and I soon discovered that a cow in the road will stop hundreds of cars, whereas a red traffic light rarely will.

I half expected the High Commission to flatly reject my request. Instead, they issued the letter straightaway for a nominal admin fee. What other purchases did they routinely approve, I wondered? Lawnmowers? Blenders? Tin openers? The letter duly acquired, I returned to Pinky, who hopped on a scooter and took the letter to the Motor Vehicle Department. He came back two hours later, regretting to inform me that our address had been found 'objectionable'. It wasn't, I was surprised to hear, because we were residing in rat-infested Ringo's but because the letter had failed to say we were *living* at the British High Commission.

'The High Commission will never agree to that. It's not true,' I explained to Pinky. Much as I wished it was – at least then we'd have had clean sheets and a guesthouse without rats. Ever unflappable,

Pinky cheerily told me to return the following day to help him get the paperwork approved.

'With you with me, sir, the vehicle department people will most definitely not say no.'

The next morning, after a breakfast of *chai* and rubbery omelette, I returned to Karol Bagh where Pinky stood ready to drive me to the Motor Vehicle Department in his dad's Suzuki. We got there at 10am – and waited until 3pm because a jobsworth underling wouldn't stamp the documents until the Deputy Director of Transport (West Zone) gave him the nod. And the Deputy Director deigned to turn up for work at 2pm. Pinky did his deferential bowing and scraping bit and words in Hindi were exchanged. Profuse thanks were lavished as we left. It transpired the Deputy Director had said no. Undeterred, Pinky, as far as I could make out, got the okay from the Ministry of External Affairs instead. The next morning he had his money and I had the registration papers, the keys and the Enfield of my dreams.

That evening Lisa and I treated ourselves to lamburgers – India's holy cows do not hamburgers make – at Nirula's, a popular fast-food franchise in Connaught Place. Halfway through eating it, I decided I didn't want any more. There's a reason Texan ranches are full of steers, not sheep. Walking back to Ringo's, we were crossing Central Park when a young boy accosted Lisa.

'Your boots dirty, your boots dirty, I clean, yes?' the lad said, brandishing a brush and a tin of polish.

We politely declined as our tan suede-effect boots would have been ruined by a coating of oily polish, but then I glanced down and saw that Lisa's right boot was indeed dirty. What's more, it was *very* dirty, with a sizeable dollop of lustrous excrement atop the toe. Lisa was appalled. I was amused. Now we couldn't say the shoe-shine boy's services weren't needed, but we were damned if we were going to accept them as we strongly suspected that, to secure our business, *he'd* been the one who'd flung the dung. Lisa was especially put out because her boots, identical to the ones I owned but wasn't wearing, were almost brand new. The shoe-shiner pursued us all the way to Ringo's, his price falling from ten to two rupees. Back in our room,

I could see a pair of boots next to Lisa's side of the bed.

'Are those your boots, Lisa?' I asked.

'Oh yeah, I forgot I put them there. I must be wearing *your* boots! Here, you can have them back.'

This meant the shoe with the shit on it was mine. It was my turn to be appalled. Lisa, of course, was greatly amused.

We decided our first stop after Delhi had to be Agra, home to the Taj Mahal, widely considered to be one of the world's most beautiful buildings, and so on the morning of our fourth day in India we donned our open-faced helmets, stowed our rucksacks in the panniers, topped up the Enfield's tank and set off south.

Once the city environs were behind us the traffic thinned out somewhat, but the risk ramped up. Along with scooters, cars, bullock carts and buses, we now faced lorries whose drivers were obviously of the opinion that it was karma, and not bad driving, that would kill you. Lights flashing and horns blaring, they insisted on overtaking everything that was slower than them and trying to overtake everything faster than them. We both had to be alert lest we become badge ornaments on an oncoming Tata truck. Lisa hung on grimly and, peering over my shoulder, kept crying out warnings.

'Be careful of that truck! Watch out for that cow!'

Twice we were forced off the road onto the scrubby, sandy hard shoulder. It was all quite mad and unnerving, and our progress was slow. And then, about 7km from Hodal, after passing a hoarding advertising 'Hair Fertiliser', the Enfield began to burn. Lisa smelled it first and frantically tapped me on the shoulder.

'Holy fuck!'

I pulled over, kicked down the stand and hastily dismounted the bike. Smoke was rising from the engine.

'Get away from the bike, it might explode!' shrieked Lisa, running into the scrub.

'You've watched too many action movies Lisa, motorbikes don't burst into flames like that. Quick, help me throw some sand on it.'

Lisa returned to the bike and we scrabbled about on the hard shoulder, managing to scrape together four handfuls of dirt, which quickly smothered the fire that had started in the engine.

Trucks rumbled by, some parping their horns, oblivious to our plight. I was fuming. 'What a piece of useless shit,' I ranted, swinging a theatrical kick at the bike, aiming to miss. 'Our first journey out of Delhi and the bloody thing catches fire and packs up. I knew I should've bought a Hero Honda.' I was having a decidedly un-Zen motorcycle maintenance moment.

Lisa, thankful for the interlude to her suffering, kept her cool and, no doubt to calm me down, shared her 'expert' opinion on the health of the bike.

'I'm sure there's nothing majorly wrong with it, Graham. It was only smoking a little. And we're on a main road so eventually someone will help us.'

Half an hour later, someone did. A passing camel-cart driver kindly offered us a lift, but we couldn't find a way to heave 200kg of machine onto his laden cart so he continued on his leisurely way without us.

We had no choice but to risk restarting the bike and limp into the nearest town or village in the hope that we'd find a garage able to fix it. Thankfully, on the outskirts of Hodal we found one, though quite why a village garage in Nowheresville would have Enfield parts in stock, just in case, remains a mystery.

For the next two hours Lisa and I sat in metal-framed chairs in the shade smoking *bidis* and watching schoolkids play cricket on a grassless field with bats made from planks of wood as the garage's resourceful mechanics, hopping crab-like on their haunches about the bike, went to work fitting a new rectifier, whatever that is. By the end of the afternoon we'd attracted a small crowd of curious villagers who, when the time came for us to leave, cheerfully waved us on our way. We hoped that if the bike caught fire again it would have the good manners to do so outside somewhere as hospitable and mechanically minded as Hodal.

An Agra-vating encounter

Three squashed vultures, the painted rear ends of umpteen trucks urging us to 'Horn OK please' and hundreds of others bearing down on us from the opposite direction were about all that we saw on the road to Agra. And countless road signs displaying ominous words of doom such as 'Undertakers love overtakers'. The truck drivers either couldn't read – or couldn't care less. Several buses and lorries sported a child's shoe tied to the bumper. I wondered whether they were lucky charms to prevent the vehicle running over children. Maybe they were the way truckers memorialised the unfortunate kids they'd tragically mown down.

By the time we reached Agra shortly before dark, we had numb bums and were covered from head to toe in grime from the traffic. So much for the romance of the open road. Trembling, I climbed off the bike. My nerves were shredded and, dreading what Graham would say in reply, I blurted out: 'I'm not getting back on this flipping bike again! I really believed we were going to die out there!'

Graham removed his goggles, unaware that he now resembled a panda. His face was sooted black save for two white circles where the goggles had been.

'Too bloody right. If all Indian roads are like this, we'll be dead before Gwalior.'

'I can't believe you ever suggested this, Graham. It was such a dumb idea. And I can't believe I ever agreed to it.'

At that very moment our dream of doing India by Enfield died. We didn't mourn its passing. There was no way we could see ourselves spending up to eight hours a day enduring white-knuckle rides and staring death-by-truck in the face at every turn. In our naivety we hadn't appreciated that, unlike on trains, you couldn't eat, snooze, chat or read on a motorcycle as every waking moment had to be spent remaining vigilant to avoid becoming roadkill. I was learning fast that uncritically accepting Graham's big ideas wasn't always wise.

We later learned that Indian roads didn't just *feel* dangerous, they *were* dangerous: at the time there were 125 road deaths a day, about 12 times the comparable rate in the UK.

The Taj Mahal was as awe-inspiring as advertised, its huge onion dome gleaming white against a pale grey-blue sky, fronted by manicured lawns and duplicated, upside-down, in its reflecting pool. All over the Taj, both inside and out, were delicate tendrils of flowers and vines either carved, painted or inlaid with coloured stones. Sadly, not everyone came to admire its sublime architecture: we watched aghast as two youths used their metal watch clasps to furtively carve their initials into the marble of one of the minarets.

After strolling in the gardens beside women in a rainbow of wafting saris who seemed to float along its paths, we posed for photos on the stone bench that a lonely-looking Princess Diana had once sat on, before taking a nap on the grass behind a row of rose bushes. Opening my eyes half an hour later, the Taj now seemed to hover over me like a pale and tissue-paper-fragile sky lantern, a haunting marble memorial to an emperor's undying love for his departed wife.

Hunger forced us to tear ourselves away. Back in Agra's traffic-clogged streets we were intercepted by a middle-aged man selling fox-handled leather bullwhips. No doubt useful in 'starting' a bullock, they were of no use to us. We couldn't fault his perseverance as he pursued us for 300m, tugging on Graham's shirtsleeve and importuning all the way.

'But it's ugly,' said Graham, trying to refuse the offending item on aesthetic rather than cost grounds.

'It's ugly,' echoed the vendor, who immediately halved the price to 150 rupees, presumably to make it half as ugly.

On and on and on it went, with Graham politely declining the ever-decreasing asking price. After Graham's 99th 'No', I cracked. I simply couldn't tolerate another second of the man's pestering. Turning on my heels I barked, 'We are *not* buying your whip under *any* circumstances. So… leave… us… alone!'

The wind was momentarily taken out of the salesman's sails, but as we strode away he rallied with a plaintive cry of 'Twenty rupees?' I didn't feel good about losing my temper, especially not with someone who was trying to scrape a living, but there is only so much Agra-vation a woman can take when she's tired, hot and very, very hungry.

The next afternoon, after biking to Fatehpur Sikri where we explored the capital that the Mughal emperor Akbar founded in 1571, we bought three train tickets back to Delhi, two for us and one for the Enfield. Indian Railways insisted that the bike couldn't just be wheeled on board and carted back to Delhi, it had to be presented to the guard as a parcel.

'A parcel? Why? You'd better check if we need to gift wrap it and tie a fancy ribbon round it, too.'

'There's no arguing with Indian bureaucracy,' sighed Graham. 'Let's go and find some brown paper and string and get rid of this bloody bike.'

Arriving back in New Delhi Railway Station, where troops of monkeys gambolled playfully in the roof girders and a billboard proclaimed 'Cleanliness is next to Gooliness', we unwrapped the Enfield and biked back to Ringo's.

Two days later Graham returned to Karol Bagh to offload the bike. Pinky wasn't surprised to see him, but it soon became apparent that he wasn't at all interested in buying the Enfield back either. Another dealer saw his opportunity and grasped it, offering 7,000 rupees less than we'd paid Pinky. After only a few minutes' haggling, Graham accepted his offer gratefully. Losing US$225, he reasoned, was a *very* small price to pay to escape with our lives.

Midnight train to Madras

 Unburdened of the fear of death-by-Enfield we did what we should have done all along, namely travel by train and use buses when there was no rail connection. We preferred overnight trains so as not to waste a sightseeing day, and chose sleeper-class carriages because, although they weren't clean or air-conditioned, they were very cheap, and they went exactly as fast as the first-class ones.

Indian Railways is phenomenal. Consider the scale of it: today its trains carry more than 23 million passengers each day on 71,000 miles of track. Judging by the seeming chaos of its antiquated ticket offices, stations and platforms and its rundown-looking rolling stock, it was hard to believe that it could all hang together but, for the most part, day after day, it did. In Delhi we pre-booked a ticket from Calcutta to Madras – a distance of 1,650km that took over 33 hours – and six weeks later our train pulled alongside its designated platform, exactly on time. To our relief, delight and astonishment, we found our names on the dot-matrix-printed passenger manifest pasted to the outside of a carriage.

We always tried to book the upper berths so we could lie down when we wanted, be above the fray when we felt we needed to be, and be closer to the sole source of cooling – the cluster of dust-fuzzed fans bolted to the carriage ceiling. Lisa learned the desirability of the top bunk the hard way when, tucked up in her sleep sheet on the lowest bunk, she was woken up when her head suddenly elevated 10cm.

'What the hell?' she exclaimed, in her sleepy state unable to work out what had happened.

'Are you alright, Lisa?' I called from the bunk above.

'A man just sat on the end of my blow-up pillow and it's lifted up my head, and his bottom's in my face right now.'

The newly boarded passenger paid no attention, so Lisa tapped him on the back.

'Excuse me, sir, please could you get off my bunk and go and find your own. This is my bunk and I'm trying to get some sleep.'

Twisting round, the man replied: 'I'm not having one. Unless I sit here, I'll have to be standing the whole way.'

'I feel sorry for you, I really do, but you can't sit so close to my head that you're actually *on* my pillow,' said Lisa. 'Can you go and sit at my feet end please?'

I lay in my bunk shaking with laughter at this exchange and wasn't in the least surprised when, in the morning, once the man had left the train, Lisa laid down a new travel edict.

'I refuse to be sat on like that ever again. And I'm not going to feel bad about telling people they can't sit on me. So if we can't get upper bunks I'd rather book onto a different train. Or else *you* can have the bottom bunk and enjoy being sat on.'

Travelling by train offered a window into India we wouldn't have had if we'd survived a road trip. We didn't need to wait until we got to Bombay to see for ourselves what we'd suspected was Kiwi John's far-fetched traveller's tale of communal crapping on Chowpatty Beach. Our first train trip, out of New Delhi, presented us with the spectacle of long rows of Indians facing the railway line and 'easing' themselves in fields. Just as we might take reading matter to the loo to relieve the tedium, watching the trains clatter by did the same job for them. Initially, we found this shocking, but then it dawned on us that these people had, quite literally, nowhere else to go. Something that we in the West take for granted was a luxury for the majority of Indians who had no option but to defecate behind trees, next to ponds, by roadsides and riverbanks, and on beaches and railway tracks.

When people spend up to 30 hours at a time in the intimate company of strangers it's hard to ignore one another for long. English reserve is as out of place aboard an Indian train as a hog roast is at a bar mitzvah. Indians don't mind their own business and frequently asked us intrusive questions, such as how much money we earned and why we didn't have children. In the spirit of conversation, we asked intrusive questions of them.

On Indian trains, it's customary for passengers to exchange food as well as small talk. Locals frequently offered us snacks and, being well-mannered, we offered something in return. Biscuits were a good choice. Indians like biscuits. Indians also like peanuts, and I can't think of a train journey where peanut shells didn't litter the carriage floor. It made for an unsightly mess but there was invariably someone, often a child, who boarded the train to earn a meagre living sweeping them up.

It was also the norm aboard Indian trains to drink copious quantities of coffee and tea.

'Coffeecoffeecoffee! *Chai, chai, chai*!' the vendors would holler as our train pulled into a station, rushing up to the carriage windows bearing large steel kettles and stacks of small earthen cups. The coffee was invariably cheap-instant awful, but the *chai* – heavily sugared, milky tea mixed with a blend of spices – was sublime.

'Quick Graham, buy me some!' Lisa would urge whenever she heard the *chai wallah*'s call. 'I can't believe I've never heard of *chai* before. It really is the most delicious drink I've ever tasted. You know I love tea, but this is taking it to a whole new level.'

As the *wallahs* poured the steaming *chai* into the tiny cups, the most delightful wafts of cinnamon, ginger, cardamom, black pepper and cloves filled the carriage. And once we were done, it was perfectly acceptable to toss the cups out of the window, where they lay piled thick on the embankments either side of the track until the monsoon rains soaked them back into the soil.

Indians stare, a lot. It took us a while to learn to ignore it, though we never quite got used to it. At Bombay's cathedral-like Victoria Terminus, as we waited for our train to depart, a middle-aged, middle-class gentleman came directly up to our carriage window and, resting his folded elbows on the security bars, stared in at us unblinkingly for ten straight minutes. What was so interesting about us I don't know: this was Bombay, where Westerners were hardly a rarity, and I was reading a book and Lisa was eating pakoras from a paper bag. The man's staring didn't bother me, even though I could feel his breath on my cheek, but it hugely irritated Lisa, who angrily draped her white sarong over her head to hide from his inquisitive gaze. Not caring that she looked for all the world like a human shuttlecock, she proceeded to moodily consume her snacks under the cloth, unwittingly piquing his curiosity even more.

Turning to him, I quipped sarcastically, 'Fascinating, isn't it?' He nodded and carried on staring.

Personal space – the two to four feet around us into which others are forbidden to enter unless invited – didn't exist when queuing to purchase train tickets. The unspoken rule was that you had to stand with your chin resting on the head of the Indian in front of you and the Indian behind you had to press his nose between your shoulder blades. This had to be repeated the length of the queue. If you didn't conform then someone would slip into the space and your fellow queuers would hiss and 'tsk'. Given that ticket queues moved very slowly and you'd have to withstand their disapproval for quite some time, you *really* didn't want this to happen.

Something else you wanted to avoid was catching the attention of the zealous officials tasked to bring order to the ticket-office throng. Armed with four-foot bamboo *lathis*, they seemed to delight in smacking the legs of those they suspected of queue jumping, or those who refused to close the gaps.

'Can you imagine the public outcry if British Rail or the South African Railways allowed their staff to treat commuters like this?' I said to Lisa.

'It gives a whole new meaning to the term "beating the rush hour",' she joked.

Death hotels

 Indian trains were safer than they were fast. It took 17 hours – and another six on a bus, during which Graham farted all the way – to get to our first stop after Gwalior, Kanha National Park, famed for its tigers and for being the setting of Rudyard Kipling's *The Jungle Book*. We may as well not have bothered. Graham was struck down with suspected giardiasis, a tummy illness where belches smell like farts and your farts smell worse than ever, so he stayed in bed in our increasingly evil-smelling hut all day reading a poorly printed, staple-bound booklet extolling the virtues of urine therapy that we'd bought from a pavement bookseller in Delhi.

Indians have been drinking urine for its purported health benefits for thousands of years, but Graham was astonished to discover that there's more to urine therapy than the classic 'wake, pee, quaff' scenario. There's whole-body urine massage, urine enemas, urine gargling – and peeing on one's feet to cure fungal infections, something that Madonna reputedly practises.

'Truly, there's a whole world of wee out there, Lisa, though I doubt that many people are going to be courageous enough to discover it for themselves. Even though India gave Britain its national dish of chicken tikka masala, I'm not at all surprised that urine therapy hasn't caught on back home. Why would we Brits drink wee when there's tea?'

Leaving Graham to suffer in his foul fug, I rose at dawn to embark on a tiger-spotting expedition in the back of a lurching Jeep and spent all morning swallowing dust and staring into the tall yellow grass while the tigers, elusive blighters that they are, stubbornly refused to be found. My mood wasn't improved when the tourists who'd gone on the afternoon safari – and who'd therefore had a lovely lie-in – later told us that they'd seen a tiger saunter across the track directly in front of their vehicle.

Fortunately, Varanasi, our next destination, was a lot more photogenic than Kanha with its camera-shy tigers. Swathes of colourful silk hung fluttering outside its shops, and its neglected but beautiful buildings tumbled down to the edge of the Ganges. Visiting in 1896, Mark Twain described it as 'older than history, older than tradition, older even than legend, and looks twice as old as all of them put together.' Indeed it did. Some Indians claim that Varanasi was founded 5,000 years ago by the Hindu god Lord Shiva, although modern historians say it's 2,000 years younger than that. The legions of cycle rickshaw drivers thronging the streets continuously trilling their bells to attract customers and warn pedestrians made for a magical, harmonious soundtrack. It was bedlam with bells.

Varanasi, however, looked considerably nicer than it smelled. There is no other way to put this: despite its wonderfully spiritual feel, the city stank to high heaven of shit and pee thanks to its over-large population of holy cows. Though off-limits to cattle, our hotel room had a similar aroma. We referred to it as 'A Room with a View of the Loo' as its smelly, doorless en suite was situated directly opposite our bed. The basket into which we had to deposit whatever we'd used to wipe our bottoms was seldom emptied, and whenever we took a shower we'd find ourselves standing in what I took to be sewage or sick that bubbled up from the shower drain. I cannot begin to describe the relief I felt when I discovered the liquid was, in fact, dishwater from the kitchen and the 'bits' in it were merely grains of cooked rice. The bedding, once no doubt white, was now 50 shades of grey, and one of the pillows was impregnated with several long black hairs and the waxy imprint of the previous occupant's head.

On the plus side, our room had an unbeatable vista of the Ganges so, despite its all-too-obvious failings, we stayed put. Seated on stools next to our window, we spent hours watching the *ghats* goings-on. The stone steps leading down to the river were crowded with palm readers, purveyors of postcards and massages and people doing their laundry. A half-naked *sadhu*, his matted dreadlocks tied up into a towering bun, strode back and forth carrying a trident that indicated he was a follower of the demon-slaying Shiva while a buffalo looked on, neck-deep in the scummy water, calmly munching on a marigold garland. Sari-clad women waded into the slow-flowing river to splash water over their heads as pilgrims bathed, worshipped, washed in and drank the fetid water, one sip of which would, I'm sure, have killed me. Held sacred, the Ganges is nonetheless one of the world's most polluted rivers: more than a billion gallons of waste from India's crowded northern plains, three-quarters of it raw sewage, flows into it each day. It's a river that functions as a canal – India's alimentary canal.

For all its liveliness, Varanasi was also a place of death, and the lingering smell of woodsmoke from the cremation fires on the burning *ghats* was ever-present. Hindus believe that by dying in Varanasi they'll achieve *moksha*, the liberation from the cycle of death and rebirth, and so come from all over India to spend their final days here.

Graham and I were in an auto rickshaw on a day trip to Sarnath, where the Buddha had preached for the first time since gaining enlightenment, when we passed a hand-painted sign on a crumbling building that at first glance I thought read 'STAY AND DINE'.

'That's about the worst spot in the whole of Varanasi to build a hotel,' I remarked. 'Who in their right mind would want to be down a stinking alleyway when there are so many places to stay and eat that have great views of the river?'

'Look again, Lisa, I think you've misread the sign.'

I saw my mistake. In a macabre all-inclusive deal, the hotel really was inviting prospective guests to 'STAY AND DIE'. This was one of the designated hotels where the old and infirm could come to await death. Some catered for those whose demise was imminent, but others set no time limit and so some souls had been waiting for decades to check out for the last time.

For people who'd checked into – and out of – Varanasi's 'death hotels', the next destination, for those who could afford it, was the Manikarnika Ghat, where open-air cremations were conducted. Shrouded bodies on bamboo stretchers draped in floral garlands were immersed in the Ganges and then set atop a wooden pyre and sprinkled with ghee and sandalwood. The deceased's eldest son, his head newly shaved, kindled the flames after the relatives had walked seven times around the pyre. This was Act One of a two-act drama: a ritualised, respectful ceremony like any funeral we'd attended.

Act Two was radically dissimilar, so much so that it was like watching a totally different play. It was perfunctory and, quite frankly, brutal. Once the wood had been consumed by the flames, the funeral attendants set to work, energetically thwacking the corpses with thick bamboo staves to dismember them, often cracking open their skulls to free the souls from their earth-bound existence. The poles were then used to spear and hoick chunks of smoking, charred body into the river where, with a fizzle of steam, they sank from sight. Waiting dogs, wild with anticipation, leapt into the water to retrieve their dinner, and youths dived from a moored boat, hoping to salvage jewellery and gold teeth.

Just then we were startled by a loud pop, followed by another a few seconds later.

'I think that's the sound of brains exploding from the heat of the pyre,' I said, shuddering.

Witnessing such a private ceremony played out in public made us uncomfortable. We wouldn't have dreamt of attending a funeral uninvited back home, but the fact that none of the mourners was weeping went a long way towards alleviating our unease. It helps that Hindus believe in reincarnation, which means that once a person is born they never die.

'Isn't it amazing how, when you have death on your mind, you imagine you can see it everywhere? You see those two logs, over there?' I remarked to Graham, pointing to two posts poking out of the water. 'They look just like knees.'

We peered at the logs for a while longer and then, as they dipped under the water, a cloth-bound head emerged. We had indeed just seen a body, bound up in the foetal position, drifting slowly downriver. No one paid it any attention except us.

A young Indian dressed in light blue trousers and a soot-speckled vest came and stood next to me. I turned to look at him and, catching my eye, he took this as his cue to recite his well-rehearsed pitch, explaining that the funeral pyres were lit with kindling from a 5,000-year-old fire that was kept permanently burning and was moved higher up the *ghats* when the monsoon rains fell and the Ganges rose.

'Not everyone is cremated. Pregnant women, babies, children, *sadhus*, lepers and victims of smallpox are wrapped in cloth, made heavy with stones and sunk in the middle of the Ganges,' he said, adding that if a family couldn't afford the wood for a cremation they'd simply throw the body in the river. That, we realised, would account for the floating corpse.

'Each burning takes 300kg of wood. Wood for burning is very expensive,' he said, gesturing to a ten-foot-high set of iron scales used to weigh it out, next to which a pair of black vultures were loping about. 'I explain the ritual, you make contribution?'

We thanked him for the insight he'd given us into the cremations and donated enough rupees to pay for a few kilogrammes of wood.

As we retraced our steps to our hotel, another youth asked for a donation. Graham told him we'd already contributed.

'What name?' asked the youth.

'Tarquin,' Graham replied.

Opening a tatty exercise book, the youth ran his index finger down a long list of names corresponding with a list of numbers.

'Clare give. François give. David give. Tarquin not give. François give 1,000 rupees. How much you give?'

'Never you mind,' said Graham.

'I think you give your money to robberman,' the youth persisted. 'I work in hospice.'

'That's what a robberman would say,' Graham retorted. 'Maybe I did give my money to a robberman, but how do I know you're not a robberman, too?'

Uncomfortable with this line of questioning, the youth sighed and shuffled off.

Continuing our way homewards we passed dozens of Indians making themselves comfortable for the night on the dung-stained *ghats*, reminding us of how lucky we were to have a bed to sleep in and a room to go back to, even if it did have something of the night cart about it. Out of the descending darkness an anonymous voice piped up, 'Good night, sir.'

To which Graham quietly replied, 'Good night.'

Freaks & flies

 The 'wheels of terror' transported us from Varanasi to Kathmandu, Nepal's capital, for the cheap-as-chips price of 200 rupees (US$6.50) each. Our tickets entitled us to a two-day trip aboard a rickety 30-seater bus so cramped that I sat with my bottom cantilevered over the aisle as only one cheek would fit on the wooden seat. We had the misfortune to sit in front of a large-bellied Nepali in a black Nehru waistcoat who belched volubly and malodorously the entire time.

The journey started out terror-free but, after we'd spent the night at a hotel at the border and purchased a visa in the morning, our bus started ascending the foothills of the Himalayas on narrow roads without crash barriers. Whenever a vehicle came the other way our driver would swerve the bus over until its left wheels were scrabbling for purchase on the crumbling edge of the road, giving us spectacular views of the precipitous slopes below.

'Oh God, why is he driving like this?' I thought fearfully.

I tried to convince myself that, as someone who drove this route for a living, our driver was an expert at navigating the hairpin bends and that no harm would befall us, but another glance down into the valley confirmed my sweaty-palmed fears: a wrecked bus, turned on its side, lay smashed and rusting in the undergrowth, and a few metres further there was a second. I closed my eyes after that and prayed that among the pantheon of Hindu gods there was one whose sole sacred task it was to tirelessly watch over bus safety.

After enduring an all-day buttock battering we motored into the mystical city of Kathmandu at 8.30pm. A ten-minute taxi haggle secured us a ten-minute ride to Jhochhen Tole, colloquially known as Freak Street, where we'd decided to stay. It acquired this moniker in the 1960s when it became a hangout for hippies drawn to its government-run hashish shops, giving an insight into how the locals really viewed the long-haired, bead-and-sandal-wearing Westerners who thronged there.

Roaming through Kathmandu's winding, brick-paved streets overhung with intricately carved wooden buildings was like stepping back into the Middle Ages. Even the curios were curious: pop-eyed replica *kapalas* (sacred cups made from human skulls decorated with metal plate and semi-precious stones) and Tibetan singing bowls that screamed in ever higher tones when stroked with a wooden stick. A few Nepalis followed us around with offers to 'Change money?', 'Ride rickshaw?' or 'Buy Chinese opium?' but, unlike in India, refusal didn't seem to offend. One or two 'No thanks' were enough to make them cease and desist. As the colourful embroidered tourist T-shirts for sale in Durbar Square proclaimed, 'No rickshaw, no hashish, no change money, no baksheesh, no problem.'

Kathmandu would've been heavenly but for its evil-smelling goats. Tethered to the steps of almost every shrine, the sour stink of their urine and droppings hung thick in the air. I hurried past, pinching my nose, suppressing the urge to throw up. The smell was so rank that for years afterwards I couldn't stomach goat's cheese, not even in quiche.

Around the corner from Freak Street was the Kumari Ghar Palace, past which we walked at least twice a day. One afternoon a group of politely applauding Japanese tourists blocked our path and we craned our necks to see what had captured their attention. At the middle of three wood-framed windows sat a five-year-old girl with dark kohl-lined eyes, dressed in a russet red cloak and matching headdress. She was looking disdainfully down on the snap-happy Japanese, as bored by them as they were interested in her, and furiously chewing gum.

'It's the Royal Kumari, who's worshipped as a living goddess,' I informed Graham. 'She lives in this palace from the age of three until she reaches puberty, when she ceases to be a goddess and reverts to being mortal again. She's only allowed out of her palace 13 times a year, and tradition dictates that her feet must never touch the ground. We're really lucky to see her.'

I could imagine the scene once the Royal Kumari went back to live with her family after a decade or so of divinity.

Kumari's mum: 'Now that you are back home, you have to tidy your room.'

Kumari: 'I did.'

Kumari's mum: 'No you didn't, it's an absolute pigsty. You were too busy skateboarding.'

Kumari: 'I don't see why I have to tidy my room anyway. Last week I had servants to do it.'

Kumari's mum: 'That was last week. Tidy your room, young lady, or I'll confiscate your Nintendo.'

Kumari: 'I'm a retired living goddess.'

Kumari's mum: 'That's right. Retired. And I want you to spit out that gum right this instant.'

The food in Kathmandu came as a blessed relief: we'd gritted our teeth through dozens of Indian *dosas*, *dhals* and *dum aloos* – despite our guidebook assuring us the food could be fantastic – so eating Western food again was sheer bliss. We went from restaurant window to restaurant window marvelling at the backlit lemon-meringue pies almost a foot deep and drooling over menus that featured home comforts such as spaghetti bolognese and pizza. For one of our first meals we feasted on lasagne and lassi.

'This tastes a bit buff,' remarked Graham. 'I suspect it's probably made with buffalo meat and buffalo milk.'

'Stop trying to put me off my food, Graham, it's delicious,' I replied, tucking in with gusto.

At 4am I woke to the sound of Graham violently spewing into the small plastic bowl we prepared salads in when taking a break from street food. Several bowlfuls later it was my turn, while Graham turned his attention to filling the more capacious white ceramic squat loo with rusty water.

'I told you that our lasagne and lassi were 100 per cent buffalo,' groaned Graham weakly from behind the curtain of our bathroom.

The next afternoon, recovered from our bout of food poisoning, we set off to find the prayer-flag-bedecked Swayambhunath Stupa, painted on all four sides with glowering Buddha eyes. Our expedition took us to the outskirts of the city where it became readily apparent why we'd become so ill. Here we came across Kathmandu's butcheries – 'fly hatcheries' as Graham dubbed them – with their wares hanging from giant iron hooks. Above a patch of ground soaked black with coagulated blood was a barbed-wire fence draped with entrails like stockings hung out to dry. Sawn-off buffalo legs were piled up on tables alongside heaps of offal watched over by severed goats' heads, tongues lolling from their retracted gums, ears flapping in the wind. Not one of the butcheries had refrigeration. The stink of warm flesh was overpowering, so we retreated to the river, where we saw an even more stomach-churning scene. On the hoof-trampled banks and in the stagnant ribbon of water buffalos grazed and bathed among hundreds of severed, putrefying buffalo forelegs. We both vowed, then and there, not to eat meat again in Nepal. Or perhaps ever.

The wisdom of our decision was confirmed minutes later when we crossed a rope-and-wood suspension bridge and saw three smartly dressed Nepali gentlemen walk down the riverbank, lower their trousers, squat and void their bowels. 'How very social,' we thought. An enormous hog loitered expectantly nearby and, as soon as the trio had finished and put a respectable distance between themselves and their business, it moved in to snaffle up a three-course meal.

Second-hand dentures

A tired Lisa is a tetchy Lisa so, when Lisa asked if she could borrow my cherished inflatable pillow for the bus journey from Kathmandu to the Indian hill station of Darjeeling, having carelessly misplaced her own, I said yes as I knew how uncomfortable subcontinental bus trips can be. But when she promptly sat on and burst it, I was not a happy bunny, especially when she went on to fall blissfully asleep for the rest of the bumpy bus ride, her head drumming incoherent Morse code against the window. How does she do that?

Darjeeling in March was misty and chilly, and we weren't outfitted for its cool, dank weather. We spent most of our time in bed, shivering ourselves warm, and stayed clean by topping-and-tailing with tepid water delivered in a metal pail. During the day, the sunshine burned away some of the cold's rawness and we layered ourselves in what thin cotton clothing we had to visit a tea plantation. There we learned how Darjeeling became famous for producing the 'Champagne of teas' that could fetch astronomical sums on the international market. We also joined the women on the terraced slopes to try our hand at picking tea. Their slender hands darted over the bushes like hungry robins to lightly pluck the choicest shooting leaves and throw them by the handful across their shoulders into the wicker baskets on their backs. Our fingers tore ineptly at the leaves. Within 20 minutes the tea-pickers had harvested enough to keep a British Army regiment in char for a week, and we'd picked maybe enough for a small cuppa each.

Chilling (literally) in Darjeeling soon lost its appeal, so we left after 48 hours. A day-long bus and train journey brought us to an appreciably warmer Calcutta, a city where life appeared to be lived on the street. People found shelter in cardboard 'homes' on the pavement, ate their meals there, worked streetside occupations, lathered themselves clean at communal pumps and probably died as they had lived, on the street. The city was alive with coconut-drink sellers, men mangling sugarcane to create ultra-sweet beverages, and *chai wallahs* surrounded by piles of shattered clay cups. A vendor of second-hand dentures, sitting on his heels, his wares set out on a cloth on the pavement, caught our eye. We wondered if his sales pitch went: 'Hello, hello, nice dentures, very cheap. How about these? One previous owner who used them only on weekends. Do you want vegetarian or non-vegetarian teeth?'

You may think that dead-men's dentures are a far-fetched proposition, but as late as the middle of the 19th century 'Waterloo teeth' – teeth pulled from corpses on the battlefield of the same name – were on sale in England. Buyers knew where they came from but didn't know if they had been pulled from the mouths of British or French soldiers.

The marble Victoria Memorial, which bore a passing resemblance to St Paul's Cathedral, was sited on one corner of the Maidan, Calcutta's green lung, where cricketing boys honed their skills after school and a sign proclaimed 'Physical and yogic exercises not permitted in gardens. Shooting (movie) not allowed'. The Memorial housed a museum whose contents were showing their age. Several portraits of Victorian royals were spattered with pigeon droppings, and a gown from Edward VII's Coronation celebration lay forlornly in a glass cabinet. Neglected for 90 years, it resembled a heap of well-rotted compost. A framed poster inside asked visitors to refrain from defacing any of the galleries: 'Do not write on the walls. Persons doing so will be liable for a fine of Rs100 to pay for painting the wall. By order.'

On the steps outside, in front of a statue of a po-faced Queen Victoria who was clearly 'not amused', an Indian asked me if I would pose for a photo with him. I obliged. Once he'd gone, I turned to Lisa. 'I wanted to tell him that my rugged good looks would make him seem exceptionally unattractive and that maybe he should pose with you instead!'

Calcutta was the last Indian city where human-drawn rickshaws plied their trade. Although there were still 6,000 of them drawn by 20,000 rickshaw *wallahs*, they were a threatened breed even in 1993, and I was curious to know what it was like to pull one. So one rainy day, as the roads lay under several inches of water, I invited one *wallah*, wearing the customary vest, *lungi* and flip-flops of his trade, to sit with Lisa and let me pay him to draw his rickshaw. I wouldn't want to pull a rickshaw all day for a living, but once I'd judged the balance and built up some momentum it was easy to maintain it, though difficult to stop or change direction in a hurry. The rickshaw *wallah* was delighted, beaming from ear to ear as he was borne through the backstreets to smatterings of applause from an amused, perhaps bemused, Indian public

Public inconvenieinces

'Mummy, mummy, please can I lick out the bowl?'
'No Johnny, flush the toilet like all the other children.'
Jokes such as this would've been completely lost on the pre-traveller Lisa because South Africans don't 'do' toilet humour. Or at least they didn't in the Jackson family. The closest they ever got to talking about toilets was Lisa's mother's tale of how she was chased down a Parisian street after failing to tip the attendant as she was unaware that it was compulsory to part with a few centimes to spend a penny.

The British most certainly *do* do toilet humour. The English language is replete with words, idioms and euphemisms for bodily functions and activities. Sigmund Freud would no doubt argue, disapprovingly, that the British never quite got over the 'anal' stage of childhood development. Perhaps toilet humour evolved alongside British imperialism, when death at a young age was as likely to come from a crap-yourself-to-death disease as it was from an indigenous spear or a wild animal. Even if Freud is correct, in its defence, scatological humour is a very effective class leveller (Hooray Henry or chav, we all shit), punctures pretension and challenges taboos. All are valuable functions.

At bottom, farting just *is* funny, one of life's guilty pleasures. Who hasn't been tempted to drop one in a lift, and who hasn't eased out a 'velvet slipper' and blamed it on the dog? Toilet humour can also be a shield and a weapon for those inevitable ugly encounters with public toilets. Once Lisa started travelling, she quickly learned to see the funny side of toxic toilets. It really was a case of laugh, or cry or retch uncontrollably.

In my family, toilet humour was not off-limits. My brother Rod, for instance, has a back catalogue of cringe-worthy toilet tales. Age 20, his work sent him to Italy to inspect a tomato-ketchup factory in a rustic farmhouse. Needing the loo rather urgently he was taken to a barn-sized room with four giant steps at one end. Climbing the steps he got a view of the loos: there were no cubicles, no screens, just three rolls of paper next to three holes sunk into the floor.

'Oh my god, what am I going to do?' he asked himself, sweat pouring off him as he stood surveying the scene in his thick woollen suit. He had no option but to unbuckle his belt, lower his trousers and crouch down into an unsteady squat. At that very moment a siren sounded, as though advertising the moment. It was lunchtime, and several dozen workers streamed in to relieve themselves. All Rod's dignity and authority as the man from head office who could shut down the production line with a disapproving shake of his head evaporated as he became painfully aware of how ridiculous he must have looked wobbling away on his haunches, his trousers gathered about his ankles. What followed was even more excruciating: he had to eat lunch with all the workers in the canteen.

It's impossible to erase the memory of the first time we used a public toilet in India. We were on our way to Jhansi and after three hours of sitting on a rock-hard bus seat we all spilled out at a service station to use the facilities and stock up on snacks. There was one loo, and I hurried over to use it. It was a concrete box with a tin roof, accessed via a rusting metal door. The stench was overwhelming as I stepped inside, patting the interior wall to locate the light switch. There wasn't one. The windowless room was barely twice as wide as its door so I could see there wasn't a toilet, only a hole in the corner that was off-the-scale unhygienic. Only it wasn't a hole anymore, but a former hole now clogged with excrement. Gagging, I had no choice – it was either get on with it or risk holding it in for Lord knew how long. Stuffing some shredded tissues into my nostrils and memorising the location of the shit pyramid, I reluctantly closed the door. In the inky blackness I did the speediest crap I've ever done, before bolting outside and sucking in great lungfuls of fresh air. Never again would I take for granted the puddle of water in the bottom of the bowl that encases and deodorises faecal deposits while simultaneously acting as a barrier to sewer gas.

But even this wasn't the grimmest WC we'd encounter in India. That dubious honour goes to a toilet block in Mandla. Our bus developed engine trouble so the driver pulled into a lay-by, whipped out a spanner and set to work fixing it. We snatched the opportunity to use the facilities, cautiously skirting the pool of white-grey scum outside the toilet building from which arose swirling swarms of flies. Piles of faeces formed brown islands in the scum. Inside there was a row of cubicles, each of which contained a groove in the concrete floor with a hole at the far end. None of them had doors, or running water, so the shit simply lay where it fell. We walked the full length of the block, trying to avoid making eye contact with those in the occupied booths, finally choosing two where the mess was less. During my very brief visit I could hear Lisa taking turns to retch and wee, to the amusement of the other users.

The squat toilets aboard Indian trains could be pretty squalid, too. On more than one occasion I had to kick turds off the footrests where they had been deposited, I surmised, as a result of the violent swaying motion of the train. That left unanswered the question, where the hell were their feet when they dropped their guts? Perhaps they'd adopted a far wider squatting stance, or had shat while hanging from the overhead fan. It didn't bear thinking about for too long. Using train loos required the balance and poise of a ballerina and the ability to press and keep the top of my head against the wall to stabilise me. This technique also saved me from inadvertently touching anything with my hands, which I'd need to eat with later.

At least our trains had toilets. Eight decades earlier, Indian carriages didn't, resulting in passenger Okhil Chandra Sen's unfortunate mishap. In his 1909 letter of complaint to the Sahibganj Divisional Office West Bengal, Okhil wrote that when his train arrived at Ahmedpur Station his belly was 'too much swelling with jackfruit' and so he'd disembarked 'to make dung'. As he was defecating, the guard whistled for his train to depart. Rushing back, water pot in hand and *dhoti* in the other, Okhil tripped over, exposing 'all my shocking to man and female women on platform' and missed his train. He threatened to go to the newspapers unless the guard was punished but, to the grateful relief of railway passengers ever since, Okhil's letter – on display at the National Rail Museum in New Delhi – instead led to the installation of toilets on India's trains.

The only thing worse than using an Indian toilet was there not being one when we needed it. Especially on the incredibly long bus journeys we had to undertake across the subcontinent. I found this out the hard way when we were heading to the hill station of Darjeeling in the foothills of the Himalayas. At the junction town of Siliguri I went to the toilet twice as a 'precaution', but as the knackered old bus started its three-and-a-half-hour emphysemic uphill struggle I suspected there was more to follow. There was. After an hour of worsening cramps I couldn't hold it in anymore. Striding purposefully to the front of the bus, I shouted 'Stop the bus! Stop the bus!' gesturing to the driver that I was about to vomit − I wasn't about to mime explosive diarrhoea in front of 20 passengers. Understanding my urgency, and wanting to keep his bus chunder free, the driver obliged, opened the door and allowed me to leap out and sprint directly for the low retaining wall I'd spotted seconds earlier that I hoped would afford me *some* privacy. I vaulted it, dropped my trousers not a moment too soon and, to a loud tearing sound, explosively ejected a not insignificant volume of runny shit.

Back aboard the bus I lasted 20 minutes before, cramping anew, I had to reprise my 'Stop the bus!' act. Making this time for a culvert almost deep enough to protect my modesty, I hopped down, squatted, and shat profusely again. This time, however, I couldn't conceal the true nature of my sickness: a cluster of curious faces watched me through the rear window of the bus. I stepped out from the ditch, composed myself, walked half a dozen paces, felt a griping twinge in my guts, turned sharply about and returned hastily to the culvert. By now I'd completely exhausted my supply of tissues and anxiously looked around to see what I could use to wipe my battered bottom. I considered using my left hand, as Indians supposedly do, but decided against it when I remembered that a Dutch traveller who'd tried this had smelt shit on her fingers for a week. All there was to hand were a few small fallen leaves. Balancing them one at a time on my index finger, I carefully and precisely wiped myself. It took a lot of leaves, and a steady hand.

Lisa, meanwhile, had given up pretending that she had no idea who I was and cringed as several concerned passengers enquired after my welfare.

'He's sick,' she told them, not wanting to go into detail about the state of my stools.

The news spread quickly.

'He's seek, very seek,' I heard them say as I clambered back onto the bus.

'Yes, and he's also very, very embarrassed,' I thought as I gingerly lowered myself onto my seat.

I'd be the first to admit, however, that some of our toilet traumas were exacerbated by my decision, as our trip's self-appointed auditor and accountant, that we couldn't afford toilet paper as it was so eye-wateringly pricey in India. A single roll could set you back the price of a meal or two. So we did as many Indians do. Not using the old left-hand trick, but newspaper cut into strips. That was until we discovered that old paperbacks were more absorbent. A particularly poignant memory of India involved wiping our bottoms with pages torn from *Duel of Eagles*, a Battle of Britain memoir by Group Captain Peter Townsend, one-time suitor of Princess Margaret. We'd read the book as quickly as we needed toilet paper. Which was quickly.

Laughter, it is said, is the best medicine. I don't disagree, but it's sadly not the cure-all some people think it is. In India, it wasn't enough to prevent my raging diarrhoea from repeatedly embarrassing me in public. That took Imodium.

The Bogeyman of Pushkar

Ah, Indian cuisine: enough to make your bowels water. We tried very hard to like it, but usually it was either dull, disgusting – or verging on the deadly. Granted, not every single thing that passed our lips was vile. If we cast our minds back, Lisa and I both agree that the *thali* we had in Khajuraho, a town that's home to a group of temples featuring exquisite pornographic sculptures, was quite delicious. Set up on a three-legged table outside an elderly couple's home, each dish in the bicycle-wheel-sized compartmented metal tray was subtly and expertly spiced. Pity that we couldn't find another like it. And we did rather enjoy *masala dosa*, cricket-bat-sized lentil pancakes stuffed with spicy potato that were widely available, until we realised they were about the *only* dish we liked, had two too many and couldn't stomach another one.

Indian food wasn't very tasty, nutritious or hygienically prepared, and we didn't want to eat it, but we needed to eat it, and when we did eat it, sooner or later it made us ill. In Varanasi, Lisa ordered an egg curry: it came as a halved, hard-boiled egg floating in a bowl of what looked like pee, with several peas bobbing on the surface. In Delhi I was served a *chapatti* that had a large ant pressed into it. In Goa we were halfway into a flavourful meal of mussels steamed in wine when I bit into one so gritty, gassy and shit-tasting that I hastily spat it into my napkin. It must have been harvested mid-way through filtering effluent.

And so it went, day after day. Soon all I could face was Western food, but most of the hideously misspelled dishes – 'fried children', 'vegetable neudies', 'egg burgle' – tasted as grim as their names were silly. I once ordered a brown bread sandwich from a roadside restaurant in Jabalpur, but when it arrived it was quite the whitest bread one could hope to find, only toasted. I called over the waiter and reminded him that I'd asked for brown bread. Taking the plate from the table he ran his finger across the inadequately toasted sandwich, pausing wherever the bread had discoloured, and said helpfully, 'Brown, here brown, here more brown.'

In Pushkar in Rajasthan we went on yet another search for non-Indian food. All the restaurants in this camel-trading town seemed to serve toast with honey but we soon found out they also had flies. Noisy swarms of them that rose from the open honey pots in humming clouds. We'd already visited and rejected on the grounds of hygiene violations every establishment along the town's main street when we entered RS Restaurant, near the Brahmaji Temple. The menu said they had toast and honey. In need of the nourishment that sweet white bread would have been stripped of, I asked the nearest waiter, dressed in blue trousers, flip-flops and a stained double-breasted chef's jacket, if they had wholemeal toast. Not comprehending, he summoned a second waiter who was indolently wiping a table with a filthy cloth. You know you're in India when a dirty cloth is used to clean something.

'Do you have wholemeal toast?' I asked again.

As the second waiter contemplated my question, quite unselfconsciously he slowly brought his left index finger to his left nostril and inserted it up to the middle joint. Looking me full in the eye, his finger distending his nose out of shape as he rooted for the only greens that children are happy to eat, he replied, 'Yes, sir, we have wholemeal.'

I looked at Lisa with a 'They have what we want, let's sit down' look. Lisa, mouth agape, looked at me with a 'The waiter is picking his bloody nose!' look and, snapping shut the menu, started crying uncontrollably. I waved the baffled-looking waiter away and asked Lisa whether she wanted to leave.

'No,' she sobbed from behind the anonymity of her sunglasses.

'Well, if we're going to stay, what do you want to order?'

'Wholemeal toast with honey. I've given up hope of finding anywhere vaguely clean. If we're going to eat flies, we might as well eat them here.'

And so we ended up devouring rack upon rack of toast, butter and honey, Lisa stifling a small sob between each bite, served, with great efficiency, by The Bogeyman of Pushkar.

Schadenfreude is not an admirable character trait, but we are all susceptible to it and, at one time or another, we've all let ourselves revel in the mean-spirited, negative pleasure of delighting in another's discomfort. This was one of the times that I decided to let schadenfreude out for air. I began softly humming a tune. Lisa looked up at me, dimly familiar with my rendition of a Jackson Five number, as if to say, 'What are you up to now?' Lisa knew that I was humming it to make fun of her, but she couldn't quite recall what it was. I gleefully continued, quietly singing the chorus lyrics with a single word substitution: '… blame it on the bogey'.

Her tears now dried into salted stains down her cheeks, Lisa removed her sunglasses and looked me in the eyes, now chuckling.

'You know, sometimes you can be such a bastard.'

Lisa wasn't the only one troubled by Indian food. Within a few weeks

I lost my appetite and started losing weight. Then I got ill, despite sitting on my left, bottom-wiping hand to remind myself to eat with my right hand. So it was definitely the food, not me. We knew it couldn't have been the water because we boiled our own every day using a plastic jug and a travel immersion heater – we calculated that during our India trip we saved a princely US$200 that way. It also meant we could steer clear of one of India's better-known scams in which fraudsters would refill discarded bottles with tap water and pass it off as mineral water.

First, I had suspected giardiasis and then repeated bouts of diarrhoea, and the pounds started to fall visibly from me. I ate what I could bear to eat to stay on the right side of soiled trousers: white boiled rice, *chapattis* with mixed-fruit jam, lemon-flavoured Limca soft drink and Thums Up spicy cola. The latter was India's answer to Coke and had been introduced to fill the gap left by Coca-Cola which had been booted out of India in 1977 by the newly elected government when it refused to divulge the recipe for its flagship product. The advertising tagline for Thums Up was 'Taste the thunder!'. I drank it to quell the thunder in my bowels. I could also stomach ice cream, but it was a risky foodstuff because if it had melted and been refrozen it could give you the squits. My favourite brand, whose name may have been an ominous forewarning of this disaster scenario, was Cadbury's Dollops.

Sometimes this dietary regime worked, but often it didn't. When it did work, I was fine and India was fascinating and fun, but when it didn't work I spent days not leaving our room, not daring to pass wind for fear of uncontrolled follow-through. We missed our overnight train to Amritsar because I shat 27 times in 24 hours, which confined me to our Delhi hotel for three days. It hurt to miss out on Amritsar's Golden Temple, the Sikh holy of holies. It hurt even more to shit so frequently. As I rallied, Lisa fell ill, spending two days reading *Duel of Eagles* while lying over the latrine hole in the floor of our bathroom, too weak to get up and go back to bed.

To have someone 'eating out of your hand' is a common expression in English to denote having someone completely under your control.

During our train journey from Ahmedabad to Udaipur it took on a completely different meaning for Lisa – a literal one. Our ticket showed the distance was 298km, which should have taken six hours but which, because the decrepit steam train kept breaking down, took 21. The seats were bum-numbing wooden slats and whenever the train stopped, so too did the ceiling fans, so it became unbearably hot. We had no food and so were entirely dependent on whatever the hawkers who boarded the train had for sale. The only one not flogging plastic combs or whistles was a genial-looking man selling salads. He was doing a brisk trade and we watched him work. From the woven basket in the crook of his wiry arm he'd take a small bowl made from dried leaves and put it on a train seat. Then he'd reach in for a small onion, a gherkin-sized cucumber, a tomato and a green mango, each of which he deftly diced in the palm of his hand and tipped into the leaf bowl. To finish, he'd add some chickpeas, a squeeze of lemon juice and open a twist of newspaper to dust the salad with spicy seasoning. It was a minimalist operation that asked at least two questions of health and safety: one about the risk to him of cutting his hand, and the other about the risk to his customers of food poisoning. But it was very hot and we were hungry and the salad was fresh and he'd served several customers already so I figured his hands were as clean as they were ever going to be. He stopped next to me.

'Do you want a salad, Lisa?'

'You've got to be kidding. He's been cutting the food in his hands. That's gross. No thank you.'

I held up two fingers, the polite 'bunny-ears' way.

'I said that I didn't want one,' snapped Lisa.

'I heard you the first time. I'm ordering two for myself.'

The vendor repeated the process and gently placed two bowls next to me on the train seat. I handed him 30 rupees and said thank you; he dipped his head in gratitude and moved to the next carriage.

Man, but that salad tasted divine and Salad Man could only have done better had he also been able to sell me an ice-cold beer to go with it. My appreciation for his simple culinary craft was evident to Lisa from the enthusiasm with which I set about devouring the first bowl. This aroused her curiosity.

'What's it like? I'm so hungry. Let me have a taste.'

'You said you didn't want one,' I objected, 'and now you want some of mine. It's delicious. No. Get your own.'

This awoke the green-eyed monster in Lisa.

'Give me the other bowl,' she demanded. 'Please.'

'Get your own.'

'Aw, please Graham.'

I can be mulishly stubborn, but I'm not immovably hard-hearted, so I passed Lisa the second bowl and walked towards the front of the swaying train to find Salad Man and purchase two more salads. He was delighted that we'd appreciated his food so much. And Lisa was chuffed to bits that she'd overcome her squeamishness and hadn't missed out on what, for her, was not only the only food she ate on that long journey but the nicest food she'd eaten in India in two months, and the best hand-made salad she'd had in her life.

Moaner Lisa

 In Calcutta we brought forward our departure date to 21 May. The heat and the hassle were getting to us and we were starting to run out of puff. We'd initially planned to stay in India for the full six months our visa allowed, but now decided we'd be lucky to stick it out for a little over half that.

From Calcutta we trained over 1,600km to Madras. Only two good things can be said of that, our longest rail journey. One, that it was necessary. We wanted to get to southern India as swiftly and affordably as possible, so were prepared to suck up the numbing tedium of spending 33 hours in a second-class sleeper. Two, at one of the stations a *hijra* came on board to solicit money from the passengers. *Hijras* – eunuchs, intersex or transgender people, invariably dressed in glittering saris, dripping in gold and with their faces heavily made up – often walked through carriages asking for money. They were Misses who were hard to miss. Many Indians believe *hijras* have the power to bless or curse, and *hijras* trade off this uneasy ambivalence. Reaching our section of the carriage, the *hijra*

stepped close to me, placed one jewellery-festooned hand lightly on my shoulder and held out the other for me to cross with silver. I reached into my pocket for loose change and dropped a few rupees into her palm. She glanced down to assess my generosity, closed her fist and her eyes and broke into mournful song. What was the going rate for a *hijra*'s blessing? I hoped that I'd been generous enough to be rewarded with a beneficent spell of the 'May your life be rich and your loins fruitful' kind, rather than a maleficent hex of the 'May your foreskin grow long like a windsock' type.

Her song sung, she had one more clever trick to wring a few extra rupees from me: standing square in front of me she clutched her sari at the knee with both hands and raised it several inches, unmistakably communicating that for an additional consideration she would reveal her 'eunuch-ness'. Her groin was at eye-level. I paid *not* to see.

By now Lisa was writing a letter to Tony Wheeler every other evening. Tony was the founder of The Lonely Planet guidebook company, and we were joined at the hip to its India guide, a dirty, dog-eared, third- or fourth-hand copy of which we'd purchased in Bangkok's Khao San Road for a hefty US$16. We were utterly dependent on The Book as we reverently referred to it, as in those pre-GPS and Google days, we'd have been lost (literally) without it. We didn't sleep anywhere without consulting it, no food passed our lips unless the establishment had been Lonely P-vetted and we didn't go anywhere unless the LP suggested it.

Much as we worshipped The Book, we soon found that it wasn't without its errors. Foremost of these was, in my opinion, inviting readers to get in touch and submit comments and corrections. 'Moaner Lisa' took this to heart, feeling morally obligated to inform Tony of every single cartographic error, overrated restaurant dish and mis-described or defunct hotel.

'Dear Tony, I hope you're well. I thought you should know that in the India Lonely Planet you have printed a map of Jhansi with Vijay's Restaurant on the left side of Railway Quarters Road, when in fact, it is on the right. This meant we took half an hour to find it. I suggest you correct this in your next edition. Also, I think you should know that Gupta's restaurant does not have a 'particularly good thali'. We ate there last night, and thali wasn't even on the menu. Yours faithfully, Lisa Jackson.'

'Dear Tony, I hope you're well. I think that you should know that the New Imperial Hotel in Hospet you recommended closed more than a year ago. On arrival, my husband and I requested the auto rickshaw take us there. The driver protested that it was closed. Suspecting that he preferred to take us to another where he would receive a "commission", we insisted he take us to the New Imperial. That wasted journey cost us Rs22. Please bear this in mind when updating your next edition. Yours faithfully, Lisa Jackson.'

Futile as I believed Lisa's efforts were, I didn't do anything to discourage her endeavours as, had she not vented her India-fuelled ire in the absent Tony's direction, she would no doubt have directed it snappily at me. For Lisa, it was a cathartic exercise. I could picture Tony's resigned trepidation as the postman delivered yet another sheaf of 'rant-o-grammes' to his Melbourne office from Lisa Jackson somewhere in India.

In Madras our first priority was to shorten our India sojourn by a further two weeks. Like an insufficiently pruned hedge, we decided the first cut hadn't been deep enough. We'd been considering it on and off but were decided when, walking down a Madras street, Lisa abruptly wheeled about and ran up and smacked an Indian man on his back with her metal water bottle. He turned around, gave Lisa an astonished ghee-wouldn't-melt-in-his-mouth look and sauntered on his way. Lisa rushed back to my side.

'Thanks a lot, Graham! Why didn't you stop him?'

'Stop him from doing what?'

'That bloody man just grabbed me between the legs!'

'What? What are you talking about?'

'Graham, are you blind? Why didn't you do something?'

'Lisa, I didn't *see* anything,' I replied in astonishment that she was having a go at me about something I couldn't have prevented.

'Did he hurt you? Are you okay?'

'I'm fine, no thanks to you. From now on, I'll protect myself, shall

I?' she sarcastically retorted, stalking off.

In India, 'Eve teasing' was and still is commonplace. The archaic euphemism sounds harmless, but it covers a multitude of offences by men against women, from catcalling and wolf-whistling to public sexual assault of the groping kind. Sometimes it's directed against men. Danish Magnus had told us in Taipei how, on a crowded bus in Trivandrum, a passenger had discreetly fondled his genitals.

From then on, whenever Lisa walked anywhere in India she repeatedly smacked her water bottle into the palm of her left hand to send out an unmistakeable don't-mess-with-me message.

Nice legs & a bitten-off toe

 From Madras, we cut inland to the ancient village of Hampi, where clutches of hardy hippies slept rough in its colonnaded bazaar and temples, sharing their space and, involuntarily, their food with the legions of thieving monkeys who'd settled there first. Though Hampi was compact, we hired bicycles so we could see the out-of-town temples, explore the hills and sluice off the dust in the river away from prying eyes. Agreeing the price and selecting our chariots we'd made 30 yards when I stopped to adjust my saddle. Graham halted next to me, his right foot on the ground and his left on the pedal. A young Indian man walking past stopped too, placed his hand on Graham's bare left thigh (he was in shorts – only children wear shorts in India so to see a grown man wearing them is a novelty), gave it a gentle squeeze and murmured approvingly, 'Nice legs'. Graham thanked him for the compliment but went on to advise against touching strangers' legs: it was a little creepy and if he made a habit of it sooner or later someone was bound to take offence. Graham thought it fair that he should know. And so did I.

Passing down from the high and dry interior to the lush coast we made our way from Hampi to Goa. For 451 years Goa was a small piece of Portugal in India until, in 1961, Indian troops forcibly took it back after a 36-hour battle. The former colony provided, as Nepal had, a welcome respite. The pace of life was slower and the food more to our taste. We tucked into fried pomfret fish whenever it was on the menu, and there was cheese that wasn't the ubiquitous *paneer* and wonderful Portuguese-style bread that wasn't *chapatti*.

In the Basilica of Bom Jesus, high above the altar, the body of the Jesuit missionary Francis Xavier lay preserved in an ornate glass-sided casket that resembled a train carriage. Once a decade the casket was brought down and ceremonially paraded through Old Goa and pilgrims had the opportunity to kiss the mummified feet of the saint. We were surprised that this was still allowed, considering that in 1554 an impassioned female Catholic bit off one of Saint Francis' toes. The booklet on the saint's life that we purchased from the gift shop, along with a postcard depicting his scary-looking skeletal hand that would've made a great cover for a heavy metal album, told of how he had got over his revulsion of dressing suppurating wounds. 'Francis wanted to run away but to overcome himself he took a little pus with his finger and swallowed it,' the booklet informed us. 'After that he felt no more any repugnance and could dress any wound, even the ugliest.'

Bedbugs were the reason we made the final change to our departure date, shaving off another week from our itinerary. We came to this decision when Graham woke one morning to find our bedding speckled with blood and his body covered in fantastically itchy bites. He insisted that I conduct a bite census: back and bottom, 30; right arm, 20; left arm, 30; legs, 6. Total: 86. The bugs took at least half a pint, he claimed. I, on the other hand, mysteriously escaped unscathed.

'Bedbugs, it would seem, are fussy eaters,' said Graham.

After Goa we caught a slow train to Bombay. Here, we paid good money to check into a better class of establishment as I was adamant that I simply could not bear another clammy night sleeping without air-con on threadbare, soiled sheets. For once, Graham didn't put up too much resistance, reasoning that shelling out a few hundred extra rupees would be a bargain if it meant not making another involuntary blood donation to India's insatiable bedbugs, who didn't even have the courtesy to give him a cup of tea and a biscuit afterwards.

The hotel was a massive step up from the kind of places we'd been patronising. It had a TV, a minibar stocked with bottles of fluorescent soft drink, and crisp, white bed linen that smelled of washing powder, not the room's previous occupants. It also had air-con of a sort, which clanked and wheezed as it puffed out not-hot air, and a Western-style toilet, complete with toilet paper, which could be made to flush. Another first for us was the lovely rooftop balcony, where residents could retire and take tea served in uncracked crockery or even enjoy alcoholic refreshments. It was on the balcony that we met Angus, a businessman from Shetland. A frequent long-distance traveller, he said the hotel compared very favourably with the more expensive one in Sri Lanka he'd stayed in a few days earlier.

'My hotel was in one of Colombo's smartest neighbourhoods,' Angus told us as we sipped the first of two Kingfishers, for cost reasons the only beers Graham allowed to pass our lips during our entire India trip, 'so I was delighted when the receptionist said that he'd upgraded me. I imagined a suite with a fresh fruit basket, but when I walked into my room I was disgusted to see that it was absolutely filthy. I wouldn't even sit on the bed, far less lie down on it.' Graham and I nodded knowingly.

'I called the receptionist and asked him to come up straightaway. When he arrived I pointed to each item of furniture in turn: "Look," I said, "Look at the carpet. Look at the bed. Look at the chair. Look at the dressing table. They're all covered in grime." He admitted they were, and offered to show me the unoccupied room directly opposite. It was no better. "You see, sir," he said, "it's filthy, too. They're *all* like this."

'Astonished, I said: "But you said you were upgrading me."'

'"I did, sir," the man replied matter of factly. "I upgraded you to a higher floor."'

Sky burials & a hair-dryer hijacking

A flock of hungry vultures can pick a corpse clean in under an hour. In a practice known as 'sky burial', Parsis expose their dead to scavenging birds on Towers of Silence rather than burying them and thereby contaminating the earth. In this way, Parsis have been practising eco-friendly disposal of their dead thousands of years before anyone conceived of recycling. Though visible to circling vultures, the Towers of Silence in Bombay's Doongerwadi Forest were invisible to us, encircled as they are by smothering foliage. It's said that, as development encroaches, people in surrounding high-rises can look down onto the towers. It's hard to imagine that this vista adds value to their properties.

Of the Big Four – the others being Delhi, Calcutta and Madras – Bombay was the most pleasant city, with wider and cleaner streets, less choking traffic, more trees and, all in all, a more monied look to it. But it was unmistakeably India: the waiters slept and cooked in the corridor outside our hotel room, and a sign in the stairwell declared, 'No spitting on the walls'.

We bought some pistachios and raisins and walked the full length of Marine Drive and Chowpatty Beach. It was way too late in the day for the dawn spectacle Kiwi John had promised.

'I didn't believe him then, and I'm not sure I believe him now,' I said. 'I can't see a single turd on this beach.'

'That's because the tide's come in and flushed them all away.'

On our third night in Bombay there was an insistent knocking on our door at 3am. Rising groggily, Graham wrapped his sarong around his waist and padded barefoot to the door.

'Who's there?'

'Police,' answered a stern-sounding voice from the other side. 'Open the door.'

Graham shot a look at me, now sitting up in bed, the sheet pulled up to my neck, and opened the door halfway. A police officer and a constable stood outside, with the hotel manager keenly peering around the latter's shoulder. The officer stiffened, looked Graham up and down and asked to see our passports, which Graham retrieved from our money belts.

'Where have you come from, and where are you going?' he asked, as he flicked through the pages of Graham's passport, obviously reluctant to enter a room occupied by a half-dressed man and a woman naked underneath a sheet.

'We've come from Goa, and we're leaving for Udaipur later today,' Graham replied, apprehensive that he might ask him about honey collecting. He'd grown so tired of registering personal details at every hotel we stayed at – details that we were sure would never be checked – that he'd taken to having a little fun with them, and in Bombay had listed his occupation as 'beekeeper'.

'Is there a problem?'

'It is okay,' the policeman said officiously, returning our passports, 'Good night.'

'What do you think that was all about?' I asked. 'It's the middle of the night.'

'I have no idea. A random visa check, perhaps. It clearly wasn't a shakedown as they never asked for any money.'

The next morning, when Graham questioned the manager about the nocturnal visit, he mumbled something about terrorism, referring to the 13 bombs that had killed over 250 people and injured over 1,400 in Bombay three weeks previously. Quite why they were suspicious of a beekeeping Brit and his South African wife we'll never know, but Graham stopped writing improbable occupations on hotel registration forms after that. He didn't mind, as he'd already amused himself quite enough by variously claiming to be a 'rock star', 'astronaut' and 'pantomime dame'.

With our Indian odyssey drawing to a close, we turned our backs on the coast and made for Rajasthan, a state famed for its majestic desert forts, opulent maharaja palaces and men sporting fabulous handlebar moustaches and outsize turbans. Even the women working picks and shovels building its roads looked as though they were glamorous extras in a Bollywood musical as they lugged heavy loads of steaming tar on their heads or sat on their haunches breaking stones in the dust as their children played nearby.

Every few days we were deposited at new destinations with names that seemed to have been dreamt up to mimic the satisfied purring of a cream-fed cat: Udaipur, Jodhpur, Pushkar and Jaipur. India was becoming a blur. The pleasure of seeing each stunning sight was now competing with the pain and persistence it took to get there. Udaipur's Taj Lake Palace, 'afloat' in the middle of Lake Pichola; Jodhpur's Brahmin houses painted different hues of blue; Pushkar's lavishly attired camels decked out in pom poms and colourful macramé ponchos; Jaipur's dusky-pink Palace of Winds and its Amber Fort with its processions of clown-like painted elephants – we saw them all. But we were growing weary.

By the time we reached Delhi a week before our departure date, we were heartily sick of budget travel. Graham had contracted yet another bout of Delhi belly and was sick of being sick. We were also fed up to the hind teeth of the endless arguing over the price of everything, and being relentlessly followed by people offering us hashish, massage, flutes, 'change money', tomato soup, boat rides, postcards, *pooja* powder, fruit, transport, horoscopes, *tabla* drums, fluorescent armadillos, bottled water, squeaking plastic mice, opium, carpets, marble, alabaster, palm readings, weight-measuring, tourist information, hotel rooms, airline tickets, soap, noisy plastic guns and straw cobras in baskets. The weeks of heat and dust and flies, the horrible food, the choking traffic and periodic debilitating sickness had finally ground us down.

Waiting for our Biman Bangladesh flight bound for Amsterdam on 30 April, we read the alarming news that an Indian Airlines 737 had crashed soon after take-off when its wheels clipped a truck carrying stacked bales of cotton. In the short time we'd been in India, four aircraft had been hijacked: one by a lone *mujahideen* guerrilla who was shot dead, and three by persons armed with, respectively, a hair dryer, oranges and pomegranates, and a ball of clay and piece of string. It was definitely time for us to leave India, possibly the world's most beautiful and beguiling, baffling and bonkers country.

Five years later we went back for a rematch.

CHAPTER FOUR

1993-1997: The Wilderness Years
Washington DC & Egypt

As newly minted travellers we took on India, not just a country but a subcontinent, and surprise, surprise, we lost. India: one; Lisa and Graham: nil.

Hugely relieved to have escaped relatively unscathed, and still both suffering the ill effects of dysentery and doing India on eight arguments a day, we arrived in Amsterdam in early spring. One of our first tasks was to take our clothes to the laundromat. For three months they'd been washed in handbasins and by *dhobi wallahs*, so when my paisley-print trousers returned they were several lighter shades of pale.

'I can't believe they're the same trousers,' I said, sniffing their born-again spring freshness. 'They're like new.'

We rushed off to buy crusty bread, tomatoes, Gouda cheese and Heineken and, overjoyed at having access to these home comforts, for the first time in our lives took photos of our food. I also photographed an emaciated Graham sunning himself in Vondelpark; his protruding ribs were so prominent I could have played them like a xylophone. The Rijksmuseum, tulips, the Van Gogh Museum, walking the canals – even though there were things to do and see, India had drained our batteries and we had to dig ever deeper to tap into our diminishing reservoir of enthusiasm. It had been ten months since I'd left South Africa and we were getting close to the end of our tether.

Though this was my first trip to mainland Europe, and the food such an upgrade on India's that I stayed up late every evening to

113

squeeze in a fourth meal, everything seemed tame, a little 'so what?' Yes, there was a moment of high drama when I was nearly knocked into a canal by a Dutch cyclist who rang her bell compulsively as if she'd been tasered when I stepped into a cycle path. But when we were in India I'd almost been trampled by an elephant. And a camel. And a holy cow. Not in a zoo but on one of Delhi's main thoroughfares. Yes, I was somewhat surprised to see brown cafés where you could freely buy space cakes and hash brownies, but when we were in Malaysia we'd been offered opium, for God's sake, the trafficking of which carried a mandatory death penalty. And yes, though the explicit skin mags, massive fist-and-forearm dildoes and nasty nipple clamps on sale in Amsterdam's red light district had been eye-opening for someone like me who'd led a very sheltered life in Pretoria, when we were in Thailand we'd seen 'death porn', for pity's sake. Against my will, I'd been turned into that most dreaded of travellers – the Greater Spotted 'When We'. A traveller worthy of a top table place on the balcony of Taipei Hostel.

There were two countries we still wanted to see: Czech Republic, then only just over four months old after splitting from Slovakia, and Portugal, where Graham had spent a happy month after completing his undergraduate degree, so after two weeks in Amsterdam we bussed to Prague. We arrived early one morning and were immediately invited to don our judgy pants.

'Are those men drinking what I think they're drinking?' I asked Graham as we pulled into the coach station.

'Yes, they're drinking beer.'

'But it's 9am in the morning! How on earth are they going to go to work after that?'

'Drunk, I suppose.'

We camped in a woman's garden out in the suburbs, and every evening we returned to find Olga watering her borders, dressed in gripper knickers and an over-sized T-shirt. It took us only a day of drinking Prague's foul tap water before we emulated the men we'd so hastily judged and began drinking beer at breakfast. At four for a dollar, beer was cheaper than bottled water.

The Velvet Revolution, aka the Gentle Revolution, had peacefully freed Czechoslovakia from Russian domination three-and-a-half years previously, and its citizens, compared with those in Amsterdam, looked poorly nourished and shabbily dressed. At Kotva, the supermarket where we bought our 'breakfast beer', a tower of greasy salami cost less than a wilted, worm-eaten lettuce and they allowed self-service. Unlike the shop on Wenceslas Square where you were issued with a ticket and when your number came up the staff would fetch the items you wanted from the shelves behind them and place them in your basket. Liberated from Russian domination the Czech Republic may have been, but not, alas, from all vestiges of Russian customer service.

Prague was my mother's and sister Loren's favourite city, so we had a long list of recommended must-sees. The guidebook they'd recommended had patently been written by a failed architect who classified every one of the city's hundreds of historic buildings according to their architectural style: Romanesque, Gothic, Baroque, Art Nouveau, Renaissance, Neo-Renaissance, Cubist, Modernist, Functionalist and Communist Era.

'Read me! Read me!' I playfully implored Graham outside the Church of Our Lady Before Týn. Tired of reading the guidebook to plan each day's excursions, I wanted it read out to me.

'I'm sick of doing all the "read me's",' said Graham miserably, staring up at the building's black-and-brooding twin towers. 'And I truly think that if I read the word "Gothic" one more time I'm going to vomit.'

'This is one of my mother's favourite churches, so stop your moaning. Give me the book.' I wrenched it from him.

'It says here that the spires inspired – get it? – Walt Disney's Sleeping Beauty Castle.'

'Tell someone who cares.'

'Oh, and you're going to love this. The interior contains the tomb of the Danish astronomer Tycho Brahe.'

'Never heard of him. What's he famous for?'

'Accurately observing the planetary positions. And maths.'

'Right...'

115

'I haven't finished. It says here that he wore a fake nose.'

'Really?'

'Yes, his was sliced off by his cousin in a drunken duel over who was the best mathematician. That's why, for his own epitaph, he wrote: "He lived like a sage and died like a fool." He died in 1601 of a burst bladder. Apparently, he was at a royal banquet and was too polite to ask permission to relieve himself.'

'Maybe that's where the phrase "I'm dying for a pee" comes from,' jested Graham, perking up slightly.

Two weeks was time enough to do Prague leisurely justice, and we then flew to Portugal. By now Graham, and to a slightly lesser extent I, had 'museum sickness', a term coined by Loren to denote the particular malaise one suffers from when traipsing from church to gallery to museum while submitting oneself to a bombardment of spirituality, culture and learning. Despite becoming increasingly jaded, I forced Graham, like a foie gras goose, to ingest not only the Feira da Ladre 'thieves' flea market, but the Bairro Alto and Chiado neighbourhoods, the São Roque Church, the cathedral, São Jorge Castle and the Gulbenkian Museum, a vast and utterly overwhelming art gallery.

'I feel terrible seeing all this celebrated art and not really enjoying it,' I said, staring gloomily at Rembrandt's *Portrait of an Old Man*. 'By the time I was six, my mother had taught me so much about the Old Masters that when I was asked to draw the Easter bunny I based my picture not on Bugs Bunny like all the other kids in my class but on Albrecht Dürer's *Young Hare*.'

'Don't sweat it, Lisa. We've been travelling too long. Sooner or later everyone gets museum sickness, even Loren, and I've got it way worse than you.'

Despite our museum sickness, Graham insisted we drag ourselves to Belém, a district of Lisbon 13km west of the centre. As a child he'd been photographed beneath the Monument to the Discoveries, a prow-like edifice jutting out over the River Tagus commemorating the 500th anniversary of the death of Henry the Navigator, the patron of Portuguese exploration. Though it featured Vasco da

Gama, the explorer who'd named Natal ('birth of Christ' in Portuguese), the South African province where I'd spent my childhood holidays, and a huge compass-and-map mosaic gifted by the South African government, my interest was not piqued. As for the spectacular Jerónimos Monastery across the road, suffice it to say that I glanced at the statue of Jesus sporting rasta dreadlocks, felt museum sick and walked out.

The sole saving grace was the next-door bakery selling delicious pastéis de Belém, custard tarts with pastry so crisp it cut the roof of your mouth. There was a lengthy queue and Graham – in a hard-wired Pavlovian response that's uniquely British – joined it. My behaviour was equally reflexive and unthinking: when Graham queues, I queue. When we got to the front after a hot 30 minutes in the baking sun, we saw that we were in the queue for takeaways and that we could have breezed into the tiled, fan-cooled café the moment we'd arrived.

'Jesus!'

'Yes, my child?'

'Graham, why the hell did you do that?'

'Do what?'

'Go and stand at the back of the queue like a sheep instead of finding out what we were queuing for.'

'Lisa, you've got eyes in your head and a tongue in your mouth, too, you know. You could have gone to investigate.'

'Yes, but you know I hate being told off, and I didn't want to be scolded for trying to jump the queue.'

'You don't speak Portuguese, so it wouldn't have mattered what they said.'

'Easy for you to say, Graham, as I think you actually *enjoy* being told off. Especially, judging by your behaviour on this trip, by me.'

'I'm never knowingly naughty, you know that.'

'Don't try to get cute with me, you bloody well know you are. All the bloody time.'

We were listless and ill-humoured. Everything had become difficult. It was wearisome even to rouse ourselves from our sleeping mats, and tiresome to have to take a shower, so we caught the train to São Martinho do Porto. Here we hoped a few days' camping at the beach eating grilled sardines would revive us, only to find that, once there, we barely had the energy to uncork the bottles of Três Marias Vinho Verde we'd bought. We were in a wine-induced slumber when our alarm woke us up at 5am so that we could catch a train to Porto.

'I can't be bothered to go,' I said groggily to Graham.

'Neither can I,' he said, rolling over and going back to sleep.

That was all it took for us to miss out on one of Europe's most attractive cities. Not even the fact that Porto was famed for producing one of Graham's choice tipples was enough to lure him from his sleeping bag.

It was then that we realised we'd just gorged on our 20th chocolate. We'd had too much of a good thing. We were travelled out. If Pope John Paul II himself had come to our tent and offered to fly us to Rome for a private tour of the Sistine Chapel, we would have told him to sod off and leave us alone. We'd binged on travel long enough. It was time for us to head back to England, to 'real life', and start starting over.

Living with your in-laws is always going to be challenging, even in-laws as lovely as mine. Predictably, the main issue was housework. Determined to be model house guests, Graham and I offered to help with the cleaning and my mother-in-law Irene patiently showed me how to use the vacuum-cleaner attachments.

'I usually hoover the whole floor or carpet first, and then I use this attachment to clean the tops of all the skirting boards and door frames,' said Irene.

I'd never heard of anyone hoovering their skirting boards or door frames, but I didn't argue.

When I wasn't helping out with the housework I was applying for jobs. I'd buy *The Guardian* and send off media-job applications and speculative letters to all and sundry. I received 120 rejections and stony silences.

'Lisa, have you seen my vacuum-cleaner attachment?' called my mother-in-law as I sat handwriting a covering letter to *BBC Gardeners'*

World magazine about how, despite killing my peace-in-the-home plant through neglect, I was nonetheless the ideal candidate for their advertised senior sub-editor role.

'No, I haven't,' I replied, realising too late that this was Irene's way of letting me know she knew I hadn't cleaned the door frames. I had to be wilier. Or do more housework.

Eventually, I found a job as production editor at *OK!* Magazine, but when holding meetings with my male boss while standing on magazine proofs depicting naked women became too much – *OK!* was a celebrity mag, but the company also published soft porn in the form of *Penthouse, Black & Blue* and *Asian Babes* – I jumped ship and went to work for British *Cosmopolitan*. For the next three-and-a-half years I worked the nine to nine: I wasn't paid overtime but, as the main breadwinner, I was so grateful to have a job that I stuck it out, even though it meant studying the complex family relationships in *EastEnders* as a condition for passing my probation. In a programme where all the cast had either slept with each other, or tried to murder one another, this was almost impossible, even though I furiously scribbled down notes and attempted to draw up a Mitchell family tree. If India had taught me anything, it was how to persevere and press on.

 Though I'd never assumed that three philosophy degrees would guarantee me a salaried place on the board of a multinational corporation, I didn't think they'd scare employers away, or worse slam the doors to jobs in my face. As the UK economy crawled out of recession, I was uniquely qualified for an academic position that never came to market – UK universities just weren't recruiting – but grossly over-qualified for the few jobs that did. Each time I caught sight of our toastie maker that, used once, now sat gathering dust on top of our fridge, a rebuke in Teflon to an impulsive decision, I dolefully thought that my years in Cape Town had been a bad investment. As if I'd apprenticed myself to an alchemist.

The only paying jobs I could find were selling jewellery part time in H Samuel and cleaning my brother-in-law's office. By then, we'd bought a house in south London – mercifully, it was still possible then to buy a modest house on one salary – and I started doing it up myself. As long as I stayed away from plumbing and electrics I'd do more good than harm. So wallpaper went up and linoleum went down; tiles were affixed to walls and coving to ceilings, and the former owners' penchant for dove grey and dusky pink colour schemes – inside and out – was obliterated by gallons of white paint. I was so grateful to the H Samuel manager Steve for taking a chance on me that I pulled out all the stops, and on Christmas Eve came home with the bottle of wine that he'd promised to the assistant who sold the most jewellery that day. Travelling had taught us how little money you needed to be happy, and as long as we could share a bottle of inexpensive Romanian pinot noir and a frozen Goodfella's pizza on a Saturday night while watching *Gladiators* and *Blind Date* on the old black-and-white TV we'd inherited from my parents, we were content.

When work allowed, Lisa would accompany me to my cleaning job so we could snatch more time together. As I dusted, vacuumed and emptied the bins, Lisa washed up the mugs and cleaned the loos. Amazingly, given her history of serial housework avoidance, she volunteered for toilet duty: I suspect her experiences in India had instilled in her a determination to never let a toilet in her care become toxic. Lisa didn't tell anyone at work about her double life – *Cosmo* girl by day, khazi cleaner by night – but it made her chuckle to think how it would have horrified her colleagues.

By now we'd given up arguing, as we knew that if we were to make it in London we needed at all times to present a united front. We did, though, have one blazing row when Lisa found out that I'd stopped applying for jobs.

'You're like someone who's fallen off an ocean liner,' she railed. 'If you keep swimming there's a chance you'll be rescued, but if you stop swimming you'll definitely drown. You cannot afford to lose hope. When was the last time you applied for a job?'

'It's all so bloody depressing. You don't know what it's like. What's the point of completing an application when I know full well I won't even get an interview?'

'I don't care, Graham. Do you want to clean offices for the rest of your life?'

Month after month, my pile of rejection letters had grown, but my mother never gave up hope, slipping job adverts she'd cut from newspapers under our front door.

'Ma, I'm not going to apply for a job as a fish smoker,' I told her.

'Why ever not, it's a good job. It pays well.'

'It says you have to have previous experience. And besides, we're not going to relocate to Peterhead.'

'Oh well, it was worth a try.'

One afternoon, another cutting from Ma appeared under our door, this time for a job as a research analyst with the Ministry of Defence. It had a ten-year residency requirement and we'd been in the UK for two, but I applied anyway and, to my surprise, landed an interview. Full of hope, I donned my hand-me-down suit and took myself off to Whitehall. Two weeks later, I got a letter. I hadn't got the job. To say I was gutted would be to under-egg it. At 31, I was running out of options.

'You won't believe this,' I said to Lisa one evening as she staggered in at 10pm, ready for the 'intravenous' gin and tonic I prepared for her when she worked overtime and needed a rapid way to decompress before going to bed.

'I got a call from the Ministry of Defence and they asked if I'm still interested in the research analyst position.'

'What, four months later?'

'Yes, apparently it takes so long to get security clearance that some of the people they offered jobs to have found other work in the meantime and have withdrawn their applications.'

'So, you've got a job?'

'I think I have, as long as I pass the security vetting.'

A wave of relief flooded over us. After two long years of filling in application forms, selling jewellery, cleaning an office, renovating our house, running Lisa's bath, taxiing her to East Croydon station and making her sandwiches to show my support for her in every way I could, I finally had a proper full-time, pensionable job I could call my own: Research Officer for Ballistic Missiles at the Defence

Intelligence Staff.

In all I waited ten months for my security clearance. In April 1995, a former Special Branch Chief Inspector came to our Croydon home to interview me as part of my vetting. He was polite, plain spoken and not *too* intrusive, and pored over our bank statements to confirm that Lisa and I weren't spending more than we were earning, took notes of my views on nuclear weapons and homosexuality and asked about my history of drug use.

'Alcohol and paracetamol. And during my student years I smoked cannabis a few times,' I'd answered.

He'd scribbled in his flip-top notebook. As I'd walked him to the front door, I'd nervously asked him if my honest admission of cannabis use had disqualified me.

'If you'd said you'd never tried it, I wouldn't have believed you,' he'd replied. 'So, no.'

Several days later, my boss at H Samuel had revealed that he'd received a phone call from the ex-detective, cross-checking on my suitability for employment under the Official Secrets Act.

'He asked if you'd ever turned up for work in women's clothing,' Steve had disclosed.

'Just as well that you can't see my bra and suspenders under my suit,' I'd replied.

The day after my 33rd birthday, I started work as one of Her Majesty's civil servants. With the same zeal that I'd sold silver-plated Beatrix Potter egg cups and £99 engagement rings, I set about making a success of my new role, and in the new year I was sent to a conference in Washington DC. I took a week's leave on the back of it and Lisa flew in to join me. At last, after three-and-a-half years in the wilderness we could travel again, and we were determined to make the most of it.

Guns Я U.S.
Washington DC

 Funny stories are like those rare gems in the 'Middle of Lidl' aisle. You pop in to buy shopping-list staples – bread, milk and a tube of Pringles – and emerge, triumphant, clutching a must-have inflatable kayak or can't-live-without work dungarees. Take Washington, for example. Every single visitor will have 'bought' the bread and milk of the White House and Capitol Hill, some may have treated themselves to the Pringles by visiting the Smithsonian museum, but few will have returned home as happy as Lisa and I did after collecting this jewel of a 'middle-aisle find' in the lobby-cum-breakfast-room of our budget hotel, where everything from the cornflakes to the quarts of tepid, tasteless liquid Americans call coffee was served in planet-killing polystyrene. It was the priceless fragment of a woman's phone conversation, following hot on the heels of a banal discussion about whether or not she should bring some corndogs home for dinner.

'I ain't taking Jerome on no more haunted-house tours,' she said as she held out her left arm to admire the stars and stripes decorating her talon-like nails. 'Uh-uh, no way. You wanna know why? Because every single time, the boy gets possessed!'

How did she know he was possessed, we wondered? Did the poor boy return home potty-mouthed, swivelling his head, *Exorcist*-like, through 360 degrees?

Our Washington DC walking tour threw up another corker. Explaining how his neighbourhood had recently become gentrified, our guide pointed to a swish glass and chrome establishment.

'This is now a classy restaurant,' he said, 'but in my youth it was a topless bar.'

This prompted a credulous Australian to ask: 'So to go inside, you had to take your top off?'

The X-Files, in which FBI agents Mulder and Scully investigated strange and unexplained cases, had nothing on our mind-bending tour of the Federal Bureau of Investigation HQ.

'Hi there, how y'all doing? Welcome to the J Edgar Hoover building. My name is Kimberly, and it's my pleasure to be taking you around today. Where are y'all from?'

Only Lisa and I were not American, and therefore to Kimberly we were curiously exotic.

'You're from South Africa and living in London England?' she repeated as a question back to Lisa.

Kimberly was an irrepressible people person. Had she worked in fast food she would have had a genuine beam and cheery welcome for every customer, never mind that she'd been on her aching feet for eight straight hours and her varicose veins were surely beginning to give her gip. Not for her the sham smile and feigned warmth indoctrinated into millions of Americans working in service industries. It was real.

'You are going to learn about the good work that the Federal Bureau of Investigation does, about how we play our part in keeping you and your families safe. The tour will take about one hour. If anyone wants to take a comfort break, please use the restrooms now.'

Three elderly visitors, one leaning heavily on a cane, peeled away from our group.

'If anyone has any questions during the tour, ask me and I'll be happy to answer them.'

'Does the CIA do tours?' asked the woman from Rhode Island.

With an hour to acquit her duty as a guide, Kimberly ushered us through the building as quickly as her short, stout legs would permit. So speedily were we shepherded from one room to the next that we still can't fathom how two of the FBI's Ten Most Wanted Fugitives had been caught when their mugshots were recognised by people taking the tour. Perhaps they'd been family members.

'Willie Sutton was once one of the FBI's ten most-wanted,' intoned Kimberly. 'You folks may not have heard of him but I'm sure you know of the robber who, when asked why he robbed banks, answered "Because that's where the money is". Well, that was "Slick Willie" Sutton.'

Kimberly reeled off rafts of statistics about the history and the work of the Bureau, the number of agents and its great successes:

Watergate, JFK's assassination, the Unabomber. Then she walked us to the FBI's gun reference library, a vast repository of over 7,000 firearms used to identify the weapons involved in gun crimes. Next up was a glass-walled lab where they examined forensic evidence – snot, spunk, splattered blood and so on – and, much like parents use nit combs to rid their kids of the horrors of headlice, painstakingly combed crime-scene clothing for incriminating fibres.

The most peculiar part of the tour was a long, preachy video about, of all things, detonators. Its message, brought home by a 1970s-era public service film cast with over-acting, androgynous long-haired children, was unequivocally 'Don't touch detonators, kids, as they can hurt you if they explode in your face, hand or pocket.' In the film, the kids find a box of detonators in Jimmy's dad's garage and, excited beyond reason, play with them. It isn't going to end well. Jimmy strikes a detonator with a hammer and loses a hand and his sight (and his dad's perfectly good hammer) and the detonator in Bobby's pocket spontaneously explodes, forever ruining his chances of dating the prom queen and obliging him to pee through a surgical straw for the rest of his life. Cut to close-up of Mary-Beth, hands on face, eyes wide, screaming.

Call me Mr Pedantic, but Bonnie and Clyde didn't hold up banks using detonators, America is not notorious for its 'detonator culture' and the Second Amendment is silent on the right to own them, so we simply couldn't see the educational value of such a film. They might as well have shown a 'Don't play with flamethrowers kids, as they can get very hot and turn your friends into a human torch' video instead, with footage of Bobby arcing a stream of sticky fire onto Jimmy as Mary-Beth screams impotently. It would have been equally gratuitous.

No one knows for sure, but at the time there were approximately four times as many guns as there are people in America. The FBI would have performed a more valuable public service had it warned children of the risks of fooling with firearms. But no. Just when we thought the tour had peaked, we were treated to a five-minute firearms demo by a handsome, steel-jawed Special Agent who blazed away with handguns and a tommy gun at a criminal-shaped target. In that moment, I looked about the firing range to see if I could identify the adult, his mental health tortured out of shape by America's many strangenesses, most likely to 'go postal', or the kid, unhinged by the lure of online infamy, who'd take his father's gun to school and blow away his classmates. As a ripple of excitement coursed through the range, I understood why America has such a deep-rooted gun culture. The young children, obviously thrilled by this fabulous display of firepower, were no doubt thinking, 'Daddy, I definitely don't want to play with detonators – but a sub-machine gun sure would be nice.'

The Terminator tour
Washington DC

 The tour of the Pentagon Lisa and I signed up for later that day was equally 'out there'. It wasn't the fact that our guide was a soldier that puzzled us – the Pentagon is, after all, the headquarters of the US military – but the way in which she conducted the entire tour walking backwards, a distance of a mile and a half. With no thought for how utterly bizarre it appears to outsiders, Pentagon guides walk in reverse for security reasons: it helps them to keep a beady eye on the tourists they're tasked with shepherding through one of America's most top-secret buildings. It was 'normal' walking backwards, not the slick moonwalk popularised by Michael Jackson or one from Monty Python's Ministry of Silly Walks, but it nonetheless must have taken a steady nerve and a lot of practice, especially when stepping on and off escalators.

The guides were stamped from the same cookie cutter. They were all dressed in crisp-pressed military uniforms, brass-capped shoes and white gloves, and passively aggressively polite and humourless, utterly inflexible and gratingly officious, as many American uniformed officials tend to be. Whether your group was led by Private First Class Lance Chuckhagen III or Senior Airman Celestina Crescencia Espinoza there were rules that had to be faithfully observed and instructions that had to be unerringly followed. They took their responsibility *very* seriously.

'The Pentagon is the headquarters of the US Department of Defense so all the work here is classified,' our steely-eyed guide dead-panned, reciting from memory a well-rehearsed script from which there could be no hesitation, repetition or deviation. 'Photography is strictly prohibited. If you take any photos, I will terminate the tour. Do not look into any of the offices as we walk the corridors. If you do, I will terminate the tour. I need this group to stick close together. If you do not, I will terminate the tour. Is that understood?'

Suitably 'scared', we meekly followed The Terminator as she explained that the Pentagon is virtually a self-sufficient city, with 23,000 employees and space to park 8,770 cars. Despite its immense size – it's about as wide as the Empire State Building is tall, and has 17.5 miles of corridors – it takes no more than seven minutes to walk between any two interior points.

'We tell the time by 4,200 clocks, drink from 691 drinking fountains and utilise 284 restrooms,' she droned in a mechanical monotone. 'Each day we consume 30,000 cups of coffee, make 200,000 phone calls and replace 250 lightbulbs. The Pentagon has a post office and a florist.'

'Fun facts never to be forgotten,' I sighed, wondering how anyone found time to conduct top-secret work while obsessively counting clocks and logging phone calls, and drinking so many coffees that the building needed every one of its almost 300 toilets.

It quickly became apparent that visitors would get to see not much more than corridor after corridor of mirror-polished floors, half-panelled walls hung with portraits of long-dead luminaries we didn't stop to identify, and identikit wooden doors. It was about as exciting as going on a tour of a Travelodge, without the miles of cheap blue nylon carpet.

We stopped next to a three-inch length of sweetcorn attached to a stick, incongruously framed behind glass.

'This is a corn cob pipe that once belonged to five-star General Douglas MacArthur. Do any of you here know who General MacArthur was?'

'Sure I do,' volunteered a retiree in sneakers and high-waisted jeans. 'He was the man who led America in the fight against the Japs in the second war. I believe Gregory Peck played him in the film about his life.'

'Gregory Peck also starred in *To Kill a Mockingbird*,' added his wife. 'Such a handsome man.'

'That is correct, sir. General MacArthur was Supreme Commander of Allied Forces in the Southwest Pacific and led America to victory against the Japanese during the Second World War. He also commanded US and UN forces in Korea during the war there.'

The Terminator omitted to mention that MacArthur, an immense egotist and self-publicist, became infamous during the Korean War for seeking to attack China, North Korea's ally – something for which President Truman, heartily tired of repeatedly begging him to 'respect my authoritah', gave him the boot. I also happened to know that MacArthur had asked to be allowed to drop atomic bombs where he pleased, and wanted to create a permanent radioactive zone across the Korean peninsula to prevent the North invading the South, but I didn't raise this with The Terminator in case she went 'nuclear' herself. Now was not the time or place for a discussion about morally ambiguous heroes.

While our guide jeopardised her physical safety by reversing along the glassy corridors without once looking back, ruthlessly determined to deter any would-be stragglers, snappers or spies, we congratulated ourselves for remaining straight-faced. The Terminator, and those who had written her 33-page script, had obviously bought into the idea that numbers don't lie, as long as they are politically neutral. In a building with 13 elevators, 19 escalators, 131 stairways and 7,754 windows, she was mercifully blessed with an abundance of those.

World Heritage Shites
Egypt

 It's sometimes the way: you visit somewhere with antiquities as old as the dawn of time and what make an equally big impression as the sights you've snapped are the shites you've crapped. Egypt was a case in point.

With Graham now earning a full-time salary we were itching to travel and trawled Teletext, the best way in those days to bag a bargain. You couldn't search for destinations, so you had to click through dozens of pages of offers, but the deals were an undoubted steal. For the princely sum of £279 each we bought our first package holiday, which included flights, transfers and accommodation in a four-star Luxor hotel perched right on the bank of the Nile. With a buffet breakfast. And a pool. With waiters. To this day it's the only four-star hotel we've holidayed in.

Our two-week trip was packed with postcard moments. We'll always remember the man at the spectacular Temple of Karnak, famed for its avenue of goat-esque sphinxes, whispering what sounded like 'Isis, Osiris, Jesus, what a business,' as he encouraged us to perform a weird 'touch your head, touch the temple, now you'll turn into a lentil' ritual. We'll never forget Dr Ragab's Papyrus Museum, floating on a boat on the Nile which, though its sign proclaimed there would be 'No hassling to make a purchase' turned out, of course, not to be a museum at all but a shop, where we were mercilessly hounded by one of his employees, order form and pen in hand, urging us to buy, buy, buy.

'This best quality papyrus. Feel. Smooth as baby's skin. How much you want to buy?'

'We don't want or need papyrus,' I protested.

'But this best-quality papyrus in Luxor.'

'No thank you.'

The harassment stopped when we crossed the gangplank. Only to be immediately picked up by the teeming vendors strung out along the banks of the river.

Luxor's colourful street life created vivid memories, too: pyramids of watermelons and baskets overflowing with assorted spices and bright red hibiscus tea; a pile of T-shirts bearing the legend '9 out of 10 men who've tried camels prefer women'; clip-clopping horses harnessed to *kaleshes*, their wheels sinking into tarmac softened by the tremendous heat; a sign nailed to a tree outside a shop called Middle Age Essence recommending that we 'Say No to drugs – if they not good quality'. And how could we forget the Head Bread

Bike Man cycling amid the chaotic traffic with one hand gripping the handlebars and the other balancing a full-size blue wooden door laden with newly baked loaves on his head? Or the first time we both ate pigeon?

'Lisa, you just want to eat pizza all the time. Pizza, pizza, pizza,' said Graham. 'You're in Egypt, you should be eating local food.'

'Okay, okay, you're probably right. How about that place by the roundabout? It didn't look too bad.'

That night we forewent air-con and sat at an outdoor table at Hussein's, with every man, woman, child, donkey, horse and internal combustion engine in Luxor passing by, picking at two plates of scrawny, bone-riddled pigeon and chips.

'I wish I'd ordered pizza,' said Graham morosely.

But for me, the standout memory was the painful experience of getting cystitis, athlete's foot and diarrhoea cramps all at the same time, in 42°C heat. It took ten minutes of excruciatingly embarrassing mime in a crowded pharmacy before I managed to procure all the necessary medications from the male pharmacist.

Most of Graham's recollections of Egypt also have a toilet theme. After running the gauntlet of importuning stallholders outside our hotel – 'motorboat, *felucca*, *kalesh*, you like? You want? Valley of the Kings, Queens, Nobles, I take you there? How many camels for your beautiful wife? I give you two, no three' – we caught the ferry across the Nile to the Valley of the Queens, where the Men's toilet was locked and we ended up in two adjacent cubicles in the Ladies. Here I loudly liberated my breakfast orally as Graham did likewise, using a more southerly orifice, the sound of which simply made me vomit all the more.

First emergency stop of the day over, we engaged the services of Gamal, a portly man wearing a stained white ankle-length *jilabīyah*. Gamal looked like everyone's favourite uncle, the one who brings the best Christmas presents and, with a conspiratorial wink, pours the 15-year-old you a glass of wine at dinner. Sadly, he didn't have the corresponding manners. Pinching the bridge of his nose and leaning forward, Gamal blasted a double-barrelled snotgun onto the hot tarmac before drawing his sleeve across his wet nose.

'Okay, you get in, we go,' he sniffed, gesturing to his knackered Mercedes station-wagon.

Gamal drove us to the Temple of Hatshepsut, a magnificent, tiered edifice built by Egypt's longest-reigning female pharaoh in the barren mountainside. Except, of course, this would soon be redubbed the Temple of Hatshepshit, as Graham's bowels once again needed voiding and there wasn't a toilet for miles. Leaping over a wall and a 'No Entry' sign he found a spot as far from the temple as possible, away from the prying eyes of several would-be temple guides, and performed an al fresco crap that he described as 'melted chocolate'.

We'd just finished reading our guidebook's description of how Hatshepsut had a penchant for what amounted to cross-dressing – she apparently insisted that she be depicted with a male body and fake beard to assert her authority – before Graham's next wave of bowel tremors struck. Thanks to the two dozen French tourists disgorged from a recently arrived coach, the 'over the wall' option was out, so Graham skirted behind the tour group, crept along a narrow ledge and shat again. Once our tour of the temple was over, we returned to the taxi and had driven only a short way when the urge overtook Graham a fourth time. Gamal stopped next to a row of portable toilets, but they were locked.

'Quick,' I said to Graham, 'nip round the back of them, no one will see you if you go there.'

But Gamal, alarmed, had a better idea and whisked us to the toilets at the rest house near the Ramesseum. Graham went in, but nothing came out. Our next stop was the Ramesseum itself, the mortuary temple of Pharaoh Ramesses II, with its colossal fallen statue of Ozymandias. No sooner had we located the 'shattered visage' Shelley had immortalised in sonnet, than an Egyptian materialised from behind a column resembling an Oscar statuette.

'Come see moomie,' he said, motioning to us that we should accompany him.

Graham wasn't keen, so he pretended he couldn't speak English by repeating '*Ek kannie Engels praat nie*' ('I can't speak English') in Afrikaans. The man wouldn't take no for an answer and eventually Graham, his resolve no doubt weakened by his bout of Pharaoh's

Revenge, relented and allowed him to lead us into a ruined mud-brick village where he pointed out a semi-mummified skeleton.

'Ooh, moomie,' was all Graham could solemnly intone, having exhausted his Afrikaans vocabulary and now unwilling to lose face by admitting that he could speak his mother tongue after all.

Here too, among the mud bricks, Graham found another place to go, but this time he produced a mere teaspoon's worth.

When a hoopoe alighted on a nearby wall, I pointed out the mohican-crested bird to Graham as he often had trouble identifying the most common fauna and flora – we're talking roses and squirrels here, not Ceanothus and pine martens.

'H-o-o-p-o-e, say after me Hoopoe,' I said.

'P-i-s-s o-f-f, Lisa, say after me piss off.'

Next up was the tomb of all tombs: King Tutankhamun's. As it was now noon, a time of day when only mad dogs and Englishmen were likely to be out, there were no other tourists. Even the two guards, stupefied by the heat, preferred to carry on snoozing on a bench in the shade rather than escort us below ground.

Graham, less fond of reading guidebooks than I, was bitterly disappointed: 'I thought King Tut was buried in a pyramid,' he complained as we carefully made our way down a narrow flight of steps into the unexpectedly small 3,300-year-old tomb.

All the same, being alone in Tut's burial chamber, decorated with frescoes of baboons and Egyptian gods that had been painted so soon before the tomb was sealed that patches of mould had grown on the still-damp surface, was a magical moment. My mother had seen the King Tutankhamun exhibition when it toured London in 1972, so I'd grown up with a special reverence for the boy king who'd died prematurely aged just 19. DNA tests have proved that Tut was the product of incest: his mother was married to her brother, meaning the world's most famous mummy's father was also his uncle, and Tut's mum was also his aunt. It's a bonsai of a family tree, is Tut's.

Feeling thoroughly temple- and tombed-out, we asked Gamal to drive us back to the ferry. And here, while Graham took a farewell photo of Gamal and me standing beside his beaten-up Mercedes,

Gamal took the opportunity to give my bottom a firm squeeze, as casually as he would have tested an avocado for ripeness. It was so utterly brazen and unexpected that, unlike in the various versions of the incident that I imagined afterwards – where I screamed at Gamal and told him exactly how unacceptable his action was – I did what millions of women do in the moment and froze.

'I need to get on the ferry *right this very minute*,' I told Graham.

Completely oblivious to what had just happened, Graham couldn't understand my insistence.

'What's wrong?' he asked, perplexed.

'I'll tell you at the hotel,' I muttered through pursed lips as we joined the throng jostling to get on board.

So, after a tour of the West Bank of the Nile that Graham will remember for its many historical shites, monumental shites and World Heritage shites, I ended my day being groped by Gamal, the lecherous little shit.

CHAPTER FIVE

1998-1999: The Year of Living Apart
Bahrain, Saudi Arabia, Jordan

 Weapons of mass destruction took Graham to Bahrain. Or rather, the UN inspectors tasked with hunting them down did, as it was his job as an employee of the UK Ministry of Defence to brief them before they flew on to Iraq. Despite their undoubted sleuthing skills and licence to tromp wherever they pleased, the inspectors never found anything more chemically or biologically hazardous than the local water. They were expelled by Saddam Hussein four months after Graham arrived, and three months after they left Baghdad he was summoned back to London.

I was initially very upset when Graham first mooted the suggestion of going to live in Bahrain without me, but he managed to convince me it would be a great professional opportunity and that the extra money he'd earn would come in handy. As he'd not stood in my way when I'd wanted to go to Taiwan, I didn't feel I could veto his request: if you wanted to be treated as an equal, I'd found over the years, you had to play fair.

'Okay, you can go,' I said tearfully, anticipating telling my Editor at *Zest* magazine, where I'd moved from *Cosmo* the previous year, that being separated from Graham was the reason I was crying into my coffee at work every day.

Before he flew out to Bahrain, Graham typed up a two-page manual for me on running the household, which I still have to this day, detailing among other things how to operate the boiler, shut off the gas and water and put petrol in the car.

'Always use unleaded fuel or you'll wreck the engine,' he wrote.

135

'Don't put the petrol cap on the roof of the car when filling up.' This last instruction was a tad unnecessary as I'd only once driven off with the cap on the roof, and the trouble I'd had retrieving it from a dual carriageway was more than enough to make sure I wouldn't make that mistake again.

Graham also left instructions on how to operate the television's remote control. In the five years I'd lived in England, I'd never used it myself: I worked such long hours that the telly was always on when I got home, and at weekends he changed the channels. Besides, there were a lot of buttons on the remote.

'Graham, I'm afraid I'm never going to get the hang of all this,' I said doubtfully.

'Lisa, simply follow what I've written step by step. You can't spend the entire time I'm away without watching television.'

'You know how much I hate learning new technical stuff,' I complained. 'And now I'm having to learn technical stuff about the TV, the boiler, the gas, the water, the car, the computer, the dishwasher, the washing machine and the VHS. It's all too much.'

'Lisa, if you really get stuck you can phone me in Bahrain.'

With the help of the manual, I managed just fine, and was proud that the only time I had to call Graham was when I forgot I'd parked our car in a pay and display bay and it was towed away. I wasn't intending to tell him about this little incident, but the vehicle pound insisted I provide evidence of ownership before they'd release our car and, as I didn't know where our paperwork was filed, I had to confess all.

'Please don't tell your family about this,' I begged, as Graham chuckled down the static-filled phoneline. 'To be honest, I didn't even want *you* to know.'

Determined to stay upbeat and stave off loneliness during our long separation, I challenged myself to do two things I hadn't done since 1990: writing and running. Besides our travel journals, I'd written barely a word since the knockback I'd received at South African *Cosmo* eight years before when the Editor had called an advertorial I'd written about an artificial sweetener 'a valiant attempt at writing'. And I hadn't run a race since I'd competed in Cape Town against the Olympians Elana Meyer and Zola Budd Pieterse in the 10K Ladies Fashion Fun Run, a race in which they'd come first and second while I'd finished 11th from last. Without Graham to entertain and distract me, I threw all my energy into both activities and became a regular contributor to *Zest* and, when the Deputy Editor Sally gifted me her London Marathon place, a marathon runner. After a lifetime of exercise-aversion this was so out of character that, despite giving him regular updates on how my training was going, Graham forgot to wish me good luck for race day. My refusal to reply to his daily emails alerted him to the fact he'd done something wrong.

'Well, if you call ignoring the biggest achievement of my life "doing something wrong", then yes, you have,' I replied coldly.

'Oh, no, I didn't,' Graham groaned. 'You haven't done London *already*, have you? I thought it was *next week*. I'm truly, truly sorry.'

I forgave him on the condition that he run the Edinburgh Marathon with me later in the year. Full of contrition, he agreed.

Our daily email contact resumed, but was interrupted once again when I received the following email: 'GET A GRIP! GET A GRIP! You can't leave the dishes to grow mould in the sink for a week. And if you don't fill in that hole, they'll die under our house, we'll be overrun with maggots and the smell will be unbearable. I'm not flying home to come and dig up the floorboards.'

This in response to what I thought were two hilarious tales from the home front. The first involved my reluctance to enter the kitchen due to the giant spider living in the sink. I'd stayed as far away from it as possible, and simply stacked my dirty pots on the draining board. It took me a week to steel myself to tackle the spider, putting on rubber gloves and grabbing a glass and piece of card with which to capture it – only to find it was a tomato stalk.

In the second story, I'd told of my terror when I heard a banging on our front door at 4am. I'd been too scared to go downstairs to investigate, so had stayed in bed with my head under my pillow until the noise had stopped. In the morning, I'd discovered a large hole under our doormat. Local foxes had tried to dig a den under our house. When I'd returned home from work, the hole had been filled in. 'What tidy foxes,' I'd said to myself, until I'd read the note left by our neighbour Jim explaining that he'd shovelled the soil back and helpfully placed some bricks on it to prevent the foxes from trying again. In my email I'd told Graham most of the story but omitted the Jim part as it detracted from the humour of the situation. Frantic that he'd return home to a kitchen completely overrun with mould atop foundations littered with the corpses of decomposing foxes, Graham had felt it necessary to make his frustration with my ineptitude known.

I was in turn displeased that he should think me unable to run the household in accordance with his exacting standards, despite neither eventuality being covered by his instruction manual.

'Give me some credit,' I wrote back. 'I've managed to put petrol in the car without any drama and I haven't called you for IT or TV support. And of course I eventually washed the dishes, and I wouldn't let a family of foxes take up residence under our house. I'm coping perfectly well. And don't ever write "GET A GRIP!" to me ever again.'

A few months later I flew out to Bahrain on holiday, keen to see the unrenovated Holiday Inn room Graham was staying in, and meet his new colleagues who, with names like Aussie John and Little Dave, reminded me of the good old days in Taipei Hostel. Our side trip to Saudi, though not as interesting as we'd hoped, nonetheless inspired our next trip, to Jordan, later that year, where we were seduced by the rosy charms of Petra and spent a magical night under a starlit sky in Wadi Rum.

When Graham returned to the UK after seven months I was a changed woman. Not only was I the proud owner of what would be the first of over 100 marathon medals, but I had several published articles to my name. And a new life skill: the ability to be able to turn on the telly, and change channels, all on my own.

Big Gerry & the airborne olives
Bahrain

The list of visit-worthy tourist sites in Bahrain was as short as a power nap – the country's first oil well, several forts and the Tree of Life, a lone 400-year-old tree that survives without an obvious source of water – and the choice of entertainment was similarly limited. Although there were a couple of cafés where you could smoke *shisha* pipes and drink coffee in the still, balmy evenings, including one overlooking the Arabian Gulf, the tranquil dark waters of which reflected the moon, I didn't care for *shisha* smoking and so was an infrequent visitor. As a Brit I tended to avoid The Warbler, a British-style pub, on the grounds that drinking there was like taking a busman's holiday. I preferred Hunter's Lodge, where my Aussie and American colleagues and I would play table football, eat buffalo wings and order jugs of Long Island Iced Tea from the delightful Maria, the ever-chatty Bulgarian bartender. For an additional two dinars we'd go 'thermonuclear' and Maria would substitute the Coke with lemonade and add Curaçao liqueur to turn the now six-spirit mix a disagreeable shade of blue.

Hunter's Lodge was popular with visiting US service personnel who, over the years, had donated dozens of framed photographs of themselves in various macho 'active duty' poses on aircraft-carrier flight decks, aboard helicopters and next to tanks. I hoped that the photos were not in lieu of tips; Maria needed money from Hunter's narcissistic clientele more than her employer needed freebie 'Check out the size of my bazooka!' wall decorations.

My American colleagues told me that, for security reasons, on their return to the good old US of A, they'd have to declare any contact they'd had with foreign nationals in Bahrain, including Maria and me. At first, I took them to be joking. Did Uncle Sam *really* think that the Bulgarian secret service sent young women to tend bars in Bahrain? Very possibly he did.

My post-Hunter's Lodge late-evening standby was the Phoenicia Hotel, where a five-girl, three-guy singing and dancing band from Belarus performed nightly in the smoky subterranean nightclub.

More adept at mangling songs than singing them, I could sometimes make out the lyrics if I listened carefully to their heavily Russian-inflected English.

'My hard vill… go ahnnn,' they'd croon the *Titanic* theme song.

The Phoenicia could be a lot of fun. It was patronised mostly by Bahraini men, though on weekends they were supplemented by Saudis who drove their monstrous 4x4s across the King Fahd Causeway to enjoy pleasures that state-sponsored Islam denied them at home. To help draw them in, the five women wore short skirts and even shorter shorts, or 'cheekies' because they were high enough to reveal two slim crescents of buttock.

The Saudis would sink a few beers – sometimes a few too many – and were happy to chat to us, though the Americans learned to say they were Canadian to deflect visceral anti-US sentiment. They loved 'buying' leis to bestow on their favourite hot-pants-wearing singer or dancer as a token of admiration or gratitude. As the young woman stepped forward and dipped her head to receive the plastic floral tribute, she'd look her benefactor in the eye and smile a charming 'Why, thank you' smile. And well she might, for at the equivalent of £8 a pop – more than the price of a pint – presenting leis was an expensive gesture. The garlands would be worn for a single song and then returned to the Filipino waitresses to be 'resold'. I once saw ten bought and presented in one go.

On my final night in Manama, three colleagues accompanied me as I went to bid farewell to the band. Gerry, a strapping, bullet-headed guard recently arrived from the US, was with us. It was his first visit to the Phoenicia, and I suspect it was also his last. As Gerry sipped his Jim Beam and Coke, one of the Filipino waitresses walked over to him and slipped a red-and-yellow lei round his neck.

'What's going on?' said Gerry. 'Why have I been given this?'

The waitress gestured to the table behind. Gerry swivelled in his seat. A short, wiry Arab in a white ankle-length *dishdasha* and *keffiyah* headdress, obviously the worse for wear, flashed him a ragged, dark-toothed smile.

'No way, dude,' said Gerry, angrily removing the garland and handing it back. Gerry returned his attention to his drink.

'So, Graham, how often have you seen this band?'

'About twice a week, I guess. Some of the other bands in town are truly dreadful. Quiz night at The Warbler can be fun, though.'

Something bounced off Gerry's broad back. He didn't seem to notice it.

'I ain't much of a quiz kinda guy. But I may go and check out The Warbler some day all the same.'

A second something pinged off Gerry's shoulder blade. He spun round in his chair to locate the origin of the missile, only to see the smiling Arab coyly inclining his head at him. The man picked up a third black olive between his thumb and index finger and flirtatiously tossed it at Gerry, this time hitting him in the chest. The olive bounced harmlessly onto the floor.

'What the fuck!' exclaimed Gerry loudly, glowering and turning away in disgust.

'Looks like you've made a new friend,' I said, winking.

Gerry glared at me, his lips moving to the words of a curse unheard over the noise of the band.

Another olive hit its target.

Gerry's sense of humour failure became catastrophic.

'This is just too fucking much!' he said, unable to put up with the man's amorous attentions any longer and rising to his feet. 'That dude is just asking for trouble. If I don't leave now, I swear I'm gonna punch his goddam lights out.'

'Gerry, calm down, it's only a bit of harmless fun,' I said.

'No way, man. I'm outta here,' said Gerry as he stalked angrily from the nightclub.

Disappointed but undaunted, the Arab bought another three leis, one for each of us who remained, which we graciously accepted. At the end of the evening I didn't hand mine back as all patrons were supposed to. I still have it, stored somewhere in our loft.

Foul fowl in Al-Hofuf
Saudi Arabia

 The Kingdom of Saudi Arabia is one of several countries where you can be jailed simply for eating. A few days before Lisa and I arrived, a man had been imprisoned for a month for snacking in public during the Islamic holy month of Ramadan, when consuming food and drink is banned until sunset, even if you aren't a Muslim. This had, understandably, made us jumpy. As did the stories we'd heard of religious police whipping the ankles of women perceived to be immodestly dressed.

Very few non-Muslim Westerners had visited Saudi Arabia because, until recently, the kingdom had been disinclined to issue tourist visas, but back in 1998 I was working at the British Embassy in Bahrain, so securing visas for Lisa and myself was straightforward. At the Saudi border post, midway across the 25km-long King Fahd Causeway, humourless customs officials searched our hire car with exacting thoroughness, looking for contraband alcohol, pornography and Bibles. We disappointed them. They looked disappointed.

'It wasn't Bibles they were hoping to confiscate,' I said.

The first three towns on the far side of the causeway – Khobar, Dhahran and Dammam – were one unremitting bleached beige sprawl of squat, flat-roofed buildings, and were surprisingly impoverished-looking. We'd expected Saudi Arabia's oil wealth to be on proud display, but wherever it was it certainly wasn't showcased here. Everything was Ramadan-closed, and there was no one to be seen. It was eerie. All we could do was drive the length of the deserted Corniche for a view of the limpid Arabian Gulf. The water was so still it looked as if it, too, had fallen into a calorie-restricted coma. We pressed 150km inland to Al-Hofuf, recommended to us by an American colleague as an 'oasis town'. It wasn't the camel-and-date-palm oasis town of Hollywood's imagining but a modern sand-blasted city of over 100,000 people.

At our £23-per-night hotel the manager insisted we prove that we were legally married before he'd book us into a double room. 'It is a requirement of law. People who are not legally married must have separate rooms.'

It hardly constituted proof, but each of us holding up our left hand to show our wedding bands was enough to satisfy him. Our twin-bedded room was sparsely and cheaply furnished, with two polyester prayer mats and a small wooden arrow high up on the wall indicating the direction of Mecca. The air-conditioner pumped ice-cold air inside and warmed the planet outside, and the grumbling minibar fridge next to the bed held two short tubes of Pringles crisps and two non-alcoholic beers. The beers were cold and we were thirsty so we drank them.

That evening we went in search of a guidebook-listed restaurant. After some head scratching and map rotating, we located the correct street and, from there, the restaurant. The owner, wearing a brown *dishdasha* and smoking a cigarette, welcomed us at the entrance and ushered us to a bare table towards the back. We felt that he was trying to hide us. A younger man brought a scrappy menu in Arabic, two glasses of water and cheap Uri Geller cutlery, the sort that bends when it encounters food more resistant than soup. The tin spoons and plates were probably rife with hepatitis A to Z. The owner spoke enough English to translate the menu for us, so we ordered *saleeg*, a rice-and-chicken combo, which arrived with eyebrow-raising promptness. The porridge-like rice wasn't a portion but a smear in the bottom of a bowl. In fact, the serving was *so* stingy that we weren't sure if they'd got confused and given us a bowl they'd forgotten to wash up. And the chicken? We've eaten chicken all over the world, but this bird was so undercooked we could swear the veins surfacing from its unappetising greyish flesh were still actively pumping blood.

As we picked over our meal of foul fowl a dirty-faced, barefoot child appeared at our table and, motioning his hand to his mouth, begged for food. In all our years of travelling, including in some of the world's poorest countries, this had never happened before. Perhaps we shouldn't have been shocked as it's unofficially estimated – the Saudi government doesn't disclose the true figures – that as many as four million of its citizens live below the poverty line on less than US$17 a day. We gave the grateful child our chicken, and were tempted to advise that, when he got home, he should ask his mum to cook it.

When the muezzin called the faithful to *Maghrib* prayer, the second last of the day, the owner told us to stay seated and he and the waiters went outside to pray, pulling the security shutter down behind them. By the time they returned we were ready to leave. It hadn't exactly been a fine dining experience.

Though Al-Hofuf was now thronged with men enjoying their post-fast evening, there was very little to do: all cinemas and theatres in Saudi Arabia had been closed in 1983 after insurgents, intent on overthrowing the ruling House of Saud, seized the Grand Mosque in Mecca in 1979, which led to a stricter enforcement of sharia law. It wasn't until 2018 that cinemas reopened in reforms that also allowed women to drive and attend sporting events. Shopping, then, was our only entertainment option.

'I saw a music shop on the way,' I said to Lisa. 'Let's see if it has any Amr Diab. He's an Egyptian heartthrob singer who's very popular in Bahrain. I think you'll like his music. Aussie John has several of his albums and I wouldn't mind buying a few myself.'

No sooner had we entered the narrow shop and started riffling through the CDs than the sales assistant hurried over and, in perfect English, told me that Lisa was not welcome, notwithstanding that she was modestly attired in the black *abaya* cloak she'd purchased in Bahrain's souk specially for our trip.

'Women are not permitted in this shop,' he said. 'You must tell your wife to leave.'

I looked at Lisa who was browsing the racks of CDs at the far end of the store. I glanced around. Besides Lisa, there weren't any other women in the shop, and besides me and the assistant there were only three other men.

'Really? We're just looking for some music.'

'She must leave,' he insisted. 'No women are allowed.'

'Alright, okay, we're going,' I snapped.

I took Lisa by the crook of her elbow, put my mouth to her ear and repeated what the sales assistant had said.

'Bloody hell, are you serious?' Lisa whispered back, indignant and annoyed. 'You mean a woman can't even *stand* next to a man who isn't her husband?'

It appeared not.

With Lisa feeling humiliated and almost in tears, we left the store to stroll through the souk, which was definitely the liveliest spot in town. Small knots of women – the first we'd seen since crossing the causeway – wearing *burkas* that covered them from head to toe and veiled their eyes, moved from stall to stall, sampling the wares and bargaining confidently and loudly with the owners. Though there was nothing we wanted to buy as the stallholders sold household essentials like saucepans, pots, groceries and clothing rather than handicrafts or souvenirs, the souk distracted us for an hour. It may have been a Ramadan-inspired thing, but the most popular stalls by far were those selling *abayas* and *burkas*. To our untutored eyes it was hard to distinguish one garment from another as, like Henry Ford's Model T car, they were available in any colour, as long as it was black.

Over breakfast of toast, jam and coffee I asked Lisa if she wanted to drive on to Riyadh.

'I don't know. After what happened last night, I'm not sure. How far is it? I don't feel welcome here.'

I said that I reckoned it was at least a five-hour drive.

'What's there to see?'

I read aloud the sights recommended in our guidebook. It took me no more than 30 seconds, possibly closer to ten. That decided it for Lisa.

'Let's go back to Bahrain.'

Diddled in the desert
Jordan

'Ooh, it's like a disco out there!' declared the BA air steward buckled into his seat in the rear galley as we flew above an electrical storm en route to Amman, the capital of Jordan.

Lisa had so enjoyed the desert sunshine in Bahrain that, a few months after I was transferred back to the UK, she suggested we holiday in the Middle East. We'd caught an overnight flight and were hoping for a quiet 40 winks but it was not to be: we were seated at the rear so, with the plane tossing us around like dried peas in a cocoa tin, we were kept awake by the crew, one of whom, a ditzy Welsh lass, incessantly spouted stream-of-consciousness inanities.

'I like blinking, me,' she volunteered. 'It can be a lot of fun, and it exercises eye muscles. People who don't blink enough get droopy eyes when they're old, sure enough. Look at that Paul McCartney.' Her colleagues, no older nor wiser, murmured their sage agreement. 'If you play Robbie Williams's *Cursed* backwards – God's honest truth, this – there is a message from Satan. People who've done it killed their whole families.'

Like a horse, her teeth probably took up more space in her head than her brain.

Arriving at Amman's Queen Alia International Airport at 6am, we freshened up and then negotiated a ride to Aqaba, a coastal city 330km to the south, with Boutros, a local taxi driver, who told me he drove a taxi to get away from his overbearing wife and four clamorous children.

Lisa was asleep minutes after we got into the taxi, but woke when we stopped for breakfast at a nondescript roadside restaurant.

'Are we there yet?'

'No Lisa, Boutros wants to eat.'

Lisa made a pillow of her hoody, put her head back against the window and instantly fell asleep.

'Come, I will introduce you to Jordanian food. You will like it.'

Boutros ushered me into the spartan establishment, sat me down and ordered *fuul*, hummus, bread and tea on my behalf. His table manners left a lot to be desired: picking a fava bean from the *fuul* with his dirty fingers, he passed it across the table to me, expecting me to eat it.

'You have this in America?'

'England. And, yes, I'm sure I could get fava beans if I wanted.'

At the end of the meal he paid the cashier without giving me sight of the bill and then asked me for seven dinars. Back in the taxi, a quick check of the guidebook confirmed that Boutros had stiffed me and that I'd paid at least twice the going rate.

Two hours after leaving Amman we pulled in at the Crusader castle of Kerak, where the French crusader Raynald of Châtillon threw (or had thrown, as nobles don't do their own throwing) various souls from the ramparts, insisting that wooden boxes be placed over his victims' heads to prevent them from losing consciousness before they struck the ground.

'I don't get how that's supposed to work,' said a puzzled Lisa.

Ray's other inventive sadistic act had been to coat (or have coated, as nobles don't do their own coating) the captured elderly Patriarch of Antioch in honey and expose his naked body to the blazing sun so that he'd be driven half mad by flies in an attempt to extort money from him.

'Now that's a form of torture I *can* see working,' said Lisa.

Following her encounter with the Bogeyman of Pushkar, Lisa knew only too well how a combination of flies and honey could be mentally destabilising.

Ray got his just deserts for his many acts of piracy, plunder and truce-breaking when, after the Battle of Hattin in 1187, he was beheaded by the great Muslim warrior Saladin.

On several more occasions we pulled over for refreshments, and Boutros would insist that I remain outside the shop as he made the purchases. Then, after initially refusing my money – 'my gift to you' – he would vituperatively declaim the Bedouin shopkeepers for charging exorbitant prices.

'Why, why they charge so much?' he would ask aloud, before proceeding to answer his own rhetorical question. 'Because these Bedo, they have zero minds. In Aqaba you pay only one-and-a-half dinars for a Coke, maybe two, here it is three dinars. "Special price" for us Christians.'

A special price for the English atheist.

Boutros would then hold out his hand so I could reimburse him for the 'gifts' he'd bought from the 'zero-minded Bedo'.

When we stopped for fuel, Boutros filled the tank for a few dinars, thereby giving the lie to his earlier claim that petrol in Jordan was prohibitively expensive. His fare to Aqaba had been explicitly calculated on the 'exorbitant' cost of petrol and the day rate for an Amman taxi driver. By now I had cottoned on to the fact that I'd been overcharged on a few occasions, and I was fast losing patience with him.

On we went, through the sun-blistered, arid terrain, sweltering in the airless car, passing Wadi Rum in the distance to our left. Lisa was still asleep, with her hoody over her face. I swear she'd sleep through Armageddon. Two miles from Aqaba, Boutros turned on the car's air-conditioning, so we had a tantalising taste of how pleasant the trip could've – but hadn't – been. Bastard!

We entered Aqaba an hour before sunset, paid Boutros the pre-agreed fare *with* a consideration – I hated myself for giving him more money, but isn't 'Thou shalt always tip thy ferryman' one of the Ten Commandments? – checked into a local hotel and found a restaurant with a view across the Red Sea to the Israeli port town of Eilat. As the sun set, Eilat's lights came twinkling on.

Aqaba's main claim to fame was that it had been captured from the Turks by Lawrence of Arabia and his Arab Revolt fighters who'd crossed the desert, believed to be impassable, to take it from behind. Turkish defences all faced seaward, so Lawrence didn't have too tough a fight. David Lean's on-screen depiction of the event mistakenly, or misleadingly, chose to omit the less-heroic fact that during the battle Lawrence was nearly killed, not by a Turkish soldier, but by his camel who threw him after he accidentally shot the unfortunate creature in the back of the head. Peter O'Toole, the actor who portrayed Lawrence in the 1962 film, had no better luck with camels. Not only was he bitten by one on set but the first time he rode a camel during shooting, blood from his tenderised nether regions oozed through his trousers, so he travelled to Beirut where he bought a thick piece of mucous membrane pink sponge to put on top of his saddle. Terrified of falling off his mount during the filming of the attack on Aqaba, poor Peter got stocious and lashed himself to his camel, and hence the entire dramatic scene was shot without him having a clue as to what he was doing. The myriad of other mishaps that befell O'Toole during filming – he sprained his neck and both ankles, received third-degree burns, dislocated his spine and fractured his skull – was likely attributable to his fondness for the bottle and smoking hash.

In the morning, we set off for Wadi Rum, a desolate red-rock-sided valley that Lawrence traversed several times during the 1916-1918 Arab Revolt. At the visitor centre we engaged a Bedouin called Zaid as our host and guide. Dressed in a white tunic and trousers, his head swathed in a red-and-white chequered *keffiyah* and with a rakish Clark Gable pencil moustache, Zaid cut a dashing figure until he smiled to reveal a mouthful of blackened, stumpy rotten teeth. He was the David Beckham of the desert: impossibly handsome as long he didn't open his mouth. As far as we could tell, he didn't seem to have a 'zero mind'. We waited in his pick-up truck as he purchased what we – or rather he – would need: tea, dates, bread, crisps and about a hundredweight of sugar. The man must have syrup running in his veins.

Our first stop was Jebel Khazali gorge with its rock drawings of people, horses and pairs of human feet. Some of the outer rocks looked like melted candle wax, others were so intricate they resembled inscriptions from the Koran.

Lunch was a plain bread roll and a cup of super-sweet tea made with condensed milk *and* sugar. Lounging on a carpet that he'd pulled from the back of his pick-up, Zaid chatted to Lisa, and on hearing that she'd done the London Marathon earlier that year said he'd run the Wadi Rum Marathon several times.

'You must come and run it with me next year,' he said.

'I'll certainly think about it,' said Lisa, 'but it may be a bit too hot and sandy for me.'

'No, you would love it. I would run the whole way with you and make sure you finished.'

The conversation turned to Zaid's family set-up. 'I am a Muslim and I have four children and two wives,' he told Lisa. 'But I want another Arab wife *plus* a French, German or English wife. Or maybe an American.'

'Oh really,' said Lisa, too polite to share her views on polygamy, and not wanting to be the one to break the news to Zaid that his bad teeth completely ruled out an American wife.

Overhearing this exchange, I wasn't sure whether or not he was hitting on Lisa but concluded that, as a South African, she didn't match his wish list and that I needn't worry.

For sunset we climbed a lookout point with great views across the Wadi Rum plain and watched as a singing man on a sauntering camel crossed the desert below. Where he had come from and where he was going only he knew. We cooled the small bottle of wine taken from our flight in one of Lisa's wetted socks, but then decided against drinking it in Zaid's presence. He may have been a pious Muslim, in which case we risked offending him by drinking it in front of him. He may not have been a pious Muslim, in which case there wasn't enough for three people.

At dusk we retired to Zaid's family tent pegged out in the desert sand at the base of the mountains.

'Zaid, can you tell me where the toilet is please?' Lisa asked.

'Everywhere,' said Zaid, smiling a black-toothed smile and sweeping his arms through 180 degrees.

And he was not wrong – judging by the turds you had to negotiate to get to the one rock, some hundred yards distant, that provided any privacy. Lisa trekked out to the toilet rock and on her way back bumped into a German tourist staying at an adjacent encampment, one who was none too happy about the prospect of spending the night sleeping on the ground under the stars.

'Isn't it lovely here?' Lisa remarked to the tourist. 'This desert is exactly how I imagined the one baby Jesus and his parents fled through on their way to Egypt. It's almost a religious experience.'

'Yes,' huffed the tourist, 'it's my idea of hell!'

'You may not be enjoying it now,' Lisa replied, 'but mark my words, you'll be telling this story for the rest of your life.'

Following a tasty dinner of grilled goat and flatbreads cooked over an open fire, we unrolled our sleeping bags on the woven carpets that Zaid had laid out on the sand and fell asleep gazing at the spangled heavens and a few shooting stars that streaked across the night sky. At 4am I was woken by the crowing of a cockerel that had taken up residence on the other side of the windbreak behind our heads. It proceeded to crow itself hoarse for about three hours, joined by the bleating of goats and Zaid's rasping snoring. Naturally, Lisa slept through it.

While waiting for the bus that would take us to Petra, an ancient Nabataean metropolis carved out of sandstone cliffs that was rediscovered by Europeans in the early 1800s, Lisa and I agreed that, although we'd been a little ripped off by good old Bedo-despising Boutros, we'd most certainly got excellent value for money at Wadi Rum. Our full-board accommodation had featured a view of one of the most spectacular lunar-like landscapes on earth, the most expansive en-suite toilet anyone could wish for and the most nerve-shatteringly efficient (unless you're Lisa) wake-up call ever. Even though there weren't any towelling robes or complimentary miniature toiletries, no hotel, we concluded, could ever come close to topping it.

CHAPTER SIX

2000 – 2010: The City Break Years
Amsterdam, Madrid, Reykjavík

 When I returned from Bahrain Lisa was an expert in using the dishwasher and washing machine, two kitchen appliances she'd previously viewed with distrust verging on distaste. 'I must write more manuals and go away more often,' I concluded.

When I asked her, however, if she'd be prepared to continue assuming her fair share of housekeeping duties, it was quite a different story.

'The problem is, I'm just not that interested in housework, Graham,' she responded.

'Lisa, 'I don't think *anyone's* that interested in housework. Most people view it simply as something that has to be done, like clipping their toenails.'

In her defence, Lisa's magazine job and the extra editing and writing work she took on, as well as all the running she now did, meant that she was incredibly busy. But every now and again I became resentful and we'd have an argument. The same one we'd been having ever since we got married.

'When was the last time you polished the bathroom tiles?' I'd say accusingly, to which Lisa always replied, 'Forget the tiles. Why don't you ever surprise me and arrange a weekend away without me suggesting it?'

Thankfully, we learned to speed-fight, omitting all the boring and unnecessary verbiage. An argument would now go like this.

Me: 'Tiles.'

Lisa: 'Surprises.'

The End.

What saved our relationship, I now realise, was my willingness to go on city breaks. Granted, I rarely suggested them, but I never refused to go on one either. Since I'd come back from Bahrain, Lisa had a bee in her bonnet about travelling as often as possible.

'From now on, Graham, I don't want to spend a single day's holiday in the UK – and that means bank holidays, too,' she'd proclaimed. Having been starved of travel for the first 24 years of her life, Lisa was keen to overindulge in it now.

'I'm not sure we can afford to do that, Lisa,' I said.

'We can do anything we put our minds to Graham. Remember how we managed to save US$8,000 in Taiwan.'

Living on one-and-a-bit salaries for three years had thankfully taught us to be frugal. Despite working alongside fashionistas at *Cosmo* and *Zest,* a health and beauty magazine, Lisa didn't feel the need to splash cash on clothes, jewellery, make-up, massages or manicures. I, too, had simple tastes: I ate homemade sardine sarnies for lunch and was more than happy to wear the suits my brother Rod handed down to me. Lisa and I were the last people we knew to buy mobile phones, and restaurants, takeaways, pubs, the cinema, concerts, taxis and even Starbucks were special-occasion treats unless we were abroad, where, as all of the above were usually less expensive than London, we heartily indulged ourselves. Likewise, we never bought each other lavish gifts, but treated each other to trips instead. Lisa gave me Cologne one birthday – and it wasn't Old Spice – and I gave her Vietnam for our tenth wedding anniversary. Unlike Lisa, I was barred from moonlighting, but indirectly contributed to our travel kitty by becoming a have-a-go hero and never paying someone else to do a job I could bodge myself, whether that was cleaning the house, ironing, gardening or DIY. And even hairdressing. Lisa took the rationing approach here, and limited herself to two haircuts a year, as her one attempt at cutting her own hair left her with a bleeding hand and a raggedy haircut worthy of Worzel Gummidge. I, however, proudly embraced the challenge and with the help of my trusty trimmers did a damn fine job, as I'm good with my hands.

'Graham, what the heck have you done to your hair?' said Lisa the first time I gave myself a short back and sides.

'I cut it.'

'But you've got sticky-out bits on top that make you look like a woodpecker, and tufty bits at the back that look like a mullet. And the sides are squiffy, too.'

'Never mind, Lisa, my colleagues are too polite to comment. And the more often I do this, the better I'll become at doing it.'

We became adept at using our annual leave thriftily, too, turning weekends into long weekends, bank holidays into mini breaks and Easter into a ten-day holiday. As a result, the game of Bin became an enjoyable way to kill time in departures. Airports the world over are the same, filled as they are with jaded and often jet-lagged adults, excitable children and overpriced shops selling tat to those whom they deliberately bore into spending money beyond sense. Reading down the departures boards, in our own private version of Snap, we'd shout out 'bin' (short for 'been') whenever the board listed a city we'd been to.

Rome. 'Bin!'

Helsinki. 'Bin!'

Berlin. 'Bin!'

Istanbul. 'Bin!'

Budapest. 'Bin!'

Barcelona. 'Bin!'

Warsaw. 'Bin!'

Brussels. 'Bin!'

Athens. 'Bin!'

In those pre-Extinction Rebellion days, we revelled in the chance to roam Europe, knowing that the money we saved during our travels by dossing in hostels and campsites could be splurged on foreign culture and cuisine. As friends and family will attest, for a decade of summers I became the polar opposite of a Pilot Light because, whenever they wanted us to come round for dinner, like an impotent man's cock I was never in.

Wild peeing
Amsterdam

 'We asked for a *mattress*,' said Graham's sister Deb to the receptionist who'd knocked on the door of our hotel room in Amsterdam bearing an armload of assorted towels. It was Deb's first trip away with us and, as a five-star kind of traveller, she'd been somewhat uneasy about the standard of accommodation we usually booked. Not wishing to disappoint her, we'd chosen a one-star, £21 triple room at the Hotel Centre on Damrak which, despite being the city's main thoroughfare, felt grubby, as if the pavements had been smeared with chip fat and mayo. Which they had, for our hotel was above one of Damrak's many *Vlaamse frites* shops.

On our first night we stayed out late, and in the morning Deb said that she'd hardly slept a wink, complaining bitterly about her uncomfortable bed. We thought she was being a drama queen, but when we took a closer look the source of her discomfort was clear. Her bed lacked a mattress. Deb had spent the night sleeping on the wooden bed base, cushioned by a tatty sheet. Clearly, the anaesthetic effect of a night spent drinking port until the wee hours had been temporary. We marched to reception where we made our displeasure known to the manager who, without apology, promised to send up a mattress that evening.

After a sobering morning at Anne Frank's House we signed up for an afternoon cycle tour led by Stuart, a dozy dopehead dressed in jeans and a black T-shirt with 'Yes We Can-nabis' emblazoned across it. Deb spent the entire tour in a state of agitation because, being half the height of the average Amsterdammer – the Dutch are the tallest people in the world – her feet barely reached the pedals and she struggled to keep up. And once she got moving, she faced the challenge of how to stop as her hands were too petite to properly clasp the brake levers.

Stuart didn't know or care much about Amsterdam's history, but he did share an eyebrow-raising anecdote from its more recent past: to prevent the 50 deaths a year caused by inebriated men falling into the canals when weeing into them, Amsterdam's city council had installed al fresco urinals. Aggrieved that their urinary needs had not been similarly catered for, the city's womenfolk had staged a massive demonstration in one of the central squares that culminated in everyone squatting down and simultaneously urinating. This public 'pee-in' did not go down too well with the authorities for, in a city that openly allows prostitution and drug-taking, so-called 'wild peeing' is one of the few fineable offences.

Ignoring Amsterdam's 700-year past, Stuart focused the final part of our tour on the city's vice trade, on which he was an expert. He informed us that there were about 400 sex workers in the red light district and that they paid €100 to €400 per day to rent their glass-fronted rooms, each of which was fitted with a panic button that would summon the police in under a minute.

'If you want to go to a window prostitute,' said a straight-faced Stuart, 'the going rate is €50 for 20 minutes.'

At tour's end, Stuart cheekily announced that in lieu of cash he would be very happy to be tipped in hash, should anyone needed to dispose of some before flying home.

Thirsty from our pedalling, we retired to In 't Aepjen (In the Monkeys), an atmospheric 450-year-old pub that had previously been a seamen's hostel. In days gone by, sailors returning from distant Dutch colonies who were short of a guilder or two would pay for their lodgings by handing over their pet monkeys, so over time the place became overrun with primates – and their fleas – and townsfolk would know by their ceaseless scratching which sailors had spent the night 'in the monkeys'.

After a few drinks followed by dinner at a nearby Surinamese restaurant, we returned to our insalubrious dosshouse and asked that the mattress we'd requested earlier be sent up to our room straightaway. Five minutes later, a knock on the door signalled that the missing item had arrived. We opened the door to find the receptionist outside with a pile of towels. When Deb insisted he take away the unwanted towels and fetch us the mattress we'd asked for, he declared that no mattress was available.

'Put these towels on your bed and you'll sleep fine.'

Deb shook her head. Ignoring her, he entered the room and started unfolding the towels and laying them one atop the other on the divan, gently chiding us that we should consider ourselves fortunate: 'Before you, five refugees shared this room,' he said. 'They slept across the width of the bed with their feet supported on five chairs.' That shut Deb up, though it didn't stop her complaining, once the receptionist had left, about the lack of cupboard space, which was a bit rich considering she'd nabbed the solitary hanger (and nail to hang it on) the moment we'd arrived. I slept soundly, but Graham was forced to sleep on the floor – on a couple of towels – as he couldn't get comfortable on our horribly saggy double mattress. And Deb? Well, as the receptionist had promised, the towels did make a difference, but she nonetheless had another sleepless night, blaming the smell of frites for keeping her awake.

The prawn puppeteer
Madrid

I was not expecting to spend an evening with a total stranger who'd told me he was freshly out of a psychiatric hospital, but that's what I ended up doing in Madrid. On the last night of a weekend break, my schoolfriend Karen and I had chosen to dine at Mejillonería El Pasaje near Sol Metro Station, a restaurant acclaimed for its mussels, strings of which adorned its walls. Minutes after we'd sat down, a tall, good-looking man with cornflower blue eyes and dark hair, who'd been sipping a beer at the bar, joined us.

'Hi there. My name is Felipe,' he said, pulling up a chair. Taken aback by his friendliness, and too polite to ask him to leave, we started chatting and allowed him to order us beers and a plate of mussels as our mispronunciation of '*mejillones*' had our waiter in stitches. Apparently, it's not 'me-jillions'.

'People in England are sad. Why do you live in England?' Felipe asked when he learned we'd soon be flying back to London.

'English people aren't as outgoing as the Spanish, but once you get to know them, they're really friendly and the weather's not nearly as terrible as everyone makes out,' I replied defensively.

As we slurped down our mussels, Felipe told us that he worked for *The Best of Madrid* tourist guide, had a sideline in breeding cats and had recently spent some time in 'what do you call where they send crazy people? I don't know how to say it, but I can write it'. Pulling a paper napkin from the metal dispenser on our table, he used a biro to write 'lunatic asylum' on it. Karen and I looked at one another with searching eyes. Felipe was the kind of handsome stranger parents warned daughters to be wary of. But he *was* charming, the beers *were* cold, and we were in a very public place so no harm, we reckoned, would befall us.

Prior to his stint in the asylum, Felipe had worked as cabin crew for Iberia Airlines.

'I got fired as I was too popular,' he said proudly. 'Too many female passengers gave me their telephone numbers. And I think I entertained the passengers too much. After one safety demonstration I got a standing ovation.'

The idea of Felipe, a deflated yellow life-vest around his neck, using exaggerated *YMCA* dance moves to a soundtrack of quick-fire lisping Spanish evacuation instructions was one that I, by now more relaxed as the beer took effect, found hysterically funny. A crew member whose performance had every passenger onboard unbuckling their seatbelt as the plane taxied for take-off is a health and safety nightmare, so no wonder Iberia fired him. It was some time before Felipe could continue with his intriguing life story.

He pulled out his pillbox. It contained a rabbit-dropping-sized piece of dope and a rainbow of assorted pills.

'I take these amino acids to make me grow. As an experiment,' he said, pointing to some red pills. 'When I was young the doctors told me I would not grow, and I trusted them. But one day I hit my head on the "walk" sign on a traffic light and realised that I'd grown. That was many years ago, but now I am trying to grow some more.'

Why someone would want to risk repeated concussion by adding even more inches to his six-foot-plus frame puzzled me – surely life was perilous enough without needing to remember to duck under every doorframe?

With seemingly no more revelations about his colourful past to disclose, Felipe issued an invitation. 'How about I take you two ladies to a tapas bar? How much would you pay to eat as many *gambas* as you want?'

Though still slightly nervous, Karen and I both love prawns so agreed to accompany him to a bar in Palos de la Frontera, a short Metro ride away. Karen had been head girl at our Pretoria high school, so I reasoned that if someone as sensible as her was okay with the proposal then I'd go along with it. What I didn't know was that she was thinking the very same thing about me.

The bar was closed by the time we arrived, but the staff reopened it for us. 'You must pay for me as I am saving money to buy a plot of land so I can farm ostriches,' Felipe declared. Eager to hear more about this latest turn in Felipe's curious story, Karen and I agreed, and we sat down on three tall, low-backed stools at the dimly lit bar.

'I love eating ostrich,' said Karen.

Felipe was immediately all ears. 'You've *eaten* them?'

'Sure, my parents run a game lodge in South Africa. But when my dad tried to breed ostriches, they all died of flu.'

Felipe looked heartbroken. 'I cannot afford to buy ostriches now, which is why I have Russian Blues. I love them because they are always smiling.' From his jacket pocket he pulled out an album of photos of grey-blue smiling cats. 'My dream is to farm ostriches, and then I will invite all my friends to come round and eat ostrich-egg omelettes. Ostrich eggs are very big so my mother says I can use her paella pan. You are welcome to come too.'

Felipe did not seem to appreciate how funny his plan was – like drilling for oil so you'd have petrol to drive your friends to the pub – and because I didn't want to pop his party balloons, I stifled my rising giggles.

Our platters of prawns arrived and we tucked in, noisily licking pungent garlic butter from our fingers.

'You like?' asked Felipe in a sinister voice, putting prawn heads on his fingers and waggling them menacingly in a marine version of Freddy Krueger's murderous mutant hands.

'Mmm,' said Karen, chuckling, 'these prawns are some of the best

I've ever had.'

Felipe looked pleased and continued telling us tales about his life in Madrid, and how he went to bed at 3am but had to get up at 8am to go to work. Siestas, he told us, were all that stood in the way of the country becoming a nation of zombie sleepwalkers. He lived with his grandparents, mother and girlfriend – 'so don't call me at weekends' – and grew hashish on his balcony.

'My mother knows,' Felipe volunteered with a wink, before we could ask.

Back outside, well past midnight, Karen and I bid farewell to our new friend. We laughed all the way back to our hotel, and probably laughed in our dreams, grateful that we'd ignored our misgivings and taken the chance to spend a weird, wonderful and wildly funny evening with Madrid's disarmingly charming, aisle-dancing, pill-popping, cat-breeding, hash-growing wannabe ostrich farmer.

Rotten *Jaws*
Reykjavík

Iceland, the land of fire and ice, is home to several different kinds of puffin. We knew because we'd read Reykjavík's restaurant menus. It's also one of the few places on earth where, should you be so inclined, you can eat whale kebabs, aka 'Moby Dick on a stick.' But *hákarl*, its national dish, is a real classic – in the ironic sense of 'classic'. To a non-Icelander *hákarl* sounds inoffensive, disguising the fact that it's rotten shark. Traditionally, it's made by burying a Greenland shark for several months in sand and gravel weighted with stones to expel the bodily fluids. The disinterred corpse is then dry-cured for several additional months and afterwards cut into sugar-cube-sized pieces that are usually consumed with Brennivín, Iceland's signature schnapps.

Anthony Bourdain described *hákarl* as 'the single worst, most disgusting and terrible-tasting thing' he'd ever eaten, and that's from a man who'd stomached his fair share of I-dare-you-to dishes including still-beating cobra heart in Saigon, roasted sheep testicles in Morocco, raw seal eyeball in Quebec and unwashed warthog anus in the Namib Desert. When TV chef Gordon Ramsay, famed for his four-letter expletives, tried *hákarl* he reacted with 'Ah shit! Damn! God Almighty! Bloody hell!' before vomiting into a bucket. Mick Jagger's response was similar. In the glare of a dozen TV cameras he popped a chunk in his mouth and just as quickly spat it out into a serviette. Unlike Chef Ramsay's, the pillow-lipped singer's piece of saliva-covered *hákarl* didn't end up in the bottom of a bucket but was snatched up by a canny fan and is now allegedly exhibited in an Icelandic museum.

Of course, having heard these tales, *hákarl* was the first thing Lisa wanted to sample in Reykjavík but, despite its notoriety, it was difficult to come by. None of the tourist shops sold it, and it was only after navigating the stalls selling vintage clothes and second-hand books in the cavernous Kolaportid Flea Market near the old harbour that we found some in a chiller cabinet next to three cling-wrapped puffins and a half dozen fillets of minke whale. As the ever-intrepid epicure, Lisa wanted to go the whole hog.

'Let's buy this one,' she proposed excitedly, holding up a 500g tub and hurrying towards the till.

I rushed to intercept her. Snatching the *hákarl* from her hand, I turned over the tub to find the price. Irritated, she huffed aloud as she waited for me to convert Icelandic króna into British pounds.

'Stop being so stingy, Graham. This is our one chance to try this and I don't really care how much it costs.'

'Jesus Lisa, this is going to set us back more than 60 quid! Find a smaller pot. If you like it, you can buy more.'

Miffed, Lisa went back to the chiller cabinet and fished out a 50g carton of ten dice-sized pieces. In her eagerness she wanted to taste it on the spot but, fearing she might 'do a Jagger', or worse 'a Ramsay', I ushered her outside into the market's car park. It was just as well that I did because what happened next wasn't exactly pretty. Lisa opened the tub, took an exploratory sniff, picked out a morsel, popped it into her mouth and started to chew. I stood ready with my camera.

'It's actually not that bad,' she said, rather chuffed with her own adventurousness. Then the true flavour of the *hákarl* came through and her tight-closed eyes, twisted face and shuddering body conveyed her revulsion at the ammonia taste that filled her mouth.

'Quick, get me some water!' she croaked, turning on the spot in helpless circles.

I was too busy chortling and photographing Lisa's grimaces to accede to her request. Desperate to end the violent affray in her mouth, she rushed back into the flea market to buy some Brennivín schnapps, hoping it would expunge the horrendous taste. It did dilute the awfulness of the *hákarl*, but it added a loathsome liquorice flavour that seared her throat and made her eyes water all the more. Its name doesn't mean 'burning wine' for nothing.

Then it was my turn to do the *hákarl* taste trial. My verdict? It's an acquired taste, is *hákarl*. And if you enjoy things that taste of ammonia and smell like bleach, you'll love it. The closest thing to eating *hákarl* that is not eating *hákarl*, I concluded, would be to munch on a sanitising block retrieved from a gent's urinal.

CHAPTER SEVEN

2000: The Breakthrough Marathon Year
Paris & Dublin

 It seems I fall in love with something new every six years. I fell for Graham aged 18 and for travel aged 24, and six years later fell head over heels for running. My entire family were athletic, but throughout my childhood I'd dodged sporty stuff as effectively as my much younger brother Mark had managed to avoid eating *boerewors*; he'd stuffed it under the wooden feet of our dining room table for many months before my mother discovered his secret hoard of shrivelled, air-dried sausage. Being teased on sports day for being a spectacularly slow runner, and never having the ball passed to me when playing netball, led to a pathological aversion to anything physical. A phantom case of athlete's foot excused me from several years of school swimming lessons, and my high-school PE teachers turned a blind eye to the way I'd perpetually sneak to the back of the rounders queue so I'd never have to bat, something that carried a risk, though small, of having to run 12 metres to first base. As an academic over-achiever I hated doing things I wasn't good at, so anything involving sweat automatically got three 'No's' from me.

My transformation from fitness-phobe to marathon maniac surprised no one more than me. The discovery, at a 5K charity race, that running didn't have to be competitive, saw me leapfrogging from that to the Great North Run half-marathon four months later and the London Marathon six months after that.

Challenging myself to do something light years outside my comfort zone, and the exhilaration I'd experienced when I'd done so, made me greedy for more. It was the whole travel bug story all over again, but this time my new obsession didn't involve planes, trains and automobiles but two things I'd previously viewed as purely decorative: my feet. And in the same way I got Graham hooked on travel by using Taiwan as a gateway drug, I got him into marathons by threatening to only forgive him for not wishing me luck for London if he ran the Edinburgh Marathon with me five months later. Running, I soon found, was a harder sell than travel, and when the wheels came off for Graham in Edinburgh at mile 20, he vowed, as most marathon virgins do, never to run one again. I made the very same vow: 'Take lots of photos of this,' I'd sobbed as Graham photographed my fairy wings and tear-stained face that was as pink as my tutu, 'because if I'm ever crazy enough to be tempted to run another marathon I want a reminder of how horrible this one was. I wouldn't wish this kind of pain on my worst enemy. I know I've said it before, but this time I really mean it: I am *never* running another bloody marathon.'

Running all the way from Dunfermline to Edinburgh city centre while chanting 'I am fit, I am strong, I will run this marathon' meant I carved 78 minutes off my London time, where an injury had forced me to walk half the course, but it also meant hobbling down stairs backwards for three weeks afterwards as my hips were so sore. But in exactly the same way that new mothers forget the challenges of labour when they gaze lovingly at the new-born in their arms, once the pain had passed I craved another high like the one I'd experienced in Scotland. I would get my next fix in Paris.

Blisters, sweat and fears
Paris Marathon, France

 'No way,' snapped Graham when I proposed that we enter the Paris Marathon. 'I'll come along to support you as I don't see why you should have lots of fun in Paris on your own – if that's what you call it – without me, but I'm not doing another marathon. It's just so boring. And painful. And besides, I hate running.'

'It's boring only because, unlike me, you don't chat to people when you're running,' I said. 'And it's painful only because you did a sum total of three training runs for Edinburgh. I told you that wouldn't be enough. And you don't hate running. You haven't done nearly enough of it to know that.'

Graham wouldn't budge, so I roped in my Aunty Rosie, with whom I'd run London, instead.

'You've got your stress face on,' observed Graham the night before the race. 'You're clenching your jaw and grinding your teeth.'

We were in the Hotel de Milan, across the road from Gare du Nord Eurostar station. Though we enjoyed drinking coffee out of soup bowls, the way they served it at breakfast, the hotel had a very Parisian laissez-faire attitude to service and upkeep. Our room boasted a hula-hoop-sized circle of mouldy carpet caused by a radiator leak, and when I sat on the corner of the bed I slipped to the floor because the mattress springs were wrecked. It wasn't the state of our room that was stressing me out, however, but the state of my knees. An osteopath had put the agonising pain in my patellas down to a leg-length discrepancy, and had recommended I put padded leather heel lifts into my left trainer. The pain disappeared, but I had my doubts about running 26.2 miles on what felt like a wobbly pile of Scotch pancakes.

'Graham, please pipe down,' I snapped. 'If you were this under-trained and injured, you'd also be feeling stressed right now. I'm going to finish that darn race tomorrow. I didn't come all this way to go home without a medal.'

To calm myself I began reading the race brochure. Inside was an article by a running expert that advised anyone doubtful of finishing to consider walking. At that time I equated walking with failing, so this was akin to suggesting that if you didn't care for the exam questions you'd been set you could make up your own. However, needs must, and so I resolved to try alternating five minutes of walking with 15 minutes of running.

After a quick dip-down behind a blade of grass somewhere near the start when my aunt and I failed to find a toilet, we excitedly made our way to the start line where tens of thousands of colourfully clad runners created an amazing Technicolor Dreamcoat all the way down the Champs-Élysées.

'Be very careful of the cobbles – if you trip on them, you'll be going home in an ambulance,' I cautioned my aunt.

Walk-running proved a godsend, and I was almost starting to enjoy myself when my left knee twanged like a badly plucked guitar string: 'Ouch,' I said, pulling up short. 'My knee's blown up and I'm not sure I'll make it to the finish. Go on ahead, Aunty Rosie, please don't let me hold you back.'

'Are you sure? I really don't mind walking to the finish.'

'No, it's really bad. And at least one of us should get a medal.'

My aunt receded into the distance and I was left to limp on without her. Having perfected my chat-running technique in my previous two marathons, I was disappointed to be so far at the back of the pack that there was barely anyone to practise it on. Usually my fancy-dress outfits – I ran as a tutu-clad fairy clutching a wand full of jelly beans in both London and Edinburgh – were enough to attract complimentary comments and company, but in Paris the streets were almost empty and what runners there were didn't seem to speak English. Or feel compelled to admire my lovely 'fairbun' costume, an outfit I'd invented by adding *Playboy* bunny ears to my traditional fairy garb.

A kilometre on, I tentatively ran a few steps and was pleased to find that my knee was no longer painful. I resumed walk-running and was amused when, every time I approached a water station, the cheering volunteers, seeing me walking, presumed I was struggling. '*Allez! Allez!*' ('Go on! Go on!') they'd chant, seeing it as their duty to encourage me to start running again. It took a lot of willpower to defy their exhortations and not run, but I knew I had to stick to my walk-run plan if I hoped to finish.

I'd been to Paris twice before. The first time was with my mother, who took me there for my birthday. We arrived almost hysterical from lack of sleep, at 5am, after spending an uncomfortable night on a coach, and I would have paid anything to curl up into a ball on a park bench and get some shut-eye. My mum was made of sterner stuff than me, so following the briefest of breakfasts we'd hit the art galleries, despatching three before nightfall, plus a boat ride on the Seine and a visit to Notre-Dame. And that was just day one. The second visit had been with Graham, earlier in the year, when we'd come to the City of Light to celebrate the new millennium. We didn't know that the Metro wouldn't be working after midnight and so, giddy with millennial optimism and a surfeit of Champagne, we'd stumbled the 6km from the Eiffel Tower to our hotel in the early hours. Thank heavens I'd left my heels at home. Now, once again, I was traversing the entire city on foot.

I'm not sure whether the organisers consulted my mum when they drew up the course, but it certainly looked like they had. A giant dog bone stretching from the Bois de Vincennes in the east to the Bois de Bologne in the west, almost every Paris landmark – the Arc du Triomphe, the Place de la Concorde, the Louvre, Place de la Bastille, Notre-Dame, the Seine, the Eiffel Tower – was en route. About the only sights not included were Montmartre and Pere Lachaise Cemetery, although if I'd been a faster runner I could have fitted them in post-race. Baron Haussmann also had a hand in making the race runner-friendly: by bulldozing the city's narrow medieval streets and alleys to make it less easy for uppity Parisians to barricade them, he unwittingly created boulevards that allowed runners to barrel down them 20 abreast.

The final unlikely contributors to the Paris Marathon's unique atmosphere were Laurel and Hardy.

'You couldn't make this up,' I chuckled as I carefully picked my way through the slippery mess of banana skins that runners had discarded at the Place de la Opera, expecting at any moment to entertain the clapping spectators with the world's most famous slapstick-comedy gag: the banana-skin pratfall.

The stretch along the *quais* was spine-tinglingly spectacular, with the river on our left and crowds of spectators tossing down cheers like confetti from the bridges above. It says a lot about the poetry that is Parisian architecture that not once did I have to resort to mantra chanting to keep me going, despite the lack of company and the painful blisters I'd developed on all of my toes.

Shortly after mile 17 the route ducked into the Pont de l'Alma tunnel. Even though I was in the middle of a run section, I slowed to a walk, almost blinded by tears. This was the tunnel in which Princess Diana had lost her life less than three years earlier. It stank of petrol fumes, and the pillars her car had crashed into were chipped and scuffed. In that moment I relived how I'd become aware of the tragic news. I'd gone to our corner shop and seen the screaming headline 'DIANA DEAD' on the cover of the *News of the World*. The newspapers in the preceding weeks had been full of pictures of her happily holidaying with her boyfriend Dodi Fayed, and she was just six years older than me. She'd been so young and full of life, how could she possibly be dead? Shocked and disbelieving, I'd stumbled over to the shopkeeper.

'Is that true?' I'd said, gesturing to the piles of Sunday papers stacked up under his magazine rack.

'I'm afraid it is,' he'd replied sadly.

Tears welled up in my eyes. I'd loved Princess Di since I was a teenager: I'd had my hair cut like hers and worn the pie-crust-collar blouses she popularised. My first visit to the UK had coincided with her fairy-tale wedding, and I'd cheered at the news that she refused to include 'obeying' her husband in her wedding vows. As an adult, I'd also had huge respect for her incredible work in helping to ban landmines and destigmatise HIV and AIDS.

That evening I'd watched Prince Charles and Diana's sisters bring her body back to England. I'd started crying, and couldn't stop, as the ceremonial guard carried Diana's flag-draped coffin to a waiting hearse. The next day I'd been one of the first people to take flowers to Buckingham Palace. As I'd laid a bunch of sunflowers against the palace railings, a TV crew had asked if they could interview me, but I'd been too overwrought to speak. When I'd got to my office I'd been reluctant to go in. As far as I knew, I'd be the only person at *Zest* mourning Diana's passing and I was embarrassed by how red and swollen my eyes were from sobbing.

'Are you okay, Lisa?' our Art Director Lucy had asked. The mournful violins of The Verve's *Bittersweet Symphony* soared in the background on our office radio.

I'd burst out crying. 'Yes, I guess. It's just that I loved Princess

Diana so much.'

'I think we all did, Lisa,' she'd said gently.

On my walk back to Victoria Station that evening, the morning's smattering of flowers had turned into an ever-expanding carpet outside Buckingham Palace, and I'd realised the truth of Lucy's words. The entire nation was in mourning, not just me.

It took me a full mile beyond the Pont de l'Alma tunnel to start feeling myself again, and my spirits were further lifted in the Bois de Bologne park by pom-pom-waving cheerleaders and a supporter who pressed a plastic cup of wine into my hand. It was here that I caught up with my aunt. She was walking.

'Aunty Rosie! My knee miraculously got better and I'm going to run all the way from here. Come with me.'

'Leecy, so wonderful to see you. This is my new friend Jeanne, she's done 52 marathons. Why don't you two go on together and I'll see you at the end. I can't run another step.'

Jeanne proved a very entertaining companion but also a speedy one, and with her help I crossed the finish line nine minutes faster than I'd done in Edinburgh, where I'd run the whole way. Exactly as I'd done there, I vowed I'd never run another marathon. But this time I meant it. Because from now on, I promised myself, I would always walk-run.

I slept in my medal that night, and even the saggy mattress couldn't prevent me from having sweet dreams.

Over baguettes and bowls of coffee at breakfast the following morning, Graham laid out our plans for the day: a leisurely stroll through the Left Bank, a hot spot for artists and literary types, which he knew would appeal to my inner bohemian, and a visit to the Sewer Museum, which resonated with his fondness for toilet humour.

'Can't we go up the Eiffel Tower instead?' I asked, less than enamoured with the idea of spending an afternoon inhaling sewer gas. 'It's lovely and sunny, so the views will be amazing.'

'I don't think you'll be able to climb the stairs,' said Graham, 'and even if you can, I'm not waiting all day for you to walk backwards down them.'

'Our guidebook says there's a lift.'

'And I've read you pay a small fortune to use it. And besides, the Eiffel Tower's so touristy. Every visitor to Paris goes there, but how many people have been to a sewer museum?'

'There's probably a very good reason why they don't.'

I knew it was a waste of time trying to persuade Graham to splurge on the Eiffel Tower lift. If there's one thing I hate about him when we're travelling, it's his ability to rapidly convert foreign prices into a disadvantageous comparison I can easily grasp.

A half-hour gondola ride in Venice?

'That's ten *bottles* of Sauvignon Blanc, Lisa.'

A Cosmopolitan cocktail at New York's Rainbow Room?

'You're kissing away three pints at The Claret.'

The cost of taking the lift versus the stairs would probably translate into ten or 20 croissants, and I knew there'd be no arguing with that. And as walking up and down 674 steps was out of the question, the Sewer Museum got my reluctant nod.

Even though my body was still complaining loudly that I'd overdone it the day before, our walk in the Paris sunshine was a tonic without the gin. During our stroll we bought a few postcards from one of the *bouquinistes* who sell their wares from metal boxes fixed to the embankment on either side of the Seine. Painted Carriage Green to match the city's park benches and the borders of its street signs, the boxes open up to reveal a treasure trove of dog-eared books, magazines and journals that Hemingway and Sartre would once have browsed through.

Much as I'm loathe to admit it, Graham's sewer safari was fascinating. Others had found it engrossing, too: in the 1920s, groups of tourists would enjoy gas-lit tours of the sewer canals in open boats drawn by flat-cap-wearing workers, the information boards informed us, though they were mute on whether there had ever been any 'open flame' incidents. Still, you wouldn't catch me striking a match down there.

Mirroring the streets above, each sewer in the 2,100km-long network had its own enamel street sign, prompting Victor Hugo to write in *Les Misérables* that 'Paris has another Paris under herself; a Paris of sewers.' Hugo was familiar with the flipside of Paris because his friend, the engineer Pierre Emmanuel Bruneseau, had spent seven years mapping it, earning for himself the dubious moniker 'the Christopher Columbus of the cess-pool'.

'His mother must have been so proud,' commented Graham. 'And I've just clocked that Bruneseau translates into "brown water". How very apt.'

The noise of thousands of litres of sewage passing under us was the soundtrack to our visit.

'It says on this information board that the equivalent of a six-storey building of brown stuff is hauled from the sewers each year,' I said. 'I'm not sure that's true as I can't see any solids bobbing by.'

We peered through the metal grille beneath our feet. Though dark, dingy and with a hint of eau de toilet, the sewers weren't in fact all that shitty, and appeared more akin to a matrix of stormwater drains than the conduit for the contents of several million Parisians' bowels.

'Come and look at this ball,' said Graham. 'You'll never guess what it's used for.'

I joined him at a six-foot-diameter metal sphere set into a recess in one wall.

'It's called a *boule de curage*,' said Graham, 'and apparently they drop it into the drains.'

'Whatever for?'

'Water builds up behind it and forces it forward, dredging the tunnels of silt and shit. Every home should have one.'

Sadly, the souvenir shop didn't stock any, so we still have to rely on our trusty bog brush.

I would go on to run dozens of marathons, but none were as seismic as the Paris Marathon, to this day my favourite city marathon, because it launched my career as an author. Unaware that Jeff Galloway had already popularised walk-running in America, I was buzzing with excitement at sharing my newfound discovery that walk breaks were the equivalent of adding a turbocharger to a marathon. It would be four years until *Running Made Easy*, the beginner's walk-running book I co-authored, was published, and a little longer before it became a runaway success, but it would be mere months until I again combined a foreign trip with a race. Like a seductive siren, the fair city of Dublin was calling me to walk-run 26.2 miles, and I was powerless to resist.

Running Wilde with a couple of swingers
Dublin Marathon, Ireland

 Riverdance, famine, leprechauns and the IRA. As a South African, what I knew about Ireland's history could more or less be summed up by those four words. I don't know why it took me so long to visit Ireland; perhaps it's because it's merely a hop, skip and a swim away from London across the Irish Sea and so I regarded it as too close to visit. A bit like people who live on the coast but never go to the beach. The Dublin Marathon seemed the ideal opportunity to plug my gaping knowledge gaps, so I invited my sister Loren to fly over from South Africa to be my cheerleader. We stayed in a garret room at a hostel down the road from the church in which the bones and blood of St Valentine, who was executed in the third century for performing Christian marriages, are interred.

'We've not any hot water at the moment,' said the receptionist. 'But a plumber has been called. You are in room number 12. There's tea and coffee in the kitchen. It's complimentary. Enjoy.'

Little did we know that this lack of hot water would very nearly land Loren and me in hot water a couple of days later.

The walking tour we went on brought us more up to speed with Ireland's tragic history, revealing that the 1840s Potato Famine forced a million people to flee and left a million dead, meaning that, though it's hard to believe, Ireland had more than twice the inhabitants prior to the famine than it did when we were there.

The next step in our education came during a tour to Glendalough, a 1,500-year-old monastic site. Our bus driver Kevin was also our guide and had us in stitches as he repeated the second half of every sentence like an echo: 'Penneys is a department store, you won't get ripped off there, won't get ripped off there,' he'd drone over the public address system. 'Carrolls is good for small gifts, good for small gifts.' Kevin didn't teach us a great deal about Dublin, but he did reveal the best place to buy plastic leprechauns.

Glendalough is a forest-fringed valley hewn by an Ice Age glacier that, like a pair of cupped hands scooping up water, contains two rust-coloured lakes. The ancient settlement here, now mostly in ruins, was founded by St Kevin, a kind-hearted, bird-loving saint. Good St Kevin didn't just throw stale bread out on his lawn to feed the birds, he turned himself into a human incubator. Legend has it that when a blackbird laid an egg on his outstretched hand as he prayed, St Kevin, in a divinely inspired game of Mannequin Challenge, remained motionless until it hatched.

Despite the busloads of tourists, Glendalough still had a sacred air about it, but was also strangely fairy tale-like. The soaring Round Tower topped by a conical roof – with a doorway halfway up that could be reached only by ladder – would've made Rapunzel feel right at home, and the roofless stone cottages could, if they'd been thatched, easily have been snug homesteads for families of elves.

After a few days of sightseeing, and a semi-sleepless night fretting about my lack of marathon preparation – three 60-minute runs in as many months does *not* count as adequate training – it was marathon day. I rose early to don my running gear, which I accessorised with a flouncy layered skirt, glittery fairy wings and a pink-feathered hat Loren had gifted me. Packed shoulder to shoulder in Fitzwilliam Square with the other marathoners, I felt a surge of excitement – even though it was my fourth marathon the sense of 'pinch-me-hard-I-can't-believe-I'm-actually-doing-this' had yet to leave me. The race billed itself as 'the friendly marathon' with good reason: thousands of Dubliners had surged onto the pavements to ensure we surfed round the course on a tide of encouragement. Sticky-palmed toddlers handed out sweets, pensioners camped out in deckchairs blew whistles, and one young man held up a poster proclaiming 'I trained for months to hold up this sign', in which case he'd trained harder than I had. Notable landmarks included Trinity College, which counted among its alumni Bram Stoker, Oscar Wilde, Jonathan Swift and, surprisingly, Courtney Love, who'd studied theology, of all things; the bullet-riddled GPO badly damaged in the 1916 Easter Rising when Irish Republicans fought a bloody battle to end British rule; and the huge expanse of Phoenix Park where, in 1979, over one million people gathered to celebrate mass with Pope John Paul II, and in whose zoo the MGM lion was born. By now, thanks to our walking tour and our own independent dawn-to-dusk pavement pounding, I was a bit of a bore on Irish lore.

'If you hurry, you can still win it!' shouted a spectator 10km from the finish in a failed attempt to transform my super-slow shuffle into a trot. Near the end, Loren popped up from nowhere and jogged alongside me to give me a quick lowdown on the remaining sights on the route so we wouldn't have to come back to see them. The moment I crossed the finish line in Merrion Square, she presented me with a Celtic cross Christmas tree decoration she'd purchased at – where else? – Carrolls, and then, even though I was blue with cold, exhausted and drenched in sweat, dragged me to see the nearby louchely reclining statue of Oscar Wilde. Looking uncannily similar to the flamboyant, floppy-haired TV presenter Laurence Llewelyn-Bowen, the sight of this green-jacketed Wilde, man-spreading on a rock, was admittedly worth the detour.

Back at the hostel I was informed that there was *still* no hot water, something that another of Dublin's literary sons, Samuel Beckett, might have appreciated. Like the mysterious Godot in his play *Waiting for Godot*, it never arrived.

'The plumber came, had a look at the boiler and went away to fetch parts. That was several hours ago. We're still waiting for him to return. Sorry about this.'

The 20 per cent discount on our bill the receptionist offered us when he saw the angry look on my sweat-caked face made topping and tailing more bearable, though a proper shower at that point would've been bliss.

Loren has the world's worst-known case of FOMO (fear of missing out) so the next afternoon we slogged around town some more, relentlessly checking off what she'd noted down as Dublin's must-see sights. We concluded the day hunting down the saucily nicknamed public sculptures the city is renowned for: the bursting-out-of-her-bustier statue of the cockles-and-mussels-seller Molly Malone (fondly known as the Tart with a Cart); James Joyce (the

Prick with a Stick) and Meeting Place, a statue of two seated women and their shopping bags (the Slags with the Bags). List-ticking really is what Loren does best.

In the early evening, Loren finally relented and said I could ease my marathon-tender feet in a pub a few blocks from our hostel. Sipping our Guinnesses underneath an etched mirror advertising Jameson whiskey and a shelf decorated with empty bottles and soda siphons, we got talking to the exceptionally friendly 60-something couple at the next table. Deirdre was a petite blond with weathered skin that spoke of a lifetime of lighting up, and Donal was leprechaun-sized with white hair and twinkly eyes. We made the usual chit-chat about what we'd seen and done in Dublin – which took quite some time, thanks to Loren's List – and then Donal, spotting only one gap in our do-Dublin-till-you-drop itinerary, made a suggestion of his own.

'You've really got to see Newgrange,' he said emphatically. 'It's an amazing tomb that's older than Stonehenge. During the winter solstice the sun penetrates right through the doorway and lights up the inside.'

At this point Deirdre, who was quite tipsy, lit a cigarette. When Donal reminded her that cigarette smoke aggravated his asthma, she jumped up and shot off outside. In her haste she overturned Donal's three-legged stool, leaving him sprawled on the pub's threadbare carpet. Unperturbed, Donal rose unsteadily to his feet and, without a word, returned to his seat to continue drinking.

On Deirdre's return a few minutes later, the conversation took a decidedly confessional – and for us uncomfortable – turn, as she related how they'd been caught *in flagrante delicto* on her mother's living room floor. They'd known one another for several years before Deirdre decided to lose her virginity to Donal, and she'd chosen him because she believed he'd know what to do. She was wrong: he was a virgin, too. Branded a 'whore' by her family, they'd married and – somewhat to their surprise – had stayed married for 40 years. Donal then embarked on a garbled story about a bisexual friend they'd met in their hippie heyday who'd decided she wasn't gay and had moved in with them.

'Why is he telling us all of this?' I thought.

'You must come to Newgrange with us tomorrow,' Donal said, abruptly changing the subject. 'We'll drive you there. And you must stay with us tonight so that we can leave first thing.'

'Oh, that's so kind of you,' I said. 'We've already paid for our hostel, so there's no need to put us up.'

'But I thought you said your hostel didn't have any hot water,' challenged Deirdre.

'It doesn't. But we're backpackers and we've put up with a lot worse than that. I've already had one cold shower so another isn't a big deal,' I fibbed.

'But our house *does* have hot water, so you don't have to put up with that,' Donal retorted.

'Well,' said Loren, 'I must admit I could do with washing my hair. It's getting so matted that I'm starting to look like a Viking.'

I frowned at Loren again. 'No, it's quite alright. All our stuff is at the hostel and we're happy staying there.'

The couple persisted and, having politely declined about a dozen times, I suggested Loren come downstairs with me to the Ladies. I'd had fewer Guinnesses than her and was starting to worry.

'Let's compromise by going to Newgrange with them,' I suggested, 'but tell them that we won't be staying with them.'

Viking-haired Loren, who'd been missing the luxury of hot water a lot more than I had, reluctantly agreed.

Back upstairs the insistent pestering began anew and I lost patience. 'We'll see you at 9am tomorrow to go to Newgrange. Where do you want to meet?'

'Why don't you trust us?' whined Donal, his face flushed pink from too much booze. 'Why won't you two come and stay with us? You don't have any hot water and we do, at our house, and you're rejecting our hospitality.'

Deirdre nodded her emphatic endorsement.

I'd had enough. Not wanting to be badgered anymore, and fearing we'd end up imprisoned in their house, I got up and strode from the pub, expecting Loren to take the hint and follow me. After a block I turned to look back and could vaguely make out Deirdre and Donal staggering out onto the pavement and slinging themselves into a taxi. Imagining they may have kidnapped Loren by pushing her into the taxi ahead of them, I ran back to the pub.

'Have you seen my sister?' I breathlessly asked the barman.

'I don't know who you mean,' he said, lifting his head and continuing to dry the inside of a beer glass with a linen cloth.

Alarm bells clanged in my head. How often did two South Africans spend an evening in a small bar speaking to two regulars?

'The South African woman I was here with five minutes ago, who was talking to the Irish couple right over there. You *must* remember her,' I explained, pointing at our vacated table and stools.

'Oh, her. She left.'

'Left? Left with who?'

'On her own,' he replied, more interested in pulling a pint than answering my questions.

I hurried outside. Still no sign of Loren. On my marathon mashed-up legs I ran all the way to our hostel. I searched our room and all of the communal areas but Loren wasn't there. It was now dark, and I resigned myself to a night of trawling Dublin's cold streets as I knew Loren had no cash on her, and no sense of direction either. Panicking, I hobbled back to the pub, where I had another look round, shooting accusatory glances at the indifferent barman and wondering if he was an accomplice in my sister's abduction. What I would tell the police? What details had the couple let slip that would help them locate Loren? My slightly booze-befuddled brain didn't provide any answers.

'Where have you been?' snapped my sister as I exited the pub.

She was standing on the pavement three paces from the entrance.

'You left me with *no* money, and *no* map! Why didn't you tell me you were leaving? Why on earth did you march away like that?'

'I hoped you'd follow me when I left,' I said hugging her, grateful that she was safe and that I wouldn't be spending the rest of the night searching for her. 'I honestly thought that if we stayed there a minute longer our natural politeness would've meant us going home with them, and I really didn't think that was a good idea.'

'I did follow you, but I got lost the moment I stepped outside and took a wrong turn.'

Relieved that we'd extricated ourselves from a situation that I strongly suspected was an attempt by two swingers to entice us into a *ménage à quatre,* we made our way back to our hot-waterless hostel, mightily grateful that we remained unswung.

CHAPTER EIGHT

2001: The Year That Changed Our World
Australia, China, Vietnam, Cuba

It was the 'hangover' year from which no one expected very much, coming hot on the heels of the previous one which had been launched by a party where the World and his Wife had, quite literally, partied like it was 1999. The Millennium Bug had turned out to be a damp squib, the world hadn't ended in 2000 as many prophets, preachers and mystics had predicted it would, and the biggest news story of 2001 looked likely to be the release of Microsoft Windows XP.

In our lives, however, it would be a very significant year: Lisa was going to turn 34 and for some time we'd been toying with the idea of emigrating to Australia. Once she reached 35, Lisa would lose so many points in the country's immigration assessment that we would be ineligible to apply. Though we were very happy in England, we were thinking of having kids and reasoned that Oz's outdoors-based lifestyle was better suited to family life. So 2001 would be the year of the recce – we would fly Down Under to explore what it would be like to live there, and later in the year make a combined trip to Vietnam and China to see what travel opportunities were available in Australia's backyard.

And then 9/11 happened. On 11 September 2001 I was the Pakistan and Afghanistan research analyst for the UK Ministry of Defence. It had been a normal day: I'd read the overnight reporting, answered the important emails and, as usual, eaten lunch at my desk. Mid-afternoon, a colleague rang.

'A plane has just flown into the World Trade Center,' he said.

I imagined a small Cessna clipping the skyscraper and spinning to the ground.

'What kind of plane?'

'It was a commercial airliner.'

'What? An airliner?'

I struggled to comprehend what I was hearing. A plane full of passengers crashing into New York's tallest building? It had to have been the worst kind of freak accident. Twenty minutes later my phone rang again.

'Another plane – also an airliner – has just flown into the second World Trade Center tower.'

The news was shocking and bewildering. The live television coverage, which many disbelieving people at first mistook for a Hollywood movie, was horrifyingly mesmerising, a slowly unfolding tragedy that aspiring terrorists cheered while humanity wept. Peter, my good friend from York University, knew several of the 658 Cantor Fitzgerald employees who died in the North Tower. Lisa had magazine colleagues in New York on a fashion shoot, and watched the TV in her editor's office in stunned silence as the burning towers sank to street level.

At work the phone rang off the hook and emails cascaded into my inbox faster than I could hope to read them, let alone answer them. I survived on barely four hours' sleep a night and grew increasingly convinced that the two-week trip to Cuba that Lisa and I had planned for early October wouldn't go ahead, either because I'd be chained to my desk or because plummeting passenger numbers made flight cancellations more likely. To my amazement my bosses decided not to cancel my leave, saying that I needed to take a break after working so hard and that it was important I return feeling refreshed as things were bound to hot up in Afghanistan as America considered its retaliatory response. And to our relief, our flight went ahead as scheduled, though it turned out to be more stressful than even Afghanistan crisis management had been.

Great Barrier Grief
Australia

 Who are these two little possums?' enquired a smiling Darlene as we presented ourselves at the reception desk of the YHA hostel on Great Keppel Island. Her long blonde hair tied up into a loose bun, her ankle-length calico dress worn thin from years of wearing and washing, she was typical of many of the Australians we'd met on our trip: warm, welcoming and down to earth. Darlene, it turned out, was not only the mother-hen manager of the hostel but also its 'poet in residence', posting her poems – 'Little deeds of kindness, little deeds of love, help to make the YHA the place we all love' – throughout the eucalyptus-shaded grounds. Big hearted and kind to a fault Darlene was; Poet Laureate she was not.

We'd flown to Great Keppel, one of several islands at the southerly tip of the Great Barrier Reef, for some much-needed R&R after sussing out Sydney (its sea and eternal sunshine got a big thumbs up from me) and doing due diligence on Canberra (its deserted streets reminiscent of a post-apocalyptic pandemic movie got a less enthusiastic reaction from Graham) as possible new places to put down roots. Researching commutes, schools, amenities and possible employers, we'd soon found, was not exactly a holiday, hence we were looking forward to a few days of snorkel and chill on an island Graham had visited as a teenager when his father was posted to Melbourne.

Our dinner on the first evening was interrupted by a voluble rumpus in the kitchen as Darlene and several guests tried to evict a real-life possum and her baby who'd ventured in to seize some snacks. The joey fled under the fridge, then made a run for it into the common room followed by half a dozen broom-wielding backpackers. Blimey, we thought, it's a baby possum the size of a large mango, not a rabid dingo. Once it had been cornered between a stack of videos and a bookshelf crammed with board games, Graham was the only person prepared to pick it up. Three times the joey shot from his grasp like a bar of slippery wet soap before

Graham succeeded in carrying it outside to rejoin its mother, who was next to a dustbin blithely munching on Froot Loops.

That night we grew less fond of cutesy possums, for the hyperactive critters kept us awake by incessantly scampering back and forth across our canvas roof. In the morning we slept in late to recover from our possum-pattering-induced insomnia and it was mid-afternoon by the time we ventured forth to go snorkelling off the nearest beach. Unlike Thailand, however, this was not a case of putting your masked face into the water to see and hear sealife scraping algae off the rocks with an audible rasping sound while neon-coloured fish nibbled at your fingers and toes. All we saw were a few clumps of white coral and the odd parrotfish.

Returning our masks, snorkels and flippers, we mentioned our disappointment to Darlene.

'It's because the coral's been stressed,' she said.

'Stressed?' I tried to imagine coral in flight-or-fight mode. Nope. Coral had an easy life. As sedentary as a toll-booth collector and as demanding as Astroturf, surely coral couldn't be stressed?

'Yeah, it's called coral bleaching. We had very heavy rainfall a few days back and that swept a lot of sediment into the sea, which stressed the coral as it likes to grow in clear water,' Darlene explained. 'When the water's muddy the coral expels the colourful algae that live inside it and give it energy. So the coral starves to death, leaving its white exoskeleton behind.'

'I've heard of anal bleaching,' remarked Graham, 'but coral bleaching's a new one on me.'

We tried not to let on how gutted we were to have flown over 11,000 miles – including the final 30 minutes in an alarmingly unstable twin-prop plane – to see the Great Barrier Reef, the largest living organism on earth, only to find the section we were looking at had died.

'Anyway,' said Darlene, changing the subject, 'you remember the two women who were ahead of you in the line to hire snorkelling gear from me? Well, one of them stood on a snake, it bit her, and the flying ambulance had to take her off the island.' Her bouncy, hail-fellow-well-met intonation didn't change.

Visibly shocked, I shot an 'I told you so' glance at Graham. Prior to leaving the UK I'd watched *Deadly Australians*, a documentary about the continent's venomous and savage creatures, and had expressed apprehension at encountering them, which Graham had pooh-poohed. I asked Darlene whether the snake was venomous.

'I dunno. I often think that I could be bitten by a snake when I'm back on the mainland mowing my paddock. I could die out there and no one would find me. The roos would eat me,' she said matter of factly, before returning to restocking the tourist brochures.

A cheery thought. We did think that as the head of a hostel in a country that's home to more deadly snakes than any other, Darlene should have been sent on a snake identification course. But as more Australians die from falling out of bed than are killed by wild animals (contrary to what *Deadly Australians* had led me to believe), maybe her employers had decided to send Darlene on a bed-danger-awareness course instead.

As we'd so far spotted fewer fish than one would ordinarily see in a dentist's waiting-room fish tank, we signed up for a sea observatory and glass-bottomed-boat tour. The next day we assembled at the wooden jetty and a small boat ferried 15 of us to the offshore underwater observatory where a spiral staircase took visitors beneath the waves for what, we were promised, would be a 360-degree view of an undersea wonderland teeming with fish and multicoloured corals. When we got below deck we were bathed in an eerie viridescent glow. I walked over to a window and peered out. At first, I surmised the windows were shuttered closed, but there were no shutters: I couldn't see a damn thing because all the glass was opaque with green algae. If a toddler-sized grouper swam within two feet of the observatory then its dim form could be seen, but otherwise nothing was visible except green.

'That's weird,' mused our guide, rubbing his stubbled chin, 'the divers were down here cleaning the windows a couple of days ago.'

Perhaps the divers cleaned the *inside* of the glass, I conjectured, becoming annoyed.

'Yeah, sorry about that folks. Let's go up top and we'll get you lot out over the coral.'

We trooped to the surface and clambered aboard a glass-bottomed boat which motored back and forth for 20 minutes above an area where our guide had assured us we'd see coral. All we saw was water. Lots of it. If the coral was there, it wasn't going to be seen 30 feet below a high tide.

'Ah, well, the tide's in so there's too much water below us to see anything,' the guide admitted. 'Best we take you back to the jetty.'

What? Was that it? We'd paid AUS$78 for the privilege of seeing one or two shadowy shapes and some green saltwater? There was no way on earth the algae could have grown back so quickly. The guide must have known we wouldn't see a single fish. And what was the point of taking us out at high tide if he knew full well it was pointless? There wasn't a murmur of dissent from the rest of the group, but Graham and I were both outraged by our guide's feeble fibs and gross incompetence, so we returned to the woman who'd sold us our tickets and asked for our money back. During several phone calls to the company's headquarters it was repeatedly explained to us that, though they'd debited our credit card in under a second when we bought our tickets, it was impossible to issue a refund unless we went to their mainland office.

'We don't have time to go there on our way back to Sydney. And there's no way we should have to make a special journey just to get our money back.'

'It's company policy,' the ticket seller stonewalled.

'Is it company policy to take people's money knowing full well that you can't give them what they paid for?' demanded Lisa.

'I'm sorry, I don't make the rules. If you want a refund, you have to go to our office on the mainland.'

Not wanting the faff and expense of that, we eventually agreed the company should send a cheque to our UK home address. 'The cheque is in the post' is one of the world's Great Lies. After nigh on 20 years, we're still waiting.

Peking duck bad luck
China

 Becoming gung-ho gastronomes is one of travel's greatest joys: the food doesn't always taste good, but some of it sure does give you bragging rights. Lisa grew up in a family where they never ate anything spicy or exotic lest it cause a flare-up of her dad's ulcer, and at boarding school I ate a bland diet of meat and boiled-to-oblivion two veg, which is why, when we travel, we feel it's important to give our palates a private education and dutifully put things in our mouths even when we know they're likely to be distasteful.

'We eat everything: everything on four legs except the table; and except for our friends and relations, everything on two,' the Chinese poet Ai Ts'ing once told the French writer Simone de Beauvoir. At Beijing's Donghuamen Night Market it seemed not to matter how many legs something had; if it could be stuck on a stick and deep fried then it could be eaten. This is where Lisa and I found ourselves on our first night in Beijing, eyeing up the stallholders' wares, trying to decide what looked least off-putting. Until that moment I had no idea anyone in the world ate scorpions, but they do in China, and that's how I ended up eating one. At this point I should make it clear that *tourists* in China eat scorpions, as throughout the evening we didn't spot a single local snacking on strange-stuff-on-a-stick. The Chinese all seemed to be there to enjoy and film the spectacle of Westerners shrieking and screaming as they gingerly bit into a lamb's testicle or a crisp-fried silkworm.

Incongruously set up near a luxury department store, the market's row of brightly lit stalls resembled exhibits at London's Natural History Museum but, instead of the specimens being displayed behind glass, they were wriggling in metal trays or threaded onto skewers and then plunged into cauldrons of bubbling oil. We took our time choosing because we were spoilt for choice: should we go for spider, seahorse or starfish? In the end we selected scorpions, to us the eco-friendliest choice. We chose three of the smaller ones because the massive shiny black ones were way too intimidating. It took me a long time to steel myself to eat mine. I nibbled the end of a pincer – so far, so good – and then, closing my eyes, popped the whole scorpion in my mouth. To my huge relief it was crunchy, dry and salty, though not so flavoursome that they'd replace Mini Cheddars as my snack of choice.

My *I'm a Celebrity* Bushtucker Trial moment over, and captured on camera, Lisa and I looked for somewhere to have dinner. Some stalls sold less alien fare, but alongside the crispy cockroaches and millipedes, even bog-standard prawns looked unappetising, which is why we retreated to a nearby restaurant where we perused the menu while trying to ignore the Chinese diner at the next table who'd pulled his oversized white undies out of the top of his trousers and who kept spitting and hacking phlegm into an ashtray. Sorely tempted by the bullfrog and duck blood soup, we settled on something familiar: fish. That was before we noticed, too late, several dead fish, floating belly up, in the fresh fish tank.

In China, where English menus were as rare as hen's teeth – or featured them – we resorted to two different tactics to ensure we didn't inadvertently eat pangolin. Or panda. We'd either take our waiter or waitress by the elbow and walk them past the seated diners, pointing to dishes that looked good, or whose contents were identifiable, and indicate that we wanted the chef to prepare the same for us. Or we'd play Pictionary with the waiting staff, drawing pictures on our paper serviettes of the foods we did, or didn't, want to eat, and for good effect I'd mimic the sounds the animal would make. My inexpert depictions of various animals and their body parts, such as snakes, pigs, chicken feet and hearts, accompanied by the hissing, oinking and clucking sounds I made, put Lisa off her food and made her '*eet met lang tande*' ('eat with long teeth'), an Afrikaans idiom for revulsion she's fond of using.

'Lisa, don't blame me. I'm doing my best – and embarrassing myself in front of the staff and patrons – to order food you're happy to eat. I think it's that article you read on the flight that's making you feel so squeamish.'

'Which one?'

'The one about the Chinese fondness for eating live monkey brain, scooped out with teaspoons.'

The article had contained the immortal lines: 'Why *live* monkey's brains? Because dead ones taste awful.'

'It's probably apocryphal,' I noted. 'That said, when it comes to food, the Chinese do have pretty catholic taste.'

Because restaurants change their chefs more frequently than they do the oil in their deep fat fryers, I have a healthy scepticism for any restaurant listed in a travel guide: all recommendations are likely to be at least two chefs out of date. But Lisa was insistent that we try what our guidebook trumpeted as 'Beijing's best Peking duck'.

Our taxi driver took us as far as he could, set us down by construction works that blocked his route and helpfully pointed out the restaurant beyond. Its entrance proclaimed: 'Hello foreign friends enjoying authentic duck in ancient Chinese courtyard'. A sign in English welcoming foreigners deepened my suspicion that this was going to be a bad choice for dinner. As did the queue of foreigners in the alley outside. The much-lauded restaurant was really tatty and dirty. This, however, didn't bother us as we like our restaurants like we like our friends – lively, unpretentious and not *too* respectable. A waitress led us to our table in the VIP private dining room – a privilege we later realised came with a price tag – without asking if that's what we wanted. The grubby walls were bare of decoration, the lighting was interrogation-room bright and the threadbare tablecloth marked with greasy stains: it had all the ambience of an operating theatre. We ordered a whole Peking duck, a couple of vegetable dishes and, because the wine was pricey, beer. When the duck arrived it did look good, its golden-yellow skin polished to a shiny glaze. Dinner was looking up. The bird was adroitly carved in front of us. Or at least the breasts were, for seconds later the remainder of the fowl was whisked from the room with indecent haste, as if it had missed an appointment elsewhere.

We'd been under the impression that Peking duck was another name for 'crispy aromatic duck', the kind we'd been savouring for years at Streatham's Mrs Wong's restaurant. It most certainly was not. *That* duck featured deep-fried skin, melt-in-the-mouth shreds of delicious meat, tangy plum sauce and freshly chopped cucumber and spring onion all wrapped up in pillow-soft pancakes. This duck, despite having been roasted over an open fire, was fatty and tasted as if it had been boiled in dishwater – and then varnished – and was served with clammy, cold pancakes and insipid black sauce. Not nice, not nice at all.

'They've ripped us off,' Lisa told me when, after an hour, the surly waitress slapped the bill on the table. Not the duck's bill – fat chance of that – but the bill for the whole duck.

I was conned out of a few more quid the following day in Tiananmen Square after we'd exited the Forbidden City. I was in an ebullient mood having made what I thought was an excellent, albeit puerile, joke. The Palace inside the Forbidden City had been staffed by eunuchs who, because it's against the teachings of Confucianism to disfigure one's body and they wished to be buried whole, carried their severed testicles in leather 'manbags' suspended from their waists. Our guidebook reported that in 1923, when the last emperor of China, Puyi, expelled the eunuchs after they'd set fire to the Hall of Supreme Harmony to cover the extent of their prodigious thieving, hundreds of them were seen fleeing the Forbidden City 'wailing in high-pitched voices with their belongings in sacks'.

'Surely,' I quipped to Lisa, 'that should have read "with their sacs in their belongings"?'

I was still chuckling to myself when I was approached by two men eager to sell us all manner of Mao Tse-tung-themed tourist tat. I already owned a plastic-covered copy of Mao's *Little Red Book* from my student days, and had found it dreary, rivalling Marx's *Das Kapital* as a soporific. Nor did we want a T-shirt, or a coffee mug or a poster, all with the same iconic image of Mao, the likeness Andy Warhol had popularised with his pop-art copies. I was interested, though, in buying a wristwatch with its face depicting Mao's face and his right arm waving back and forth as if he was acknowledging an adoring revolutionary crowd.

'One for the drawer,' Lisa muttered, trying to dissuade me from buying the tacky timepiece in the same way that I tried to discourage her from taking touristy photos in the 'propping up the Leaning Tower of Pisa' vein.

'It's cheap as chips,' I said, thrilled that I'd managed to bargain the price down from the equivalent of £20 to £11. By the time we arrived at Beihai Park 30 minutes later the watch had stopped working. By thumping it repeatedly on a café table I caused the hour hand to spin through 24 hours several times and Mao's arm to resume its hand-waving rhythm for another hour, during which time it lost ten minutes. The Good Chairman continued to wave and tick in his erratic time-losing way for three hours until he stopped for good, like Mao himself had in 1976.

Manning up to a feather-filled egg
Vietnam

 We combined our trip to China with one to its neighbour Vietnam, and found that it, too, had its share of freaky foodstuffs. It had some terrific food, too, though. The ten raw spring rolls stuffed with rice noodles and fragrant herbs that we bought for a dollar from a Hanoi pavement vendor, who nimbly rolled them up like hand-made cigars as her baby quietly did a poo in the gutter, were, Lisa and I both agreed, the best dollar we've ever spent. And the fried spring rolls, cooked on a paraffin stove set up on the doorstep of an old woman's Ho Chi Minh City home, were so crisp and succulent that we've reminisced fondly about them for years.

But almost every market had, somewhere amid the riot of brightly coloured vegetables and exotic fruits, a section given over to meat. By which I mean meat catering to, and displayed for, local tastes. So not rump steaks and burger patties, as seen in a British butcher's window, but trays of sloppy beef entrails and bull penises, stacks of gaping fish heads, bowls of pigs' tails and frogs, and splayed chickens with embryonic eggs attached to their insides. Such a sight tends to be too much for Lisa who will first visibly blanch and then, if she doesn't remove herself forthwith, start to heave. A fresh food market is no place for heaving: it's not hygienic and besides, it's really bad for business.

After visiting Ho Chi Minh City's Reunification Palace where, in April 1975, North Vietnamese tanks dramatically crashed through the gates and ended the Vietnam War, we popped into an eatery we'd walked past earlier. Passing up the chance to order 'fish dropping soup' – please tell me it's not salmon shit broth? – we ordered fish served in a steamboat, a pot filled with stock atop a charcoal burner, to which we added bamboo shoots, assorted greenery and noodles. The eel-like fish rose to the bubbling surface before being drawn back under as though they were swimming unsuccessfully to escape the hot broth.

'Watching those fish is making me feel sick. I'm sorry Graham, but I can't eat any more,' a grimacing Lisa said, putting down her chopsticks and taking a swig of beer. 'They look as though they're being boiled alive.'

I happily ate Lisa's share. A diner at the next table in flip-flops, shorts, vest and sweat, toasted me with shots of firewater.

In Hanoi's Old Quarter, each street was devoted to a single trade. There was Silver Street (now selling sinks, extractor fans and the like), Gravestone Street (the street of stonemasons), Paper Offerings Street, and so on. With changing times, many street names no longer accurately reflected the merchandise on sale as modern wares such as computers, watches and toys had muscled in. On the pavements, restaurants had been set up under the trees and we dined at one of them on our first night in Hanoi. Seated at a low plastic table on children's plastic stools, our knees almost up to our chins, it was like being back at kindergarten, only with better food and with draught beer. The joint was heaving. As we waited to order, kids zig-zagged through the diners hawking lottery tickets, mousetraps, popcorn and *poppadoms* the size of bicycle wheels, and vendors in conical palm-leaf hats strolled past selling towering piles of bananas and clothes from baskets suspended from wooden yokes on their shoulders.

The menu was not in English, but the proprietors had helpfully divided it into sections illustrated with a picture of the generic source of the dish. So our prawns with chilli came from the list of options below the picture of a prawn, and our vegetables with garlic from the section underneath a picture of, we think, a spring onion. There was also a menu section given over to man's best friend. The image most resembled a Labrador. I'll try most but not all foods and, as a dog-loving Englishman, puppy-in-a-pot was definitely a beagle too far. To end our repast, which we washed down with lashings of *bia hoi*, a refreshing freshly brewed lager, we chose fish, and nearly choked on our chips when a whole carp arrived: the brute was as long as our table was wide.

Across Vietnam, bottles of rice wine containing snakes and scorpions were ubiquitous. Snake wine is touted as a cure for various ailments, including arthritis, leprosy and hair loss, and as a rejuvenating pick-me-up tonic. In Vietnamese culture, snakes symbolise masculinity and are associated with male potency so, inevitably, snake wine is also marketed as a sexual stimulant. Venomous snakes can be used because their poison is neutralised by alcohol. Since it's believed that the venom has medicinal qualities, the more venomous the creature the more the brew is touted to perk up the one-eyed trouser snake. A bottle of rice wine with a yellow-spotted keelback would be the bedroom-readying equivalent of oysters, whereas one containing a cobra is liquid Viagra.

In 2013 a Chinese woman named Liu was reportedly bitten when the viper she'd put in a bottle of wine and fermented for three months sprang out.

'Before the wine could have any effect on me,' Liu reported, 'I was sent to the hospital for a snake bite.'

It's thought that, as long as the bottle is not airtight, snakes can survive quite some time by lowering their metabolism.

There must be a lot of snakes in Vietnam, or at least there were. The only live serpents we saw were in a perforated cardboard box on the back of a bicycle, presumably awaiting their turn to be preserved in cheap alcohol.

In Hue, a city on the Perfume River that was Vietnam's capital for about 150 years during feudal times, we chanced upon the grossest of gross-out foodstuffs when we bought two boiled eggs from a woman selling them from a woven palm basket next to a kerosene brazier on the pavement. We'd already had dinner, but I love eggs and bought them for breakfast. They were large eggs, but I assumed they came from a big chicken. Morning came and Lisa and I ambled over the road from our hostel to Sinh Café, where we'd grown fond of the friendly owner Hien. I ordered a pot of coffee and a freshly baked baguette with butter and, using the back of a knife, split open one of the eggs.

'Jesus!' I exclaimed, recoiling in horror and shoving the offending plate away.

The hand holding Lisa's coffee halted midway to her mouth.

Curled up inside the shell was a feathered duckling embryo: beak and webbed feet, filaments of dark veins and bulbous, black unopened eyes and all. Before it had been boiled it was about a week short of hatching.

When Hien saw the appalled look on my face, she almost wet herself laughing.

'You did not know?' she chortled.

'How was I to know? I thought it was just a normal egg.'

'This is *hôt vit lôn*. I myself do not eat this egg,' Hien said. 'Many Vietnamese men, they like it a lot.'

Consumed as a beer snack, some men prefer to eat *hôt vit lôn* with an embryo that is more developed, the logic being that the more duck-like – and therefore gross – the foetus looks, then the more masculine the eater. A culinary testosterone test, if you will. *Hôt vit lôn* is said to be nutritious and to taste like creamy chicken, although in some instances the bones require mastication, so like creamy and sometimes chewy chicken.

'Prove to me that you're a real man and eat your foetal duck egg,' dared Lisa.

'Not a bloody chance. I would rather go through life with my manhood impugned than put that monstrosity in my mouth. Tell everyone that I have a micro-penis and that I pee sitting down, I don't really care.'

If the man who first ate an oyster was brave, then the man who first ate *hôt vit lôn* was braver. Call me unadventurous, but I'm sticking to peanuts with my beer.

Taking off with a terrorist
Cuba

 I didn't like the look of the sweating bearded man who, the moment the seatbelt signs pinged off after take-off, rose and made his way past us to the toilets at the rear of the plane, agitatedly rubbing his neck and head and looking from side to side as if sizing up his fellow passengers. When he returned to his seat half a dozen rows in front of us, it may have been my imagination, but he seemed to take an unnaturally keen interest in the movements of the cabin crew. On a flight this empty, his unusual behaviour drew attention to him, so I pointed him out to Lisa and told her of my misgivings. Several minutes later he passed by a second time, again seeming to study the passengers.

'What worries me is the way he keeps making eye contact with everyone,' Lisa said. 'Who does that when they walk to the toilets?'

The 9/11 atrocity had occurred ten days previously, and our Air France flight to Havana was less than half full because many passengers had cancelled their travel plans for fear that al-Qaeda might strike again and they'd find themselves aboard a hijacked plane flying towards a skyscraper. All the newspapers carried reports of how such a tragedy could be prevented again: pilots would be locked into their cockpits and armed air marshals would fly on every plane to ensure passengers had some chance of surviving a hijacking. The prospect of a shootout at altitude on a pressurised plane was hardly a comforting one.

Though unnerved, we'd stuck with our plan to travel to Cuba as we wanted to go there before American multinationals flooded in to Coca-colonise Havana in the name of McWalmart. A colleague of Lisa's had raved about her fortnight there, telling of Havana's crumbling colonial architecture, the painstakingly preserved two-tone 1950s 'Yank tanks' that cruised its streets, and the city's vibrant salsa scene which spilled out of every doorway like overfilled burritos. She'd spoken, too, of how she'd mistaken doctors hanging about at traffic lights for hookers until she'd spotted their stethoscopes – their salaries of about US$20 a month weren't enough to run a car, so they hitchhiked to and from work. She'd told of being asked for paracetamol and sachets of hotel shampoo as commonplace drugs and toiletries were so scarce. And how, if you wanted to make an avocado sandwich, you had to use coupons and queue up at three almost-bare shops, one for bread, one for butter and one for the avocado.

Now, seated 34,000ft up in a half-empty plane and spooked by the odd behaviour of the pacing passenger, we were beginning to question the wisdom of our decision. Lisa thought the best plan of action would be for her to closely monitor him, so she began following him to the toilets. He made three trips in 30 minutes. Each time she stood guard outside, nervously wondering what he could be doing in there that could be taking so long. Assembling a smuggled gun? Pulling explosives from his rectum? Each time he emerged, he was carrying his shoes. It never once crossed our minds that he wasn't a *jihadi* nutter but a very nervous flyer with prostate trouble and sweaty feet. 9/11 had dramatically changed the mindset of every airline passenger. In the past, complying with a hijacker's demands meant you would probably get out alive – albeit in Beirut rather than the airport of your choice – but now it was imperative to fight back from the get-go.

Lisa began to think how, if the need arose, we'd 'take him out'. 'What could we use to subdue him?' she whispered.

'A sock filled with sand makes a handy cosh,' I replied.

'What?'

'Or billiard balls, if there's no sand.'

'I'm serious!' she snapped.

'I don't know. We haven't got anything,' I said, looking for possible weapons and seeing only our blow-up neck pillows, a paperback and a box of duty-free Jelly Babies, none of which seemed likely to be lethal.

'I know, we could use this to strangle him,' Lisa said, touching the short length of nylon string around her neck from which hung the small padlock keys for our rucksacks.

'That would never do it. We'd have to break his neck.'

'Do you know how to do that?' asked Lisa, half-hoping that I'd learned something life-savingly practical on one of my Ministry of Defence training courses.

'No. But I've seen it done.'

'Where?'

'In the movies.'

'Oh, for fuck's sake…'

We were both incredibly relieved when the plane landed unscathed in Cuba at about 10pm, but our anxiety wasn't about to abate quite yet. Hailing a clapped-out taxi, we asked to be taken to Habana Vieja, the capital's old quarter, where we'd booked a room in a *casa particular*. There was no lighting, so the streets were dark. The yellow light cast by our taxi's one functioning headlamp illuminated the facades of dilapidated buildings that were propped up with wooden struts and that teetered forward at crazy angles, threatening to topple into the street. As our taxi waddled its way down the deserted, potholed roads we could vaguely make out broken-down apartment stairwells with rats' nests of power cables and tangles of phone lines cascading down them. Convinced that we were being taken somewhere remote to be beaten, robbed, raped or murdered, or possibly all four – and not necessarily in that order – Lisa said aloud, 'Oh God, why on earth did we come here?'

The driver slowed to a stop and announced that he'd found our address, pointing to the unlit entrance of a mansion block.

Instructing me to stay in the taxi in case it made off with our luggage, Lisa cautiously ascended the cracked concrete stairs leading up to our homestay apartment. She'd climbed no more than four when a raven-haired woman in a nightdress and curlers appeared on the first-floor landing, looked down and cried out 'Jack-sonne?'

Lisa shouted back '*Oui*. I mean, *sí.*'

When linguistically challenged Lisa – who studied French on four separate and unsuccessful occasions – always defaults to French as though it's her factory setting. In Brazil? French. In Italy? French. In Turkey? French. But in France or Francophone West Africa she inexplicably lapses into Afrikaans.

Delighted to see us, the woman told us she'd suspected we'd

cancelled our trip because of 9/11, like most of her guests had. Apologising for the bags under her eyes caused, she said, by an allergic reaction to hair dye, she introduced herself as Marisol and showed us to our high-ceilinged room furnished with antiques, and with a balcony view of the 17th-century Santa Clara convent.

Exhausted, we caught up on the sleep denied us on the plane and after Lisa had returned from a dawn run along the Malecón, deserted but for a few early-bird fishermen casting off from the sea wall, we joined Marisol for a late breakfast. In the corner of her sitting room, Marisol's television was permanently on. At breakfast, it was broadcasting the preparations for one of Fidel Castro's addresses to the people.

'There has been this 9/11, and it is very bad. But el Presidente will speak the same things as he always does,' sniffed Marisol. 'We are poor and life is difficult and Castro will tell us we must continue on the path of revolution: socialism or death!'

Marisol was one of the more fortunate few. Part of Cuba's dollar economy, she rented rooms to overseas visitors, something the communist government permitted despite the fact that it was a capitalist enterprise.

'America treats us very badly because we are communist. We do not want to be told what to do. Castro will say some strong things against America. In some he will be right. We are a proud and independent people, but Cubans want a better life.'

In certain respects, Castro's revolution had delivered. Cuba's literacy rate was sky high and healthcare was free and universal and as good as it could be given the country's dire economic circumstances. Yet, like so many revolutionary societies, the regime was tightly retentive and didn't know how to begin relaxing all-pervasive controls without risking an ideological prolapse that would make a mockery of nearly 50 years of struggle. The collapse of the Soviet Union in 1991 had been an object lesson in how change threatened control.

As we began eating the scrambled eggs Marisol had prepared for us, there was a loud knock on the front door.

'Shhh!' hissed Marisol. 'Keep quiet, don't speak.'

We froze, and the banging got louder.

'Ignore it,' Marisol whispered, calmly pouring us another coffee.

The hammering was hard to turn a deaf ear to, but within about two minutes it fell silent.

'They're gone,' said Marisol coolly. 'It was the police.'

'The *police*?' Lisa and I said in unison, our hearts thumping almost as loudly as the cops had hammered on the door.

'*Sí*. As the owner of a *casa particular* I must have a licence if I want to serve food – and I don't have one. The police are always trying to catch me serving my guests breakfast. Cuba is very bureaucracy, very red tape.'

We continued eating our delicious, illicit breakfast.

'Now,' asked Marisol conspiratorially, 'do you want me to cook you lobster for dinner? Ten dollars each.'

Lisa has a strange relationship with Ernest Hemingway. But probably not quite as strange as the ones he had with his four wives. She first encountered him at school when she was tasked to read *The Old Man and the Sea*. Though English literature was her favourite subject, and the book only 128 pages long, she never managed to finish it, and relied on summary notes from study guides to pass her exam. She had a similar encounter with *Heart of Darkness* at university which, at 78 pages was hardly going to take up too much time that could otherwise be spent sleeping or buying incense and ethnic earrings at Greenmarket Square.

'*The Old Man and the Sea* was just so boring, Graham,' she said, defending her lack of academic application. 'Nothing at all happens. In fact, I think I can summarise the summary notes I read as follows: man catches fish, sharks eat fish man caught. How was I supposed to read a book like that?'

I remembered all the weighty, impenetrable philosophy tomes I'd had to wade through to get my own undergraduate degree, and said nothing. Lisa's admission was one of the reasons why I found her obsession with visiting every spot in Havana where the great man had so much as paused to ask for directions so puzzling. By the time we went to Cuba in 2001 Lisa still hadn't read more than two pages of Hemingway in the original, but she could reel off dozens of facts about his colourful private life. Like how he'd installed a urinal from Sloppy Joe's, one of his many favourite bars, in the garden of his Key West home where his many cats used it as a drinking bowl.

'Hemingway said he'd pissed away so much of his money into that urinal that he owned it,' she informed me over our watery, mouthwashy mojitos in La Bodeguita del Medio, the first stop on our Hemingway-pub pilgrimage. The bathroom-sized bar was rammed with tourists knocking back the same, despite the fact that the sole 'proof' Papa had ever drunk a mojito there was a forged handwritten note saying 'My mojito in La Bodeguita. My daiquiri in El Floridita.'

At our next port of call, the more upmarket El Floridita, the smirking barman exchanged our dollars for two under-chilled and overpriced daiquiris.

'You know that famous photo, the one where Hemingway looks like Moses?' Lisa asked.

I nodded, imagining the iconic photo of the great man staring moodily into the distance, his bearded head balanced on the thick roll of a turtleneck sweater like a hirsute egg in a woollen eggcup.

'Well, his fourth wife Mary bought that jumper for him. It was designed by Christian Dior and she paid a fortune for it, but it was worth every penny as it made him look so manly and epic and sealed his reputation as a literary lion.'

For our final stop of our pub crawl Lisa wanted to go to Dos Hermanos, yet another bar where Hemingway had performed serial liver abuse, but I instead insisted we go to La Lluvia de Oro, not a Hemingway haunt but a lively joint where the beers were brain-freeze cold and the band, Quinteto Lira Habana, so toe-tappingly good that we shelled out for their CD.

Relaxing with our drinks on the fan-cooled terrace, we bought a copy of the English-language paper *Granma* for a dollar from a vendor who'd thrust one through the burglar bars. It should have cost its cover price of ten cents, but it's not easy demanding change through burglar bars. Reading our paper and watching the world go by to the sound of a live band straight from *Buena Vista Social Club* felt oh-so boho, oh-so literary luvvie, and Lisa was in her element.

It was late in the evening when I paid a visit to the gents. After doing what I needed to do, I flushed and, to my consternation, saw that – how should I put this? – my fudge refused to budge. I waited for the cistern to fill and flushed again. Still it stood stiffly to attention, like a Marine on parade. There was no toilet brush inside, and a fierce-looking little toilet attendant outside. The imperative to leave a public convenience cleaner than one found it, when there's a witness to its before-and-after state, is a peculiarly English neurosis. A less complex Continental – Karl from Dusseldorf, for instance – would own the situation.

Karl: 'Janitor person, come please. In this cubicle I have blocked the toilet.'

Toilet attendant, peering into the bowl, blanching: '¡Ay, caramba! It smells of pistachio and gravy.'

Karl: 'It is a good health stool. See, it is smooth, the colour is consistent and the tapering is symmetrical.'

Toilet attendant: 'It is *grande*... very big.'

Karl: '*Ja, danke*. It is a Hindenburg, as we call it in Dusseldorf. You will please deal with it.'

Toilet attendant: 'I may need some help. And some fresh air.'

Karl: 'Here is a dollar. Also, you should know that putting a bowl of mints inside a public convenience is very unhygienic.'

But being English Graham not German Karl, I felt I had no option but to dismantle my deposit myself. Wrapping toilet paper around my hand I gingerly set about this repulsive task, trying my best not to retch *too* loudly in case the attendant became curious. Chunk by chunk I pinched it into pieces and flushed again. Yes! This time it did go down. I swiftly exited the cubicle, hastily washed my hands and rejoined Lisa.

'What took you so long?' she enquired, annoyed, I think because she'd had to wait to order another round of beers.

'Nothing,' I said. 'I'll tell you later.'

'What's that on your arm?' she asked.

'What? Where?'

'That, there,' she said, pointing to a brown smear half the length of my forearm. Horrified, I flew back to the scene of the grime, where I scrubbed my arm red-raw. *A Farewell to Arms*? At that point I would most definitely have welcomed that.

POSTSCRIPT

 After our trip to Cuba I feared it would be many years until we holidayed abroad again. The fact that terrorists had turned planes into piloted missiles that could be launched from any airport seemed to herald the end of air travel. Not long after the Twin Towers collapsed, Swissair, Belgium's Sabena and Australia's Ansett did the same, and we weren't sure how many airlines would survive the industry downturn. The second, more personal reason I believed our travelling days were behind us was because we'd agreed that in my 35th year we'd decide whether or not to have kids. Graham's struggle to find a permanent job and our love of travel had seen us push this life goal into the future, but now we had a home and careers and some money saved it was time to review our priorities.

The Children Question had cropped up early in our relationship. After we'd dated for about two weeks we'd gone for a walk around Rondebosch Common, a large stretch of open land blotted with white arum lilies at that time of year.

'Imagine us walking here one day holding the hands of a little Lisa and a little Graham,' said Graham. 'That would be pretty cool.'

'Yes, wouldn't it,' I'd replied, totally smitten and already dreaming grown-up dreams of marriage and babies.

It was after our engagement that we became huge fans of the comic strip *Calvin and Hobbes,* featuring a mischievous and precocious six-year-old and his alive-only-to-him stuffed toy tiger, Hobbes. Calvin's fictional surveys to show his dad how his approval ratings among six-year-olds and tigers were plummeting – as a way to extort a later bedtime and more pocket money – was a tactic I'd adopted for managing Graham when travelling.

'Bad news, Graham, your polling is at an all-time low. You rate especially poorly among twenty-something women travelling in India. If you want them to improve, I'd suggest you allow me to order a beer.'

'I don't take any notice of polls, Lisa. Being your husband is not an elected position.'

'Not elected? You mean you can behave autocratically, issuing orders with impunity?'

'The short answer is yes.'

'In my opinion, you don't have any hope of staying in office.'

'I'm confident that not many people want this job.'

'Sarcastic comments have a way of haunting candidates, Graham.'

Calvin had been the name we'd chosen for our future son. Hobbes – handily the surname of a notable 17th-century philosopher Graham had once studied – would be the name of our second son. And if we had a daughter? Well, we thought, we could go for Calvinia, the name of a South African town famed for its wildflowers. With the idea of children twinkling in our eyes, we'd spent most of the money wedding guests had given us on a video camera to film our kids' adorable antics, if I ever figured out how to turn it on.

2002 would be the year we'd make the two toughest decisions of our lives: whether to emigrate to Australia and whether to start a family. By then, we'd had a decade of travelling to look back on and I'd discovered the joy of running. Though we'd met travellers with very young children in tow – a couple who stayed in the same bone-cold guesthouse in Darjeeling and another with a one-year-old in Egypt – we knew that the places we liked to travel to weren't known for being particularly child friendly. I'd have been worried sick about Calvin contracting pneumonia from inadequate heating or being struck down with Pharaoh's Revenge. And I simply couldn't see how Hobbes would cope with museum sickness when it sometimes took Graham and I less than half an hour until we'd had enough and would run screaming for the exit.

Neither of us had been to South America, I was keen to visit Burma and we still wanted to go to Ghana, Graham birthplace.

These were not countries where we saw ourselves carrying kids in slings, even though other travellers assured us it had all worked out perfectly well for them. I knew my mother, in particular, yearned for grandchildren. She told us so every time we went back to South Africa. If we didn't have kids, we'd break her heart.

But I also appreciated how hard having children in London could be. My harried boss always shot off at one second past 5.30pm, desperate to fetch her children from nursery on time to avoid punitive fines so eyewatering that they could wipe out half a day's pay if she was 30 minutes late. And with childcare costs gobbling up most of her salary, I knew that at least until her children went to school, almost all her cash went straight into the nursery's coffers and there was scant to spare for non-essentials such as holidays.

'Lisa, we need to be sure we get this right,' said Graham as we watched the New Year's Eve fireworks over the Thames. 'We need to think long and hard about Australia as it will mean living a long way from our families. And on the Calvin front, I just don't think we can afford for you to give up your job. I'm not earning enough for you to do that, and if I stay at home my career will stop before it's barely started.'

'I know,' I replied. 'I'm also very unsure about the whole Australia thing – it's just so far away from everywhere else. And to my mind, having kids and paying someone else to care for them is like buying a Porsche and then hiring a chauffeur to drive it. I want to be as hands-on as my mum was. *Cosmopolitan* always said women can have it all: a career *and* children. But I'm pretty sure the women it was talking about didn't have travel seekness.'

THE END?

Thank you for reading to the end of *Travel Seekness*. We hope you've enjoyed the time you spent with us as much as we've loved sharing our experiences with you.

Keen to find out what happened next? Look out for our forthcoming sequel, *Travel Agents: More Japes, Scrapes and Narrow Escapes,* where you'll hear more hair-raising tales we didn't want to tell our mothers about. Like when we braved blazing barricades in riot-torn Bolivia, helicoptered to the most dangerous place on earth, met a bottom-pinching voodoo priest in Benin, were interviewed by the secret police in Iran and had a 'torture massage' in North Korea. If you travel with us, the fun never stops, and neither does the 'squaddling'!

Whether you loved *Travel Seekness* or loathed it, we'd be chuffed to bits if you'd write us a short review on Amazon and Goodreads. Reviews can be as short as 'Hilarious' or 'Tedious in the extreme'. Little Bandit Books is our own imprint and we don't have an advertising budget, but your review will help to ensure that Amazon does our marketing for us, which means we'll be able to raise more money for lung cancer research.

If you want to meet us in virtual 'real life', see photos from our travels or get an update on how much money this book has raised for mesothelioma research, you'll find us on Facebook (track down Little Bandit Books) and Twitter (@LISAJACKSON43).

And please, don't be a stranger: why not drop us a line at lisaamjackson@gmail.com? We were brought up well, and love getting emails from fellow travellers rather than from scammers or the bank, so we will always write back.

Lisa & Graham

PRAISE FOR *TRAVEL AGENTS*

Travel Agents is an absolute belter of a book. **Vassos Alexander, Virgin Radio sports presenter & author of *Don't Stop Me Now***

No way would I ever want to join a trip Lisa and Graham organised, but I'd absolutely help hold the Iranian nightmare guide Milad down while they strangled him. **Lonely Planet co-founder Tony Wheeler**

An awesome collection of travel tales that will enthral, terrify and perhaps appal you. At times I choked on my jam on toast, at others I laughed out loud. Lisa and Graham are living proof that anyone can be the hero of their own life. **Jamie McDonald, adventurer & author of *Adventureman***

A brush with death on one holiday is bad luck; doing it on two trips is either careless – or the basis of a fantastic travel book! I raced through the chapters, swinging between thinking 'Thank god I haven't done that' and envious thoughts of 'Why haven't I done that?' **Helen Foster, travel writer & Differentville.com blogger**

Cracking stories need a cracking storyteller, and they get them here. You'll soon feel that Graham and Lisa have stuffed you in their backpacks on a journey that is warm, witty, wise and endlessly engaging. **Phil Hewitt, author of *Outrunning the Demons***

The world needs more travel writing like this; a surge of dromomania sprinkled with love, wonder and unexpected hilarity that only travel uncovers. Curl up at home and travel the world with a big grin on your face. **Dave Cornthwaite, founder of the YesTribe**

Dramatic! Unputdownable! Riveting! Make a movie of this book! But please Lisa and Graham, don't ask me to go on 'holiday' with you. Ever. For once, I'd prefer to sit on the sidelines and cheer you both on! **Kathrine Switzer, author of *Marathon Woman***

ABOUT THE AUTHORS

 Lisa Jackson is a latecomer to almost everything: sushi, mobile phones, social media. She only started travelling at 24, previously having set foot outside her native South Africa just once, as a surly, sulky teenager. Aged 31 she discovered marathon running and, never one to do things by halves, combined this new interest with her post-pubescent passion for travel, going on to run over 100 marathons and ultras, almost half of them abroad.

A London-based hypnotherapist and health journalist, Lisa is the best-selling author of *Your Pace or Mine?* and *Running Made Easy* and a columnist for *Runner's World*. On the road Lisa will always favour a backpacker hostel over a swanky hotel because, she reasons, if you're going to spend money it's always better to do so with your eyes open.

 Graham Williams is a research analyst for the British government. Terrified of turbulence, he nonetheless braves the scary skies in devoted service to Her Majesty. Graham's job has taken him to one or two hairy places such as Afghanistan and the Khyber Pass, but as a longtime resident of the London Borough of Croydon, he reckons he's acquired the street smarts to get out of any trouble.

To help fund his travels, Graham cuts his own hair – less expertly than Lisa would like – and hasn't been sighted in a sandwich shop for many years, preferring to lunch on tinned sardines instead. Despite bouts of diarrhoea so bad he needed penicillin to cure them, Graham still maintains that if you can't peel it or boil it or wash it you should eat it anyway, for it may well be very tasty.

Married for almost three decades, Lisa and Graham live in Croydon, south London, with a tame squirrel called Pecan, two over-fed wood pigeons called Fletcher and Sedaris, and four very noisy foxes who visit from next door.

Printed in Great Britain
by Amazon